Educating for Well-Being in Law

Bringing together the current international body of knowledge on key issues for educating for well-being in law, this book offers comparative perspectives across jurisdictions, and utilises a range of theoretical lenses (including socio-legal, psychological and ethical theories) in analysing well-being and legal education in law. The chapters include innovative and tested research methodologies and strategies for educating for well-being. Asking and answering the question as to whether law is special in terms of producing psychological distress in law students, law teachers and the profession, and bringing together common and opposing perspectives, this book also seeks to highlight excellent practice in promoting a positive professional identity at law school and beyond resulting in an original contribution to knowledge, and new discourses of analysis.

Caroline Strevens is Reader in Legal Education and Head of the Law Department at the University of Portsmouth and Chair of the Association of Law Teachers. Caroline's academic career was preceded by a career in legal practice as a Solicitor. She established the suite of qualifying law degrees and was appointed the first Head when the Department was formed in 2008. Caroline's primary research area is legal education. Recently, she has been investigating links between motivation, well-being and ethical decision-making. Her most recent publication entitled 'Perceptions of Wellbeing in Law Teachers' has been published in the *Law Teacher*. Caroline continues to work with international collaborators to promote well-being in legal academics and junior lawyers.

Rachael Field is Professor in the Law School at Bond University, co-director of the Bond Dispute Resolution Centre, a member of the Executive of Bond's Centre for Professional Legal Education and co-founder of the Australian Dispute Resolution Research Network. She is an Australian Learning and Teaching Fellow and a Senior Fellow of the Higher Education Academy. In 2010 Rachael established the Australian Wellness Network for Law, which holds annual Forums on well-being issues in legal education and legal practice. Rachael volunteers at the Women's Legal Service in Brisbane and has been president of the Service since 2004. In 2013 Rachael was named Queensland Woman Lawyer of the Year.

Emerging Legal Education

Series Editors:

Paul Maharg, *Osgoode Hall Law School, York University, ON, Canada*,
Elizabeth Mertz, *University of Wisconsin-Madison/American Bar Foundation, USA* and
Meera Deo, *Thomas Jefferson School of Law, San Diego, CA, USA*

Emerging Legal Education is a forum for analysing the discourse of legal education and creating innovative ways of learning the law. The series focuses on research, theory and practice within legal education, drawing attention to historical, interdisciplinary and international characteristics, and is based upon imaginative and sophisticated educational thinking. The series takes a broad view of theory and practice. Series books are written for an international audience and are sensitive to the diversity of contexts in which law is taught, learned and practised.

Other titles in this series:

Educating for Well-Being in Law
Positive Professional Identities and Practice
Edited by Caroline Strevens and Rachael Field

Promoting Law Student and Lawyer Well-Being in Australia and Beyond
Edited by Rachel Field, James Duffy, Colin James

Legal Education in the Global Context
Opportunities and Challenges
Edited by Christopher Gane and Robin Hui Huang

Legal Education
Simulation in Theory and Practice
Edited by Caroline Strevens, Richard Grimes and Edward Phillips

Forthcoming:

Emotion in the Law School
Transforming legal education through the passions
Emma Jones

www.routledge.com/Emerging-Legal-Education/book-series/ELE

Educating for Well-Being in Law

Positive Professional Identities and Practice

Edited by Caroline Strevens and Rachael Field

Routledge
Taylor & Francis Group
LONDON AND NEW YORK

First published 2020
by Routledge
2 Park Square, Milton Park, Abingdon, Oxon OX14 4RN

and by Routledge
605 Third Avenue, New York, NY 10017

Routledge is an imprint of the Taylor & Francis Group, an informa business

First issued in paperback 2021

British Library Cataloguing-in-Publication Data
A catalogue record for this book is available from the British Library

Library of Congress Cataloging-in-Publication Data
A catalog record for this book has been requested

ISBN 13: 978-1-138-47756-8 (hbk)
ISBN 13: 978-1-03-224076-3 (pbk)
ISBN 13: 978-1-351-10440-1 (ebk)

DOI: 10.4324/9781351104401

Typeset in Galliard
by Apex CoVantage, LLC

Contents

Contributors

Joanne Atkinson is Principal Lecturer in the School of Law at the University of Portsmouth. After completing an LLB at the University of Nottingham, she qualified as a solicitor in 1999. Joanne practised both in private practice and in-house before joining the University of Portsmouth in 2011. She has been involved in the development, teaching and assessment of a range of units and programs, including Commercial Law, Company Law and Negotiation Theory & Practice. Joanne is responsible for the School of Law's LLM programs. Her research interests include widening access to the professions.

Lydia Bleasdale is Associate Professor and Director of Community Engagement at the School of Law, University of Leeds. Her research covers clinical legal education, criminal law, and student well-being and resilience. In 2016–17 she was seconded – alongside Sarah Humphreys – to the Leeds Institute for Teaching Excellence, where they undertook a year-long research project into undergraduate student resilience. The project covered six disciplines, examining the similarities and differences between the students from a resilience perspective, as well as how the resilience of students might best be supported by universities.

Carol Boothby was until recently Associate Professor in the Law School at Northumbria University in Newcastle, England, and is now engaged in doctoral studies, focused around clinical supervision. For 16 years, she taught in the Student Law Office, one of the longest established law clinics both nationally and internationally. She was Director of the Student Law Office for 8 years, helping to establish an outreach service and providing pastoral support and supervision to students. Under her leadership, the work of the Student Law Office received numerous accolades including the Queens Anniversary Prize, the Attorney General Award for promoting access to justice, and the Higher Education Academy's Collaborative Award for Teaching Excellence award in 2017, to name but a few.

Carol is a Principal Fellow of the Higher Education Academy. Her research is in the area of legal education, including assessment, professional skills and clinical supervision. She has been an active member of the Legal Education and Professional Skills research group at Northumbria and led the group's response to the recent Solicitors Regulation Authority consultation on the changes to qualification as a solicitor. Carol is also a part-time tribunal judge in the social security chamber.

Margaret Castles is Senior Lecturer and Director, Clinical Legal Education at the Law School at Adelaide University in South Australia. She teaches civil litigation, dispute resolution and clinical legal education. Margaret has a background in legal practice, tribunal membership, and has been involved in the provision of pro bono legal support to refugees seeking safety in Australia. In 20 years managing the CLE program at Adelaide Law School Margaret has established three legal advice services, within the homeless community and in the Magistrates Court at Adelaide, at the Equal Opportunity Commission of SA, as well as running a clinical externship placement program. She is an active member of the Justice Access and Civil Litigation Committees of the SA Law Society, the South Australian Legal Aid Forum, and works with the courts and other organisations to develop better resources for litigants in person in SA.

As part of her teaching practice Margaret incorporates the theory and practice of wellness for students and professionals across her teaching portfolio, and in extra-curricular activities with the Adelaide Law School's 'Lex Salus' wellness in law program. Her research is in the areas of applied legal ethics, legal education and interactive curriculum design, justice access, online tools for reflective learning and capturing client narrative in legal representation.

David Catanzariti is Lecturer at the Australian National University's Legal Workshop where he has convened and taught a number of subject areas which form part of the Graduate Diploma of Legal Practice Program. Prior to joining the Legal Workshop David practiced as a Solicitor in New South Wales before moving to join a mid-size commercial law firm in Canberra.

After joining Legal Workshop, David obtained his Masters of Higher Education from the ANU and has taken a keen interest in flexible learning and educational technology, leading to appointments on the Vice-Chancellor's Flexible Learning Working Party, the Learning Management System Selection Panel as well as chairing the Web Conferencing Selection Panel. David was also part of a team which received the Vice Chancellor's On-Campus Award for Innovation in IT Application.

David chairs the Legal Workshop Rural, Regional and Remote Financial Assistance Committee which reviews applications from students who are seeking financial assistance for the purpose of undertaking legal experience placements in legal environments outside of the major capital cities. David is currently part of a team working on a qualitative research project involving undergraduate and graduate Diploma of Legal Practice students and early career commercial lawyers concerning their attitudes and reflections towards commercial and corporate law.

Anthony Cullen is Senior Lecturer in Law at the School of Law, Middlesex University, London. He currently teaches Public Law, International Criminal Law, and International Humanitarian law. Prior to taking up this position, he was a Research Fellow at the School of Law, University of Leeds (2011–2013) and a Research Fellow at the Lauterpacht Centre for International Law, University of Cambridge (2007–2011).

Anthony was previously employed on the joint Customary International Humanitarian Law Project of the British Red Cross and International Committee of the Red Cross. He also served for a period in the Human Rights Unit of the Irish Department of Foreign Affairs during Ireland's presidency of the European Union.

In addition to his position at Middlesex University, Dr Cullen is also a Visiting Professor at the University of Bordeaux and an External Examiner at the University of Exeter.

His research focuses on the areas of international humanitarian law, international human rights law, the use of contemplative methods in higher education, and student well-being.

Nigel Duncan is Professor of Legal Education at City, University of London. His teaching includes a live clinical option that involves students in representing real clients in the employment tribunals. He is a University Teaching and Learning Fellow, a National Teaching Fellow and a Principal Fellow of the Higher Education Academy. He is a member of the Education and Training Committee of the Bar Standards Board and a founder member of the UK Clinical Legal Education Organisation and the Global Alliance for Justice Education.

Nigel is Convenor of the Legal Ethics Forum of the School's Centre for the Study of Legal Professional Practice within which he convenes Teaching Legal Ethics UK, a community of practice including members from many different law schools and some practitioners, which holds regular workshops. Recent workshops have addressed issues of wellness in students and practitioners and have included an interdisciplinary perspective. He is consultant editor of *The Law Teacher*, a member of the Editorial Advisory Board of the *Legal Education Review* and of the International Advisory Panel of the *International Journal of the Legal Profession.*

His many publications and conference presentations are predominantly in the field of legal education, professional development and ethics.

Anneka Ferguson is Senior Lecturer at the ANU School of Legal Practice (formerly ANU Legal Workshop) and a Senior Fellow of the Higher Education

Academy. In her time with the school, Anneka has been both the Director and Sub-Dean of the Graduate Diploma of Legal Practice/Masters of Legal Practice, and a Convenor of the Professional Practice Core, Practice Management, Ready for Practice, Trust Accounting in Practice and Lawyers, Justice and Ethics subjects. Prior to joining ANU in 2007 Anneka worked in personal injury litigation in private and government practice, as well as a range of roles within Health, Family and Community and Regional service. Anneka's teaching motivation derives from her early years in legal practice wherein she realised how little was taught at university about operating, surviving and thriving in legal practice. As such, she is absolutely dedicated to providing all law graduates with the opportunity to practise and develop the real skills, attitudes and well-being they will need for practice.

To support her sound teaching practices, Anneka has developed (in conjunction with Stephen Tang) a comprehensive action and empirical research framework to both evaluate whether ANU Law's core Professional Legal Education course is creating practice-ready, professional, ethical and well graduates to enter the legal profession; and provide an environment to trial novel practices based on sound theory. A sample of Anneka's recent presentations and publications include 'Into the Rabbit Hole: Valuing the Dissonance' at the Future Directions in Legal Education Conference 2018 hosted by CUHK, and 'Regulating for Wellbeing' at the 8th International Legal Ethics Conference in Melbourne in 2018.

Rachael Field is Professor of Law in the Bond Law School, and a member of the Executive of Bond University's Centre for Professional Legal Education. She is an Australian Learning and Teaching Fellow and a Senior Fellow of the Higher Education Academy. Rachael teaches first year law threshold concepts and transition as well as dispute resolution. She has received national recognition for teaching excellence through a national citation in 2008, a national teaching fellowship in 2010 and a national teaching excellence award in 2014. Rachael is the founder of the Australian Wellness Network for Law, which is now expanding internationally. Her areas of research expertise include dispute resolution, family law, domestic violence and legal education. She is also co-founder of the Australian Dispute Resolution Research Network. She has a portfolio of more than 85 scholarly publications, and is co-author of five books. Since 1994, Rachael has volunteered on the management committee of Women's Legal Service in Brisbane, and she has been president of the Service since 2004. In 2013 Rachael was named Queensland Woman Lawyer of the Year.

Caroline Gibby is Principal Lecturer, Solicitor and Head of Department at the University of Sunderland. She has taught law and has been involved in teacher education for far more years than she cares to remember. Her current teaching includes teaching students who are preparing to enter the client clinic and solicitor tutor in the Legal Practice program – focusing on private client issues, with specific reference to vulnerable clients. She has also taught on the BPTC program focusing on Professional Ethics.

Caroline is Fellow of the Higher Education Academy and holds a professional Doctorate in Legal Education. She is a member of the ALT, SLS and SLSA, as well as a member of BERA, LERN and Teaching Legal Ethics UK community. Her recent conference papers have addressed liminality in legal education considering the concept of emotional labour, intelligence and well-being in legal educators and students. She has also presented papers exploring theories and teaching methods to support and develop student resilience and wellness in their studies drawing on inter- and multi-disciplinary approaches.

Freda Grealy is Solicitor and Head of Diploma Centre, Education Department, Law Society of Ireland and provides continuing professional development courses in specialised areas of law to the solicitors' profession. She qualified as a lawyer in Ireland in 1997 and worked in private practice, including criminal defence litigation and general practice before joining the Law Society in 2006. She is qualified as a solicitor in England in Wales and also qualified as an Attorney at Law in New York State. Freda received her PhD from UCL in 2018 under the supervision of Professor Avrom Sherr. Her thesis focused on an empirical intervention study with trainee solicitors in the area of teaching ethics and developing professional identity. She is a member of the Curriculum Development Unit of the Law Society of Ireland (LSI) and leads the LSI Public Legal Education initiatives. She is the founding member of the Irish Rule of Law Initiative group 'Irish Lawyers Legal Education Partnership Project – South East Asia' and has taught professional legal skills in Vietnam and Myanmar and presented at a number of IJCLE and Global Alliance for Justice Education Conferences.

Vivien Holmes, Associate Professor, teaches and researches in the fields of legal ethics, legal education and the legal profession at the ANU College of Law. She is currently Associate Dean (Education) for the ANU College of Law. Prior to joining ANU, Vivien worked as a litigation solicitor in private and government practice, as a government legal policy officer, the Registrar of the Northern Territory Supreme Court, the NT Registrar of Probates, the NT Deputy Coroner and a Judicial Registrar of the NT Magistrates' Court. She has been a member of the Social Security Appeals Tribunal and is currently a member of the ACT Law Society's Complaints Committee. Vivien is a Senior Fellow of the Higher Education Academy.

Sarah Humphreys joined the University of Leeds School of Law in January 2016 as Co-ordinator of the Legal Advice Clinics, supporting students in a range of clinical legal education volunteering opportunities in the local community. In 2016–17 she was seconded on a part-time basis – alongside Lydia Bleasdale – to the Leeds Institute for Teaching Excellence, where they undertook a year-long research project into undergraduate student resilience. Prior to joining the University, Sarah spent ten years working in Further Education with some of the hardest to reach adult learners, specialising in offender learning. Sarah has a particular interest in improving access to education through addressing barriers to learning. She is Chair of the Equality, Diversity and Inclusion committee for the School of Law.

Colin James has been a solicitor since 1989 and a clinical legal educator since 2001. He has researched and published in many fields associated with domestic violence, family law, legal education, legal history, legal practice and the well-being of law students and lawyers. He has qualifications in law, history, tertiary education and psychology, and he currently teaches family law and practice and supervises in professional development courses at the ANU College of Law. Colin presents at national and international conferences and his recent publications include as a contributing editor of *Promoting Law Student and Lawyer Well-Being in Australia and Beyond* (Routledge), *Being Well in the Law: A Guide for Lawyers* (Law Society NSW), 'Did He Ever Hit You? Exploring the Attitudes of Lawyers in DV Cases' *Australian Journal of Family Law* (*AJFL*) and 'Legal Practice on Time: The Ethical Risk and Inefficiency of the Six-Minute Unit' (*Alternative Law Journal*). He has supervised PhDs and DBAs on topics ranging from domestic violence and sexual assault survivors, industrial ethics and worker safety practices, and first-responders' powers of detention in a mental health emergency.

Emma Jones is Senior Lecturer in Law at The Open University in the UK. She is currently Teaching Director for the Law School, overseeing the undergraduate and postgraduate curriculum. Her former teaching interests focused on the development of The Open University Law School's Open Justice Centre, including chairing the clinical legal education module offered to students and acting as a supervising solicitor. Emma was previously in private practice as a solicitor and is also a qualified teacher in post-compulsory education and training. Her PhD focused on the role of emotion within undergraduate legal education in England and Wales. Her current research focuses on the role of emotion and well-being within legal education and the legal profession. Recent empirical work includes investigating the well-being of distance learning law students, looking at the emotional competencies of solicitors and researching the perceptions of the LLB held by law school admission tutors.

Emma is an Academic Fellow of the Inner Temple and a Senior Fellow of the Higher Education Authority. She is a member of various committees involved in legal education and co-editor of the *Journal of Commonwealth Law and Legal Education*. She is also co-convenor of the Socio-Legal Studies Association's law and emotion stream, co-founder of the UK's law and emotion network and co-Chair of the UK Chapter of the International Society for Therapeutic Jurisprudence.

Lughaidh Kerin is Senior Lecturer and Director of Clinical Legal Education at Middlesex University School of Law in London. He lectures on Alternative Dispute Resolution and Legal Ethics. He has coached various moot court teams as well as prepared Middlesex teams for negotiation, mediation and client interviewing competitions, both nationally and internationally.

Prior to his appointment at Middlesex University, Lughaidh held a Lectureship in Law at the National University of Ireland Galway. He is a multi-jurisdictionally qualified lawyer (Ireland, England and Wales and New York, USA), and has been involved in the provision of pro bono legal services. He, in conjunction with colleagues, founded the Middlesex University Legal Advice Centre (Mdx LAC) in 2014.

Lughaidh additionally has expertise in arbitration and mediation. He is a Fellow of the Chartered Institute of Arbitrators, whom he has examined for, as well as being a certified Mediator. He has a particular interest in sports arbitration and was appointed to the panel of Arbitrators of the Gaelic Athletic Association Dispute Resolution body, Disputes Resolution Authority (Córas Eadrána), in 2011.

The current focus of Lughaidh's research is legal education and diversity, well-being and resilience in the legal profession and among law students.

Rachel Spearing is Barrister at Serjeants' Inn Chambers in London. She has a wide civil and criminal practice covering Regulatory, Financial and Disciplinary Law. She co-founded the Well-being at the Bar Program with the General Council of the Bar, and has worked with leadership in the UK, Australia, Singapore and the US to implement culture change towards mental health and well-being in law. She is a Director of Wellness for Law UK a 'not for profit' organisation supporting charitable research, education and training for lawyers in the area of health and well-being.

Rachel holds Academic appointments as Fellow of the Dispute Resolution Centre at Bond University Australia, and is Senior Consultant to the Singapore Academy of Law. She is featured by 'The First Hundred Years' initiative as part of their 'pioneering women in law' series. Rachel sits on the executive of the General Council of the Bar. She is a Mediator, an active Trustee and NED of Charities and was appointed a Governing Bencher of the Honourable Society of the Inner Temple in 2015.

Caroline Strevens is Reader in Legal Education and Head of Department of Portsmouth Law School in the Faculty of Business and Law at the University of Portsmouth. Caroline's academic career was preceded by a career in legal practice as a Solicitor. She joined the University of Portsmouth in 2001 to establish the suite of qualifying law degrees and to expand the LLM programs and was appointed the first Head of Department when the School of Law was formed in 2008. Caroline takes on the role of Chair of the Association of Law Teachers in the spring of 2019.

Caroline's primary research area is legal education including experiential learning through simulation and through live client clinics and more recently she has been investigating how principles of positive psychology may influence well-being of staff and students in Higher Education. Her most recent publication is entitled 'Perceptions of Wellbeing in Law Teachers' has been published in the *Law Teacher*. Caroline continues to work with international collaborators investigating the well-being of law legal academics and junior lawyers.

Dr Stephen Tang is a lecturer at the ANU School of Legal Practice and an interdisciplinary scholar who applies psychological theory and methods – especially from clinical psychology, experimental psychology and decision science – to understand and reform legal regulation, legal education and the legal profession. Stephen has led quantitative and qualitative empirical work on projects investigating the psychological well-being and mental health of law students and lawyers. In addition to his legal qualifications, Stephen holds a PhD (Clinical Psychology) from the ANU Research School of Psychology. His research has included extensive psychometric research investigating personal and institutional factors associated with improved and impaired well-being (with Anneka Ferguson and A/Prof Molly Townes O'Brien). Stephen is also involved in a multi-stage project on the development of ethical professional identity and capability in newly admitted Australian lawyers (with Prof Tony Foley, A/Prof Vivien Holmes and Margie Rowe). With Prof Tony Foley, Stephen has been examining the positive role of uncertainty and ignorance in legal education and practice. He is also actively involved on research in emerging and interdisciplinary fields such as behavioural legal ethics, therapeutic jurisprudence, mental health law and empirical methods in legal regulation and evaluation.

Barry Yau has been a lecturer at the ANU School of Legal Practice since 2012, where he convenes Commercial Practice online to students based across Australia and internationally as they prepare for admission as Australian lawyers. Barry is also Senior Fellow of the Higher Education Academy. Since 2013 Barry has led a qualitative research project that is examining the attitudes and reflections of early career commercial lawyers, practical legal training students and undergraduate students relating to commercial and corporate law. The project is also researching the relationship of this area with legal ethics, wellness and work-life balance, and how these issues shape and influence the perceptions students and lawyers hold towards the study and practice of commercial law. Before joining the Australian National University full-time in 2012, Barry practised as a lawyer for over a decade in private and public practice, including a two-year stint as an Australian Volunteer Abroad lawyer in Papua New Guinea.

Preface

The practice of law is a noble endeavour contributing to peace and order in society, access to justice and the efficacy of our liberal democratic systems through upholding the rule of law. However, the work of lawyering is often complex, high stakes and requiring fine attention to detail and perfectionist traits. Lawyers must deal with difficult matters and difficult clients, always with an eye to what might go wrong, minimising risk and maximising the client's best interests. Practice is still very competitive and adversarial in many ways, and each day offers new ethical dilemmas for which there is often no clear-cut correct response. These are some of the reasons why legal practice will always be stressful and challenging. It is why we need to educate our new lawyers for well-being and inculcate in them positive professional identities and practices – helping them to enter the profession with the knowledge, skills and attitudes to cope with the inevitable stressors associated with lawyering in all its diverse forms.

The task of educating for well-being is made difficult however by the fact that law school itself is a stressful and challenging environment for both law students and legal academics alike. Knowledge and awareness in relation to wellness, legal education and the legal profession have grown significantly in recent years, and there is now a substantial body of scholarship in the US, Australia and the UK and beyond that evidences that concerns are justified about the high levels of psychological distress being experienced at law school, in the legal academy and in the legal profession.

This work contributes to that body of scholarship by bringing together international perspectives on educating for well-being in law in a volume that allows for comparisons across jurisdictions, so as to inform understandings of diverse ways to achieve excellent practice in the promotion of well-being in law. Our hope is that, in developing and taking forward the thinking on well-being for law, this work will make an important contribution to the future sustainability and relevance of both legal education and of professional legal practice. Our ultimate goal is to contribute to achieving the necessary structural and cultural change within the profession by starting with fundamental approaches to the efficacy of legal education.

The chapters of this work synthesise the current international body of knowledge on key issues for educating for well-being in law. Some chapters offer comparative teaching perspectives and techniques across different jurisdictions, others illustrate the range of theoretical lenses that are helpful in analysing well-being and the law (including socio-legal, psychological and ethical lenses), and others offer new empirical research data to inform strategies for educating for well-being. The chapters bring together common and opposing perspectives resulting in an original contribution to knowledge, and new discourses of analysis. We ask and seek to answer the question as to whether law is special in terms of producing psychological distress in law students and the profession, and also seek to highlight excellent practice in the promotion of well-being.

This book provides a useful resource to anyone wishing to understand the complex issues and challenges in terms of educating for well-being in law, including the development and maintenance of a positive professional identity for lawyers. The book has relevance for the global legal profession, including students of law, legal academics, the practising profession and the judiciary across a range of jurisdictions. In particular, the book will be valuable for legal academics who seek to apply theories of legal pedagogy in practically purposeful ways that will work to support the well-being of their students, and consequently, of the profession. Through the use of concrete examples, the book offers suggestions for change based on proven practice in the field. More broadly our hope is that this book will be of interest to anyone, including students, with an interest in positive psychology, ethics and experiential learning.

Acknowledgements

We dedicate this book to our colleagues in the Wellness Networks for Law in the UK and Australia who are passionately committed to addressing and alleviating the distress experienced by law students and legal practitioners, and work enthusiastically, positively and collegially to put in place initiatives at law school and in the profession to promote well-being. We honour all those who take a leadership role on this issue, who have the courage to speak out and call boldly for the institutional, professional, structural, cultural and societal changes that are necessary for well-being, and for educating for well-being, to be possible. We commend those who model resilience and coping skills by actively maintaining their well-being and making psychological health a priority in their lives.

We acknowledge the predecessor to this work – *Promoting Law Student and Lawyer Well-Being in Australia and Beyond* (Routledge, 2016) by Rachael Field, James Duffy and Colin James – and the important contribution to the scholarship on well-being in law made by the chapter authors of that book. We thank the professional societies and associations in both the UK and Australia for their growing commitment to the promotion of well-being for legal practitioners. We particularly want to thank Marie and George Jepson who founded the Tristan Jepson Memorial Foundation (now Minds Count) for their significant contribution to the field in honour of their son Tristan.

Each of the chapters in the book was blind peer-reviewed and we thank the reviewers for their generosity in giving their time and expertise to this work.

On a personal level we thank our families for their unquestioning and enduring love and support without which this work would not have eventuated. Caroline particularly thanks Brian, Harry, Alice and Joe; and Rachael particularly thanks Hiro, Hugo, Oscar, Barbara, Terry and Anna.

1 The ethics of well-being

Psychological health as the vanguard for sociological change

Colin James

Introduction

The discourse on well-being of lawyers and law students over recent decades is advanced and robust and has enjoyed support within most of the legal profession and academia. For more than a decade, researchers have evidenced issues for concern, criticised current practices in legal education and legal practice, and lobbied for changes towards best practice in sustaining and enhancing the overall well-being of law students and lawyers.[1] Several critiques of the wellness discourse have provided opportunities for pause and reflection on the goals and validity of the claims made. Baron for example argues the 'well-being movement' has been duped by the 'dominant neoliberal discourse' into shielding law firms from responsibility for the experience of their employed lawyers, locating blame for each individual's experience at their own feet, so that 'the structural causes of depression and distress, including public policies that undermine people's wellbeing, are not addressed'.[2] Parker agreed, saying the wellness discourse may have been co-opted by 'powerful interests' to keep the focus on individuals and their failure to cope rather than important socio-political questions and opportunities for system and institutional change. The focus on 'resilience' for example

1 Judy Allen and Paula Baron, 'Buttercup Goes to Law School: Student Wellbeing in Stressed Law Schools' (2004) 29 *Alternative Law Journal* 285, 287; Norm Kelk et al., *Courting the Blues: Attitudes towards Depression in Australian Law Students and Lawyers* (Brain and Mind Research Institute, 2009); Minds Count https://mindscount.org/ (formerly Tristan Jepson Memorial Foundation www.tjmf.org.au/) accessed 7 May 2019; Wellness Network for Law <http://wellnessforlaw.com/> accessed 7 May 2019; Sharon Medlow, Norm Kelk and Ian Hickie, 'Depression and the Law: Experiences of Australian Barristers and Solicitors' (2011) 33 *Sydney Law Review* 771; Molly Townes O'Brien, Stephen Tang and Kath Hall, 'No Time to Lose: Negative Impact on Law Student Wellbeing May Begin in Year One' (2011) 2(2) *The International Journal of the First Year in Higher Education* 49; Wendy Larcombe and Katherine Fethers, 'Schooling the Blues? An Investigation of Factors Associated with Psychological Distress Among Law Students' (2013) 36(2) *UNSW Law Journal* 1; Rachael Field, James Duffy and Colin James (eds), *Promoting Law Student and Lawyer Wellbeing in Australia and Beyond* (2016, Routledge).

2 Paula Baron, 'Sleight of Hand: Lawyer Distress and the Attribution of Responsibility' (2014) 23(2) *Griffith Law Review* 261, 280.

reflects the 'over-individualising and medicalising [of] more serious, social, economic and political problems in the legal profession and legal ethics'.[3] Parker also argued that some of the wellness discourse publications show methodological limitations and that there is no clear evidence of a 'well-being crisis' among law students compared to the rest of the population.[4]

Similarly, Margaret Thornton has contributed a series of articles that amount to a withering critique of neoliberalism, exposing its effects on law students and lawyers and alleging it has been eagerly adopted by universities.[5] Deepening the critiques of the well-being movement, Thornton claims that 'the individualisation of psychological distress effectively deflects attention away from the neoliberal agenda'[6], which privileges a new form of 'hypermasculinity' in the focus on power, acquisitiveness and competitiveness.[7] Thornton condemns the 'neoliberal turn', which she describes as a sharp move to the right in politics, which 'insidiously transformed higher education from a public to a private good',[8] departing from the egalitarian values of social liberalism.[9] In legal practice, many workplaces offer flexible work arrangements but often the milieu or stigma discourages lawyers from accessing them.[10] Thornton notes that instead of improving the conditions for lawyers, some law firms provide legal staff with free counselling services or 'resilience' training.[11] In legal education, universities, like big business, accept the pursuit of profit as the new common sense.[12] Similarly critical of the system,

3 Christine Parker, 'The "Moral Panic" Over Psychological Wellbeing in the Legal Profession: A Personal or Political Ethical Response' (2014) 37(3) *UNSW Law Journal* 1103, 1107.

4 Ibid 1104. Parker makes three broad claims: that psychological distress scales have been misused to create clinical categorisations, that studies use non-representative sampling, and that studies claim evidence of law school and legal practice experience causes depression. Specifically, Parker claims the well-being discourse falsely concludes lawyers and law students suffer clinical depression disproportionately to the general population, and that it is caused by 'the traditional adversarial idea of legal professionalism in practice and education' (1104), that errors are produced by 'slippage' in language (1115), exaggeration in conclusions (1116), non-representative sampling (1116), commercial bias in selecting participant groups (1118), self-selection bias in surveys (1119), and causation bias (1120).

5 Margaret Thornton, 'Law Student Wellbeing: A Neoliberal Conundrum' (2016) 58(2) *Australian Universities Review* 42; Margaret Thornton, 'Squeezing the Life Out of Lawyers: Legal Practice in the Market Embrace' (2016) 25(4) *Griffith Law Review* 1; Margaret Thornton, 'Work/Life or Work/Work? Corporate Legal Practice in the 21st Century' (2016) 23(1) *International Journal of the Legal Profession* 2.

6 Thornton, 'Law Student Wellbeing' (n 5) 42.

7 Margaret Thornton, 'Hypercompetitiveness or a Balanced Life? Gendered Discourses in the Globalisation of Australian Law Firms' (2014) 17(2) *Legal Ethics* 153, 156; See also Margaret Thornton, *Privatising the Public University: The Case of Law* (Routledge, 2012).

8 Thornton, 'Law Student Wellbeing' (n 5) 43.

9 Ibid 44.

10 Thornton, 'Work/Life' (n 5) 12–15.

11 Ibid. The Law Society of New South Wales set up a counselling service for its members rather than discussing or acting to address causes of distress such as overwork, discrimination and bullying in law firms. Leanne Mezrani, 'Lawyers Get a Lifeline' *Lawyers Weekly* (26 June 2014).

12 Thornton, 'Law Student Wellbeing' (n 5) 44; Thornton refers to the Vice Chancellors in Australia who were almost unanimous in accepting the government's suggestion of fee

Richard Collier and Hilary Sommerlad claim that legal education pushes graduates into a practice that maximises workloads and competition in the pursuit of profits, leaving lawyers with little control in their lives and no hope for security in the future.[13]

In legal practice under neoliberalism therefore, individuals must care for themselves. Law firms are authorised to consider employed lawyers dispensable and their well-being a superfluous cost, because profitability has become legitimised as their sole purpose. The buy-off for the individual under neoliberalism is 'autonomy', but not in the sense of self-determination theory that aligns it with competence and connecting with others in shared enterprises.[14] Here, autonomy is the 'freedom' to accept or reject the job, and with it the harsh realities of long hours, aggressive billing and a competitive atmosphere.[15] The method, drawing on Foucault, has led to individual lawyers being under increased surveillance and control with competitive billing practices using electronic time recording and monitoring of performance, misnamed as 'productivity'.[16]

In defence of methodology

Rather than striving for mathematical precision, many quantitative studies are limited by statistical representations and practical and ethical restrictions on recruitment. Reports typically acknowledge their limitations and authors are often careful not to make claims outside their evidence.[17] In addition, many

---

deregulation in the pursuit of higher profits; Stephen Parker, 'Vice Chancellor of Canberra University, ABC' *Radio National Sunday Profile* (26 April, 2015).

13 Richard Collier, '"Love Law, Love Life": Neoliberalism, Wellbeing and Gender in the Legal Profession – The Case of Law School' (2014) 17(2) *Legal Ethics* 202; Hilary Sommerlad, 'The Commercialisation of Law and the Enterprising Legal Practitioner: Continuity and Change' (2011) 18 *International Journal of the Legal Profession* 73.

14 Edward L Deci and Richard M Ryan, 'Self-determination Theory: When Mind Mediates Behavior' (1980) 1(1) *Journal of Mind & Behavior* 33.

15 Christine Parker and David Ruschena, 'The Pressures of Billable Hours: Lessons From a Survey of Billing Practices Inside Law Firms' (2011) 9(2) *University of St. Thomas Law Journal* 619; Susan Saab Fortney, 'I Don't Have Time to Be Ethical: Addressing the Effects of Billable Hour Pressure' (2003) 39 *Idaho Law Review* 305.

16 Lois McNay, 'Self as Enterprise: Dilemmas of Control and Resistance in Foucault's the Birth of Biopolitics' (2009) 26(6) *Theory, Culture & Society* 56; Colin James, 'Legal Practice on Time: The Ethical Risk and Inefficiency of the Six-Minute Unit' (2017) 42(1) *Alternative Law Journal* 61; Maryam Omari and Megan Paull, '"Shut Up and Bill": Workplace Bullying Challenges for the Legal Profession' (2013) 20(2) *International Journal of the Legal Profession* 141.

17 For example, without attempting to comprehensively list the limitations acknowledged in the well-being discourse, O'Brien states 'While there are many possible reasons that law school may increase psychological distress, this chapter will focus on what students cited in dialogue as their grievances': Molly Townes O'Brien, 'Connecting Law Students to Health and Wellbeing' in Field, Duffy and James (n 1); also 'Direct comparisons cannot be made, as the two groups were from different cohorts' from O'Brien, Tang and Hall (n 1) 55; 'Notwithstanding the limitations of the study design, the findings from the present study make an

reports confirm that law is in fact a 'special case' in posing a greater risk for individuals than in other professions. Several cross-sectional studies evidence that law students do experience higher levels of psychological distress than other students.[18] While students in other professions can experience high stress, including medical students,[19] arts and veterinary students,[20] and psychology students,[21] only in the legal profession do studies repeatedly show the vulnerability may continue through university to graduation and into professional practice.[22] In a study suggesting otherwise by Larcombe and colleagues at Melbourne Law School, the authors point out several demographic indicators that limit the significance of that conclusion.[23] Some researchers have moved on from quantitative and descriptive analyses and many now explore causation and solutions.[24] For

---

important contribution to the developing evidence base', from Larcombe and Fethers (n 1) 25; Kelk states 'It is important to note here the nature of the measures of depression, distress and other mental illnesses used in this survey . . . the K-10 and SPHERE surveys do not lead to a diagnosis of depression or any other mental illness': Kelk et al. (n 1) 'Courting the Blues' 6; according to Norm Kelk, Sharon Medlow and Ian Hickie in 'Distress and Depression among Australian Law Students: Incidence, Attitudes and the Role of Universities' (2010) 32 *Sydney Law Review* 113: 'It remains to be seen whether stress, in both the presence and absence of depression, is or is not a significant problem among this (law student) population', 121; and according to Beaton Consulting and Beyond Blue: 'It is important to note that high scores on the depression scale (i.e. moderate or severe) would not alone indicate a clinical diagnosis of depression, further assessment would be required', in 'Mental Health in the Workplace: A Joint Initiative Between Beaton Research & Consulting and BeyondBlue', <https://tinyurl.com/y8uq658o> accessed 7 May 2019.

18 For example, Catherine Leahy et al., 'Distress Levels and Self-Reported Treatment Rates for Medicine, Law, Psychology and Mechanical Engineering Tertiary Students: Cross-Sectional Study' (2010) 44 *Australian and New Zealand Journal of Psychiatry* 608, where law students reported the highest proportion of psychological distress at 58%, compared with the all-student average level of 44%.

19 Ibid.

20 Wendy Larcombe, Sue Finch and Rachel Sore, 'Who's Distressed? Not Only Law Students: Psychological Distress Levels in University Students Across Diverse Fields of Study' (2015) 37 *Sydney Law Review* 243.

21 Nabil Hassan El-Ghoroury et al., 'Stress, Coping, and Barriers to Wellness Among Psychology Graduate Students' (2012) 6(2) *Training and Education in Professional Psychology* 122.

22 Christopher Kendall, *Report on Psychological Distress and Depression in the Legal Profession* (The Law Society of Western Australia, 2011); Adele J Bergin and Nerina L Jimmieson, 'Australian Lawyer Well-being: Workplace Demands, Resources and the Impact of Time-billing Targets' (2014) *Psychiatry, Psychology and Law* 427; Omari and Paull (n 16).

23 Larcombe, Finch and Sore (n 20). The authors acknowledged that i) law students at Melbourne University are post-graduates, making them older on average than many of the comparison undergraduates in the other schools, ii) 28% of the non-law participants were caring for family members while studying compared with only 17% of law students, and iii) 20% of non-law participants spoke a language other than English at home, compared with only 8% of law students.

24 Sally Kift and Rachael Field, 'Addressing the High Levels of Psychological Distress in Law Students Through Intentional Assessment and Feedback Design in the First Year Law Curriculum' (2010) 1 *The International Journal of the First Year in Higher Education* 65; David Jaffe et al., 'The Path to Lawyer Wellbeing – Recommendations for Positive Change (The

example, several studies have identified causal connections between legal education and practice and mental health concerns.[25]

Rather than a 'moral panic' law schools should examine the research and respond appropriately, including to the possibility of a legal risk if they do not act effectively to inform and protect students in their care.[26] In legal practice, the main offenders are large corporate firms that prioritise profits and benefit from their privileged position in the neoliberal economy. Clearly law firms have not only participated in Western society's neoliberal turn but fuelled and defended it.[27] However, the critique against 'big law' is not new and the reputation of some firms and their senior partners suffered significantly from ethical and legal breaches in the late 20th century.[28]

Some authors have observed that 'moral panic theorists' are quick to construct sociological critiques, but slow to present strategic interventions.[29] The critiques of the well-being discourse have side-stepped serious questions: If not through informed, empowered and resilient individuals, how can neoliberalism be challenged? Parker's nod to legal ethics as being 'most helpful in addressing discontent' could be the start of a discussion, but as a strategy for real change, it

---

Report of the NTF on Lawyer Well-being), Part II Recommendations for Law Schools' (2017) Washington College of Law Research Paper No 2017–19.

25 Rebecca Michalak, *Causes and Consequences of Work – Related Psychosocial Risk Exposure. A Comparative Investigation of Organisational Context, Employee Attitudes, Job Performance and Wellbeing in Lawyers and Non-Lawyer Professionals* (PsychSafe Ltd, 2015); Lawrence S Krieger and Kennon M Sheldon, 'What Makes Lawyers Happy: A Data Driven Prescription to Redefine Professional Success' (2015) 85 *The George Washington Law Review* 554; Orygen, *Under the Radar: The Mental Health of Australian University Students* (The National Centre of Excellence in Youth Mental Health, 2017).

26 For example, law schools have an ethical, fiduciary and legal duty to 'do no harm' through legal education according to Penelope Watson and Rachael Field, 'Promoting Student Well-being and Resilience at Law School' in Sally Kift et al. (eds), *Excellence and Innovation in Legal Education* (LexisNexis, 2011) 390–419, 395; Peter Handford, 'Liability for Work Stress: Koehler Ten Years On' (2017) University of Western Australia – Faculty of Law Research Paper.

27 Daniel Stedman Jones, *Masters of the Universe: Hayek, Friedman and the Birth of Neoliberal Politics* (Princeton University Press, 2014); John Story, Graeme Salaman and Kerry Platman, 'Living with Enterprise in an Enterprise Economy: Freelance and Contract Workers in the Media' (2005) 58(8) *Human Relations* 103; Susan Halford and Leonard Pauline, 'Place, Space and Time: Contextual Workplace Subjectivities' (2006) 27(5) *Organization Studies* 657.

28 Dan Ackman, 'Enron's Lawyers: Eyes Wide Shut?' (2002) *Forbes* <https://tinyurl.com/y7ynay8p> accessed 7 May 2019; Mark Westfield, *HIH: The Inside Story of Australia's Biggest Corporate Collapse* (John Wiley, 2003); Ben Hills, 'Sins of the Fathers' (2004) *Sydney Morning Herald*, 2 October; William Birnbauer, 'I Helped Tobacco Firm Destroy Documents: Lawyer' *The Age* (Melbourne, 26 September 2004); Philippe Sands, 'Torture Team: The Responsibility of Lawyers for Abusive Interrogation' (2008) 9 *Melbourne Journal of International Law* 365; Christine Parker, Suzanne Le Mire and Anita Mackay, 'Lawyers, Confidentiality and Whistleblowing: Lessons from the McCabe Tobacco Litigation' (2018) 40 *Melbourne University Law Review* 999.

29 Catharine Lumby and Nina Funnell, 'Between Heat and Light: The Opportunity in Moral Panics' (2011) 7(3) *Crime Media Culture* 277.

could only happen through students, researchers and lawyers who are fit in body, competent, self-aware, emotionally informed and psychologically resilient.

Resilience is about meaning

Resilience, according to some wellness critics, is a 'right winger's ploy'[30] where 'each individual is held responsible and accountable for his or her own actions and wellbeing'.[31] They restrict the concept to 'bouncing back' from adversity and merely surviving the harsh realities of contemporary legal practice.[32] In fact, the wellness discourse engages resilience broadly, with rich capacities not merely to survive difficult experiences and harsh conditions but to identify and resist ethical challenges, to recognise opportunities for change and improvement and to challenge inequalities, bullying and unfair practices.[33]

Central to resilience is a lawyer's sense of meaning and purpose.[34] Best practice legal education helps students identify and develop this capacity with opportunities to practice mindfulness, to reflect and articulate sincere answers to powerful questions, such as 'Why am I studying law?' and 'How do I see myself being described upon my retirement?'[35] Reflection is the key. Although students' responses to such questions may change as they develop, their self-awareness generated by the reflective process can promote a resilient quality in their professional identity, empowering more intrinsic values and enabling them to be less tolerant of unethical situations and more likely to challenge them. As one researcher observed:

> Reflective capacity is a crucial enabler of innovative thinking, and it undergirds approaches to encouraging individual and systems change emerging from the organizational learning and innovation literature.[36]

30 Vlad Mykhnenko, 'Resilience. A Right-Wingers' Ploy?' in Vlad Mykhnenko, *Handbook of Neoliberalism* (Routledge, 2016) 190.

31 David Harvey, *A Brief History of Neoliberalism* (Oxford, 2005) 65; Matthew Ball, 'Self-Government and the Fashioning of Resilient Personae: Legal Education, Criminal Justice, and the Government of Mental Health' (2011) 23(1) *Current Issues in Criminal Justice* 97.

32 Yu Niiya, Jennifer Crocker and Elizabeth N Bartmess, 'From Vulnerability to Resilience: Learning Orientations Buffer Contingent Self-esteem from Failure' (2004) 15(12) *Psychological Science* 801.

33 Penelope Watson, 'Using Peer Assisted Learning to Develop Resilient and Resourceful Learners' in Field, Duffy and James (n 1); Colin James, 'Resilient Lawyers: Maximising Well-being in Legal Education and Practice' in Field, Duffy and James (n 1); Prue Vines, 'Working Towards the Resilient Lawyer: Early Law School Strategies' (Conference Paper presented at the First Year Experience Conference, Gold Coast, 2 July 2011).

34 Bruner argues forcefully how meaning is not found but constructed in what we do, our processes and transactions: Jerome S Bruner, *Acts of Meaning* (Harvard University Press, 1990).

35 Scott Rogers, 'The Mindful Law School: An Integrative Approach to Transforming Legal Education' (2012) 28 *Touro Law Review* 1189; Mike Myatt, 'The 50 Most Powerful Questions Leaders Can Ask' *Forbes Leadership* (12 June 2016).

36 Michele L Leering, 'Enhancing the Legal Profession's Capacity for Innovation: The Promise of Reflectice Practice and Action Research for Increasing Access to Justice' (2017) 34(1) *Windsor Yearbook of Access to Justice* 189.

Encouraging students to reflect positively, supported by supervision and without ruminating, can enhance awareness of their personal and professional strengths, including their values and ideals. We create meaning by identifying our values in the context of experience and then we choose how to act. Guided mindfulness practice helps students learn to appreciate the benefits of identifying their *intrinsic* motivations and moments of meaningfulness during their day (see also Chapter 12). They benefit from opportunities to critique inequities and discover their power to speak up and to act. Reflecting on these experiences informs their development as well as their career decisions as graduates about where and how they work and the extent they accept the conditions of their employment or plan to change them. On the other hand, without a positive reflective capacity, research suggests lawyers may be less resilient, motivated by extrinsic rewards and risk avoidance, and *pretend* their work is meaningful which can be harmful both to the lawyers themselves and their clients.[37]

Many authors have shown how individuals can identify and develop their own sense of meaning as a crucial part of their professional development.[38] In the US, law schools have been urged from both within and outside the legal academy to inculcate in students a sense of professional identity and purpose.[39] One suggestion is to shift emphasis from the vague notion of values and motivate the courage in students to develop specific ideals, such as justice, beauty, goodness and truth: 'Ideals have enormous power. They give you the strength to resist the seductions of status and wealth and success'.[40] Others have found meaning arises from contemplative practices such as supported reflection that not only helps to overcome anxiety from legal study and practice, it improves self-awareness by identifying individual values, intrinsic motivations and personal priorities.[41]

A resilient lawyer is not necessarily insensitive, 'thick skinned' or indifferent to the rigours of assertive legal practice (see also Chapter 11). A truly resilient

37 Catherine Bailey et al., 'The Mismanaged Soul: Existential Labor and the Erosion of Meaningful Work' (2016) 27(3) *Human Resource Management Review* 416; according to Rachel Clements, 'It's a challenge within the profession to really destigmatize mental and physical ill-health. . . . It has definitely shifted a huge amount, but it can shift a lot more.' Quoted in Dominic Rolfe, 'The Human Cost of Corporate Life' (2018) 41 *Law Society Journal* 37, 39.

38 Jeff Goins, *The Art of Work: A Proven Path to Discovering What You Were Meant to Do* (Nelson Books, 2015); Christian Helms Jorgensen, 'The Role of Meaning of Vocations in the Transition from Education to Work' (2013) 11(2) *International Journal of Training Research* 166; Tom Godwin, 'We Need to Teach Our Children to Dream' *GQ Magazine* (12 January 2017); Dan P McAdams, 'The Psychological Self as Actor, Agent and Author' (2013) 8 *Psychological Science* 272.

39 Roy Stuckey et al., *Best Practices for Legal Education: A Vision and A Road Map* (CLEA, 2007); William M Sullivan et al., *Educating Lawyers: Preparation for the Profession of Law* (Jossey-Bass, 2007).

40 William Deresiewicz, *Excellent Sheep: The Misdirection of the American Elite and the Way to a Meaningful Life* (Free Press, 2014) 103.

41 Prue Vines and Patricia Morgan, 'Contemplative Practice in the Law School: Breaking Barriers to Learning and Resilience' in Field, Duffy and James (n 1) 169.

lawyer may be a sensitive person, not in the sense of fragile, but able to recognise nuance and meaning that others fail to see and may therefore be enabled to initiate change, to speak up against discrimination, to call-out unfair billing practices and to resist a client's instructions to threaten a commercial competitor. In this richer sense, resilience implies self-awareness and enables an enhanced motivation for fairness and equality.[42] Brene Brown describes the resilient qualities of *vulnerability*, which might be counter-intuitive for some, but are born of self-awareness and compassion in an individual and is demonstrated by the best and most courageous leaders.[43]

Many Australian studies have emphasised the importance of developing resilience through self-awareness, to help students understand why they are studying law, to identify the signs of anxiety and depression and to discover how they can respond.[44] As legal practice evolves with new technological systems and automation, resilient lawyers are adapting by enhancing their 'human' abilities in communication, compassion and emotional intelligence.[45] As lawyers develop their professional identity within a connected community, the more they can leverage their values and sense of purpose in choosing where and how they practice, and how effective they will be in bringing change about.

Achievements of the well-being movement in legal education and practice

In the US, Susan Daicoff, one of the earliest proponents of law student well-being, argued in 1997 that the legal profession was experiencing a 'tripartite crisis' involving de-professionalism, low public opinion of lawyers and lawyer distress.[46] Similarly, Larry Krieger drew on research to conclude that law students and lawyers should focus on intrinsic values, which will not only enhance their personal well-being but also their performance, achievements and professional success as a lawyer.[47] Daisy Hurst Floyd argued that after students begin law

42 Colin James, 'Law Student Wellbeing: Benefits of Promoting Psychological Literacy and Self-Awareness Using Mindfulness, Strengths Theory and Emotional Intelligence' (2011) 21 *Legal Education Review* 217.

43 Brene Brown, *Daring Greatly: How the Courage to Be Vulnerable Transforms the Way We Live, Love, Parent, and Lead* (Avery, 2015).

44 James (n 42); Vines and Morgan (n 41); Tania Leiman, 'Building Resilient Professionals in an Age of Automation', Paper presented at the National Wellness for Law Forum: Rehumanising the Law and Legal Education, Adelaide Law School, February 2017; Watson and Field (n 26) 389.

45 Thomas D Barton, 'Re-Designing Law and Lawyering for the Information Age' (2016) 30 *Notre Dame Journal of Law, Ethics & Public Policy* 1; Alexander Ross Davis, 'Rage Against the Machines: Artificial Intelligence and the Future of Legal Practice' (2017) 15 *Thomson Reuters: Legal Insight* (online); Melissa Coade, 'Modern-day Lawyers Have Evolved to Become So Much More' *Lawyers Weekly* (8 March 2018).

46 Susan Daicoff, 'Lawyer, Know Thyself: A Review of Empirical Research on Attorney Attributes Bearing on Professionalism' (1997) 46 *American University Law Review* 1337.

47 Lawrence S Krieger, 'What We're Not Telling Law Students – and Lawyers – That They Really Need to Know: Some Thoughts-in-Action Toward Revitalizing the Profession From

school, many lose their sense of purpose, leaving them open to accepting unfulfilling work conditions because they think there is no option.[48] Marjorie A Silver maintained how emotional intelligence is essential for good lawyering and that it could be cultivated in law schools.[49] Silver drew on the work of Salovey and Mayer to show how lawyers' ability to perceive emotions is a motivating factor for purposeful activity,[50] and the work of Antonio Damasio to demonstrate lawyers' rational decision-making is related to their emotional awareness.[51] In the Introduction to *The Affective Assistance of Counsel*, Silver observed:

> The lawyer's navigational tool kit should include basic knowledge about psychology and emotions. Just as important, though, are self-awareness and self-care, without which we might lose our way. Although few of us received any training about such matters in law school, there is reason for optimism that this is changing.[52]

Since then the well-being discourse has contributed to developments in legal practice including community lawyering,[53] therapeutic jurisprudence,[54] restorative community justice partnerships,[55] and health-justice partnerships[56] which

---

Its Roots' (1998) 13(1) *Journal of Law and Health* 1; see also Lawrence S Krieger, *The Hidden Sources of Law School Stress* (Lawrence S Krieger, 2006).

48 Daisy Hurst Floyd, 'Reclaiming Purpose: Our Students' and Our Own' (2003) 10 *The Law Teacher* 1.

49 Marjorie A Silver, 'Emotional Intelligence and Legal Education' (1999) 5(4) *Psychology, Public Policy and Law* 1173. See also Felicity Wardhaugh and Colin James, 'A Client-Focused Practice: Developing and Testing Emotional Competency in Clinical Legal Interviews' (2014) 20 *International Journal of Clinical Legal Education* 633.

50 Silver (n 49) 1181. Peter Salovey and John D Mayer, 'Emotional Intelligence' (1990) 9(3) *Imagination, Cognition and Personality* 185.

51 Silver (n 49) 1181. Antonio R Damasio, *Descartes' Error: Emotion, Reason and the Human Brain* (Putnam GP, 1996).

52 Silver wrote this introduction after interviewing lawyers who had volunteered to work with survivors of the September 11 attacks in New York. Marjorie A Silver, 'Emotional Competence and the Lawyer's Journey' in Marjorie A Silver (ed), *The Affective Assistance of Counsel: Practicing Law as a Healing Profession* (Carolina Academic Press, 2007) 51.

53 Karen Tokarz et al., 'Conversations on "Community Lawyering": The Newest (Oldest) Wave in Clinical Legal Education' (2008) 28 *Washington University Journal of Law & Policy* 359.

54 David Wexler, *Rehabilitating Lawyers: Principles of Therapeutic Jurisprudence for Criminal Law Practice* (Carolina Academic Press, 2008); David B Wexler, 'TJ Across the Law School Curriculum' (2011) Discussion Paper No. 11–17 Arizona Legal Studies.

55 Susan L Brooks and Rachel E Lopez, 'Designing a Clinic Model for a Restorative Community Justice Partnership' (2015) 48 *Washington University Journal of Law & Policy* 139; Jacqueline Joudo Larsen, 'Restorative Justice in the Australian Criminal Justice System' (2014) 127 *Research and Public Policy Series* v; Tony Foley, *Developing Restorative Justice Jurisprudence: Rethinking Responses to Criminal Wrongdoing, International and Comparative Criminal Justice* (Routledge, 2016).

56 Liz Curran, *Health-Justice Partnership Development Report* (Victorian Legal Services Commissioner, 2016) <http://lsbc.vic.gov.au/?p=5002> accessed 7 May 2019; Liz Curran, *Evaluation of the RLC's Health Justice Partnership with Royal Prince Alfred Hospital* (Redfern Legal Centre, 2015) <https://tinyurl.com/ybcjzf2a> accessed 7 May 2019.

help skill students in a range of alternatives to mainstream legal dispute resolution such as mediation, appreciative inquiry and 'generative' dialogue.[57]

The well-being discourse has achieved mainstream recognition and its influence continues to grow. Law schools, law firms and workplaces, as well as law societies and bar associations now take well-being seriously and are introducing new policies and practices to enhance the well-being of lawyers and law students. In Australia, in addition to the Best Practice Guidelines published by Minds Count (formerly the Tristan Jepson Memorial Foundation)[58] and the National Wellness for Law Forum annual meetings,[59] there are significant publications and resources by law schools and universities,[60] law societies,[61] bar associations,[62] regulatory bodies,[63] and the judiciary.[64] Specific topics are numerous but include vicarious trauma,[65] drug use,[66] burnout,[67] bullying,[68] and alcoholism.[69] One impact of this

57 Lisa Lynn McCorquodale, 'Mindfulness and Professional Practice: A Generative Dialogue' (2015) 16(2) *Reflective Practice* 230.

58 Minds Count (n 1), TJMF Workplace Wellbeing: Best Practice Guidelines for the Legal Profession (ND) <http://mindscount.org/wp-content/uploads/TJMF-Legal-Workplace-Guidelines.pdf> accessed 7 May 2019.

59 Wellness Network for Law <http://wellnessforlaw.com/> accessed 7 May 2019.

60 See for example, Field, Duffy and James (n 1). Rachael Field, 'Wellness Education Vital to Future of Legal Profession' (February, 2018) *Bond University* Law Faculty News <https://tinyurl.com/y9hglbve> accessed 7 May 2019; ANU College of Law, 'Wellbeing and Support' <https://tinyurl.com/yca6qejw> accessed 7 May 2019; ANU Coffee Courses, Day 1: Student Wellbeing, <https://tinyurl.com/y7uh5hbx> accessed 7 May 2019; Melbourne University, 'Enhancing Student Wellbeing' <http://unistudentwellbeing.edu.au/> accessed 7 May 2019; Macquarie University, <https://tinyurl.com/ybod8sk3> accessed 7 May 2019; Monash University <https://tinyurl.com/y8lhjevt> accessed 7 May 2019.

61 The Law Society of NSW Young Lawyers, *How to Survive & Thrive in Your First Year of Law: A Realistic Guide to the Study and Practice of Law* (NSW Young Lawyers, 2010); Laura Helm, *Mental Health and the Legal Profession: A Preventative Strategy* (Law Institute of Victoria, 2014); The Law Society of South Australia, *Well-Being and Resilience Online Program* <https://tinyurl.com/y9vv7d3p> accessed 7 May 2019; Tony Foley et al., *Being Well in the Law: A Guide for Lawyers* (The Law Society of New South Wales, 2016).

62 NSW Bar Association, 'Wellbeing at the Bar' <https://tinyurl.com/ydhf8sgm> accessed 7 May 2019.

63 Law Council of Australia, *Policy Agenda: Mental Health and Wellbeing in the Legal Profession* <https://tinyurl.com/yahg2mso> accessed 7 May 2019.

64 Judicial College of Victoria <https://tinyurl.com/y9fyfu6b> accessed 7 May 2019.

65 Anna Verney, 'Lessons on Vicarious Trauma and Wellbeing from a Royal Commission' (2018) *Law Society Journal* 41, 26; Colin James, 'Vicarious Trauma in Legal Practice', Paper presented to the Wellness for Law Forum (2018) *Bond University Faculty of Law*, 15–16 February 2018.

66 Alan Sinclair, 'The Major Drug Problem of the Legal Profession in Australia' (2015) *Safework Laboratories* (10 November) <https://tinyurl.com/ycjj8xl8> accessed 7 May 2019.

67 Thea O'Connor, 'Are You Burning Out' (2018) *LSJ: Law Society of NSW Journal* 41; Randall B Christison Attorney at Law, 'Burnout: A Necessary Part of Lawyers' Lives?' *Wolf Management Consultants, LLC Newsletter* <https://tinyurl.com/y7atmf4x> accessed 7 May 2019.

68 Suzanne Le Mire, 'Addressing Bullying in the Australian Legal Profession' (2015) 18 *Legal Ethics* 69.

69 Mark Abernathy, 'Combating Alcohol Problems in the Legal Industry' (2016) *Australasian Lawyer* (14 July) <https://tinyurl.com/y96xpgwv> accessed 7 May 2019.

growing discourse has been to expose the risks as foreseeable, which is helping employers understand and accept they have a duty of care to their employed lawyers. According to Anna-Louise Bouvier: 'As employers, the risks associated with work practices that have long been considered "acceptable" in legal firms may no longer be so'.[70] According to one industrial law expert:

> Aside from good practice, it's an extension of the fact that an employer must ensure, so far as is reasonably practicable, the health and safety (and welfare) of employees. That necessarily entails having these types of training and services provided, because the risks are plainly foreseeable.[71]

Change from the bottom up

As neoliberalism fades as the dominant explanatory theme for business, many lawyers will continue to feign selfless objectivity and participate in its defence. However, as legal education adopts more reflective and transformative practices, graduates will emerge more informed and developed, motivated to make a difference and have a meaningful life. These lawyers will be key to broader changes, using their courage, enhanced sense of meaning and resilience to engage justice systems, challenge inequity and lobby for fairness and reforms to market-dominated structures. The opposition to reform will of course be well-resourced, so lawyers will need to envisage a different future.[72] Most importantly, lawyers will need to be psychologically competent, aware of their personal strengths, values and ideals, resilient, curious and courageous.

Law schools have a big role to play in the coming changes through curriculum design and teaching methods and strategies as development opportunities. Individually, students will continue to critique or model teachers, adopting or rejecting their approach to legal practice and the need for change.[73] Clinical legal education with real or simulated clients is most effective in helping students develop their resilience and professional identity, and there is likely no doctrinal subject that can't be improved with a clinical or experiential component.[74] Exposing students

70 Anna-Louise Bouvier, quoted in Rolfe (n 37) 37.

71 Jack de Flamingh, quoted in Rolfe (n 37) 38.

72 World Economic Forum, *The Future of Jobs: Employment, Skills and Workforce Strategy for the Fourth Industrial Revolution* (World Economic Forum, 2016) ('WEF Report') 54; Kate Galloway, 'Disrupted Law Degree: Future Competencies for Legal Service Delivery' (17 July 2017) SSRN electronic journal: <https://tinyurl.com/yddvypx4> accessed 7 May 2019.

73 Marjorie A Silver, 'Commitment and Responsibility: Modeling and Teaching Professionalism Pervasively' (2004) 14 *Widener Law Journal* 329.

74 Adrian Evans and Ross Hyams, 'Independent Evaluations of Clinical Legal Education Programs: Appropriate Objectives and Processes in an Australian Setting' (2008) 17(1) *Griffith Law Review* 52; David F Chavkin, 'Experience Is the Only Teacher: Bringing Practice to the Teaching of Ethics' in Michael Robertson et al. (eds), *The Ethics Project in Legal Education* (Taylor and Francis, 2010); Leah Wortham et al. (eds), *Learning from Practice: A Text for Experiential Legal Education* (West Academic Publishing, 2016); Peter A Joy et al., 'Australian Best Practices: A Comparison with the United Kingdom and the United States' (2017) Washington University Law, Legal Studies Research Paper Series.

to the emotions and complexity of legal practice, with informed, positive and supportive supervision, helps them develop capacities for emotional regulation and fast-tracks their professional development by connecting theory and practice, ideas and conflicts, legal problems and human solutions.[75] Legal education is increasingly informed by the well-being discourse and already is inspiring new lawyers to identify opportunities for change, to develop the courage and self-awareness to resist bullying, to call-out inequities and counter discriminatory attitudes by speaking up and initiating change.

Conclusion

Neoliberalism is the way post-industrial societies do business/politics/law and it constructs 'the market' as the sole, and therefore ethical, legitimising principle. Theories of market-as-common-sense have infected non-economic areas of life, a field that could trigger new forms of resistance.[76] However, now is the time to envisage and design strategies for a future that might seem impossible but could later prove inevitable.[77] The legal profession can demonstrate it does not serve as a mouthpiece for power and can lead a cultural recovery from 'common sense' to 'good sense'.

In legal practice we can draw on the psychology of well-being to exploit market-thinking priorities and re-articulate the product law firms sell to clients; instead of time units or legal advice, it can be 'relational support'.[78] Contemporary legal education is no longer silent about the risks of legal practice; it has accepted the 'certainty of uncertainty' in life rather than telling students they can work out the correct answer in every case, and it no longer presumes cultures and values don't change.[79]

Since change is the only constant, neoliberalism will pass like other historical phases. Already driving the change are individuals who act both alone and collectively in courageous exposure of ethical compromise at every level. It is only individuals who decide to ask powerful questions, to challenge discourse and engage media in organising action for change. Just as law schools and legal

75 Tigran Eldred, 'Insights from Psychology: Teaching Behavioral Legal Ethics As a Core Element of Professional Responsibility' (2016) 757 *Michigan State Law Review* 757; AJ Arielle Scoglio et al., 'Self-Compassion and Responses to Trauma: The Role of Emotion Regulation' (2015) 33 *Journal of Interpersonal Violence* 1.

76 Christina Scharff, 'Life as an Enterprise: Ten Ways Through Which Neoliberalism Is Experienced on an Emotional Level' (2015) *The London School of Economics and Political Science, British Politics and Policy* <https://tinyurl.com/yca62fqg> accessed 7 May 2019.

77 Raymond Williams refers to struggles by alternative movements as 'the emergent', quoted in Stuart Hall, 'The Neo-Liberal Revolution' in Sally Davison and Katharine Harris (eds), *The Neo-Liberal Crisis* (Lawrence & Wishart, 2012) 13, 30.

78 Bob Murray, 'The Law Firm of the Future' *Lawyers Weekly*, 20 June 2016, <https://tinyurl.com/y8h6drlr> accessed 7 May 2019.

79 Rebecca Huxley-Binns, 'Tripping Over Thresholds: A Reflection on Legal Andragogy. Lord Upjohn Lecture 2015' (2016) 50(1) *The Law Teacher* 1; Stephen Tang and Tony Foley, 'The Practice of Law and the Intolerance of Certainty' (2014) 37(3) *UNSW Law Journal* 1198.

workplaces increasingly recognise their ethical duty to care for the well-being of students and staff, individuals are accepting they have an ethical responsibility to look after themselves *in order* to be effective agents of change. There is no neutrality option.

Idealism is impotent without action. Action starts with the individual and requires integrity in mind and body. As we learnt from feminism decades ago, the personal is political; and the most effective political action is personal, starting here and now, from where we are individually in this moment.

2 Self-care as a professional virtue for lawyers

Caroline Strevens, Rachael Field and Nigel Duncan

Introduction

The practice of law can be rewarding and fulfilling, but also involves significant stressors. In the context of working in a stressful, risk-averse profession, lawyers in Western common law countries have a paramount professional duty to the court and to the administration of justice, followed by a duty to serve the interests of their clients.[1] The professional persona of lawyers is portrayed as one of resilience, stamina, strength and fortitude.[2] These are possible reasons to explain why the concept of self-care for lawyers and attention to their welfare and psychological well-being have not until recently been a focus for the legal profession. Indeed, the promotion of self-care might even appear as anathema to some legal professionals, particularly the more senior members of the profession who may perceive the concept of self-care as indicative of weakness or being 'soft'[3].

In this chapter we argue, however, that self-care is in fact a professional virtue for lawyers and an important element of a positive professional legal identity. Using Self-Determination Theory (SDT) and the work of Sheldon and Krieger,[4]

1 Lord Neuberger of Abbotsbury, 'Reforming Legal Education' Lecture in Honour of Lord Upjohn (Delivered to Association of Law Teachers, 15 November 2012) 4–17 <www.supremecourt.uk/docs/lord-neuberger-121115-speech.pdf> accessed 7 May 2019.

2 For evidence of this view see the Judgment of Lord Justice Flax in *SRA v James et al.* [2018] EWHC 3058 (Admin).

3 There is little direct research to support this assertion, but the growing move from lockstep to 'eat what you kill' remuneration approaches in law firms suggests a culture shift in this direction: Jonathan Ames, 'Will "Eat What You Kill" Replace Lockstep?' *Financial Times* (London, 8 September 2011). See also Richard Collier, 'Naming Men as Men in Corporate Legal Practice: Gender and the Idea of Virtually 24/7 Commitment in Law' (2014) 83 *Fordham Law Review* 2387.

4 Kennon M Sheldon and Lawrence S Krieger, 'Does Legal Education Have Undermining Effects on Law Students? Evaluating Changes in Motivation, Values, and Well-Being' (2004) 22(2) *Behavioural Sciences and the Law* 261; Kennon M Sheldon and Lawrence S Krieger, 'Understanding the Negative Effects of Legal Education on Law Students: A Longitudinal Test of Self-Determination Theory' (2007) 33(6) *Personality and Social Psychology Bulletin* 883; Lawrence S Krieger, 'The Most Ethical of People, the Least Ethical of People: Proposing Self-Determination Theory to Measure Professional Character Formation' (2011) 8 *University of St. Thomas Law Journal* 168; Lawrence S Krieger and Kennon M Sheldon, 'What Makes

we situate an intentional commitment to self-care within the realm of legal professionalism, arguing that lawyers who engage in self-care, and are supported to self-care, are better positioned to behave professionally and to make ethical decisions. The chapter begins by explaining the notion of self-care and why it is important for the legal profession. We then analyse some of the key stressors of contemporary professional legal practice and use SDT to explain their detrimental impact on lawyer well-being. We conclude that whilst self-care is a professional virtue for contemporary legal practitioners, the legal profession, and particularly its leaders, have a primary responsibility to address the structural, cultural, political and social issues that underpin the stressful nature of modern lawyering.

What is self-care?

There are many possible ways to conceive of the notion of self-care. The Oxford Dictionary defines self-care as 'the practice of taking action to preserve or improve one's own health'.[5] Myers et al. define self-care practice as 'engagement in behaviors that maintain and promote physical and emotional well-being' including 'factors such as sleep, exercise, and use of social support'.[6] Others see self-care as involving specific positive cognitive elements such as 'self-awareness, self-regulation or coping, and a balancing of self and others' interests'.[7]

The concept of self-care is at the heart of positive psychology. Positive psychology is a relatively new branch of psychology that shifts the focus found in traditional psychology on treating or responding to disorder, illness and dysfunction, and on assessing and curing individual suffering and damage,[8] to constructive human development and positive personal characteristics, such as values, strengths, virtues, pleasure and talents.[9] Seligman and Csikszentmihalyi define positive psychology as 'the scientific study of positive human functioning and flourishing on multiple levels that include the biological, personal, relational,

Lawyers Happy? Transcending the Anecdotes with Data from 6200 Lawyers' (2015) 83 *The George Washington Law Review* 554.

5 Oxford Dictionary online: <https://en.oxforddictionaries.com/definition/self-care> accessed 7 May 2019.

6 Shannon B Myers et al., 'Self-Care Practices and Perceived Stress Levels Among Psychology Graduate Students' (2012) 6(1) *Training and Education in Professional Psychology* 55.

7 Shauna L Shapiro, Kirk W Brown and Gina M Biegel, 'Teaching Self-Care to Caregivers: Effects of Mindfulness-Based Stress Reduction on the Mental Health of Therapists in Training' (2007) 1(2) *Training and Education in Professional Psychology* 105, 106. See also Ellen K Baker, *Caring for Ourselves: A Therapist's Guide to Personal and Professional Wellbeing* (American Psychological Association, 2003).

8 Martin E Seligman and Mihaly Csikszentmihalyi, 'Positive Psychology: An Introduction' (2000) 55(1) *American Psychologist* 5, 6.

9 Martin E Seligman, *Authentic Happiness* (Free Press, 2002). See also, for example, David G Myers, 'The Funds, Friends, and Faith of Happy People' (2000) 55(1) *American Psychologist* 56.

institutional, cultural, and global dimensions of life'.[10] Through promoting the regular enactment of positive characteristics and 'signature strengths', positive psychology pursues well-being, taking a preventive and future-focussed view to assisting people to nurture what is best within themselves, to create their own conditions for increased psychological well-being and for a 'life well-lived'.[11]

An important theory of positive psychology is Self-Determination Theory (SDT). SDT is a complex meta-theory,[12] based on the overarching premise that human beings have an inherent orientation towards growth, adaptation and development. The experience of unsupportive conditions, however, results in a vulnerability to amotivation and psychological ill-health.[13] SDT was developed using empirical studies by the eminent positive psychologists Deci and Ryan,[14] and enhanced by many further studies.[15] Essentially it seeks to explain human motivation, engagement and well-being, and the implications for well-being of intrinsic and extrinsic goals, values and motivations. The theory offers a useful lens through which to conceptualise self-care, particularly in the context of arguing for self-care as a professional virtue in law, because through identifying the positive elements of well-being, and predicting 'social conditions that promote high-quality development and performance',[16] measures can be adopted to assist lawyers to cope with professional stressors, with the consequence of creating favourable conditions for promoting optimal individual well-being.

An important sub-theory of SDT, which has been identified by Vansteenkiste et al. as a 'unifying principle within SDT', is Basic Psychological Needs Theory.[17] The three basic psychological needs for well-being have been identified as

10 William C Compton and Edward Hoffman, *Positive Psychology: The Science of Happiness and Flourishing* (Cengage Learning, 2nd ed, 2013) referring to Seligman and Csikszentmihalyi (n 8) 5.

11 Aristotle followed Socrates and Plato in defining virtues and happiness as central to a life well-lived. See for example, his ethical treatises: *Nicomachean Ethics* and *Eudemian Ethics*. See also, for example, Martin E Seligman (n 9); Myers (n 6) 56.

12 SDT's five sub-theories of motivation and human behaviour are: Cognitive Evaluation Theory, Organismic Integration Theory, Causality Orientations Theory, Basic Needs Theory and Goal Content Theory. See Maarten Vansteenkiste, Christopher P Niemiec and Bart Soenens, 'The Development of the Five Mini-Theories of Self-Determination Theory: An Historical Overview, Emerging Trends, and Future Directions' in Timothy C Urdan and Stuart A Karabenick (eds), *The Decade Ahead: Theoretical Perspectives on Motivation and Achievement* (Emerald Group Publishing Limited, 2010) 105.

13 Christopher Niemiec, Richard Ryan and Edward Deci, 'Self-Determination Theory and the Relation of Autonomy to Self-Regulatory Processes and Personality Development' in Rick Hoyle (ed), *Handbook of Personality and Self-Regulation* (Wiley-Blackwell, 2010) 169, 174 and 175.

14 Edward E Deci and Richard M Ryan, *Intrinsic Motivation and Self-Determination in Human Behaviour* (Springer Science & Business Media, 1985).

15 For a useful repository of the areas in which this theory has been applied and developed see <http://selfdeterminationtheory.org/theory/> accessed 7 May 2019.

16 Edward L Deci and Richard M Ryan, 'The "What" and "Why" of Goal Pursuits: Human Needs and the Self-Determination of Behaviour' (2000) 11(4) *Psychological Inquiry* 227, 263.

17 Vansteenkiste, Niemiec and Soenens (n 12) 131.

autonomy, competence and relatedness.[18] Autonomy is a complex need which refers to an individual's subjective experience of living a life true to the personal values that give one's life meaning. The need for autonomy is the need to experience a sense of being self-governed and of being able to engage in volitional behaviours that are congruent with one's true beliefs, values and interests.[19] An autonomous person knows what is important to them, is able to make decisions for themselves and does not experience a sense of being controlled. The need for autonomy is not satisfied in 'controlling' environments, requiring instead 'autonomy-supportive' conditions.[20] Competence involves the need to experience a sense of ability, capability and mastery in relation to managing tasks and challenges.[21] Competence is supported in well-structured, affirming environments and is neglected in 'chaotic and demeaning' environments.[22] Relatedness refers to the experience of meaningful and reciprocal connections with other human beings who are key.[23] Relatedness is supported in environments that are 'warm and responsive', rather than 'cold and neglectful'.[24]

Sheldon and Krieger summarise the three basic needs as follows:

> According to SDT, all human beings require regular experiences of autonomy, competence, and relatedness to thrive and maximize their positive motivation. In other words, people need to feel that they are good at what they do or at least can become good at it (competence); that they are doing what they choose and want to be doing, that is, what they enjoy or at least believe in (autonomy); and that they are relating meaningfully to others in the process, that is, connecting with the selves of other people (relatedness). These needs are considered so fundamental that Ryan (1995) has likened them to a plant's need for sunlight, soil, and water.[25]

Another important aspect of SDT concerns the relationship between motivation and well-being. Deci and Ryan distinguish between intrinsic and extrinsic motivation. When a person is intrinsically motivated they engage in activities due to having an interest and/or deriving enjoyment from that activity.[26] On the other

18 Richard M Ryan and Edward L Deci, 'Self-Determination Theory and the Role of Basic Psychological Needs in Personality and the Organization of Behavior' in Oliver P John, Richard W Robins and Lawrence A Pervin (eds), *Handbook of Personality: Theory and Research* (Guilford Press, 3rd ed, 2008) 654.

19 Niemiec, Ryan and Deci (n 13) 169, 176.

20 Vansteenkiste, Niemiec and Soenens (n 12) 131–132.

21 Krieger (n 4) 168, 172.

22 Vansteenkiste, Niemiec and Soenens (n 12) 131–132.

23 Niemiec, Ryan and Deci (n 13) 176; Krieger (n 4) 172.

24 Vansteenkiste, Niemiec and Soenens (n 12) 131–132.

25 Sheldon and Krieger, 'Understanding the Negative Effects of Legal Education on Law Students' (n 4) 883, 885.

26 Ryan and Deci (n 18) 654, 660–661; Edward Deci and Richard Ryan (eds), *Handbook of Self Determination Research* (University of Rochester Press, 2002).

hand, extrinsic motivations are typically a means to an end, primarily predicated on some form of external recognition.[27] Deci and Ryan developed their theory, using empirical studies, to explain that if the three basic psychological needs are satisfied this will enhance intrinsic motivation, encourage intrinsic goal setting by individuals, and support motivation for inherently less satisfying tasks where intrinsic motivation is absent.[28] This will result in higher levels of well-being. SDT indicates that if the three components are absent there will be adverse consequences for mental health, persistence and achievement.

SDT covers both what a person's goal is and why they are motivated to act. Beliefs, goals and values are all linked to the theory of motivation. A person can be said to have intrinsic goals when their goal is 'intimacy, community, and personal growth' as opposed to external goals, which they are not able to control, such as riches and renown.[29] Similarly a person is intrinsically motivated when they act from the enjoyment such action brings; for example playing a musical instrument. Sheldon and Kreiger explain that: 'motivation for behaviour is distinguished based on the locus of its source, either "internal" (the behaviour is inherently interesting and enjoyable, or it is meaningful because it furthers one's own values) or "external" (behaviour is compelled by guilt, fear, or pressure, or choosing to please or impress others)'.[30]

The empirical research undertaken in America by Sheldon and Kreiger in 2015 confirmed the importance of lawyers' experience of the three basic needs in their professional work context. Furthermore, it identified the importance of intrinsic motivation for professional well-being for lawyers. The hypothesis for this research was that 'internal (self-determined or autonomous) reasons for choosing work – interest, enjoyment, or effectuating core values – would be another critical factor for attorney well-being'.[31] This hypothesis was confirmed by the data. Further, it was found that satisfying the basic needs 'facilitates natural growth processes including intrinsically motivated behavior and integration of extrinsic motivations, whereas those that forestall autonomy, competence, or relatedness are associated with poorer motivation, performance, and well-being'.[32]

Krieger and Sheldon also explored the link between high levels of well-being and ethical behaviour, highlighting the importance of values for lawyers:[33]

> Beyond the importance of values for attorney well-being, values have a crucial significance for professionalism and ethical behavior. Intrinsic values

27 Edward L Deci et al., 'Self-Determination Theory: An Approach to Human Motivation and Personality' (2013) <www.selfdeterminationtheory.org/theory> accessed 7 May 2019.

28 Richard M Ryan and Edward L Deci, 'Self-Determination Theory and the Facilitation of Intrinsic Motivation, Social Development and Well-being' (2000) 55(1) *American Psychologist* 68.

29 Sheldon and Krieger, 'Does Legal Education' (n 4) 261, 264.

30 Krieger and Sheldon, 'What Makes Lawyers Happy?' (n 4) 554, 565.

31 Ibid 579.

32 Deci and Ryan (n 16) 227.

33 Krieger (n 4) 168. See also Deci and Ryan et al. (n 13, 14, 16, 18).

include self-understanding and improvement, positive interpersonal relationships, helping others, and building community; such values would logically lead to introspection, honesty, cooperation, respect, and altruistic behavior. These values, then, would tend to promote integrity, candor, dedication to a client or cause, and respectful interactions with clients, opposing parties, and others, thus elevating an attorney's ethical and professional conduct. By contrast, none of the extrinsic values (achieving high earnings, status, appearance, or influence over others) appear to relate directly to professional or ethical behavior, and such values could actually lead to unethical or unprofessional conduct if perceived as helpful to attain the desired end.[34]

Sheldon and Kreiger's research emphasises the importance for lawyers of experiencing autonomy support in legal practice. Autonomy support requires, for example, understanding of the stressors of practice, acknowledgement of lawyers' needs and feelings, the provision of support when faced with obstacles and the provision of an ability to make choices.[35]

In the next section we highlight the professional virtue of self-care by exploring some of the stressors of legal practice and use the lens of SDT to explain the negative impact they may have on lawyer well-being. We also note however, how important it is that the legal profession at large takes responsibility for enacting professional structural and cultural change; for example, by better attending to the provision of autonomy support for lawyers.

Understanding the legal profession and its stressors

The legal profession is one of the traditionally recognised 'professions', ancient and ubiquitous, with various manifestations in diverse jurisdictions and cultures all around the world.[36] 'The word profession is derived from the Latin *professio* or *professionem* which means to make a public declaration'.[37] Along with

34 Krieger and Sheldon (n 4) 581.

35 Edward L Deci and Richard M Ryan, 'Optimizing Students' Motivation in the Era of Testing and Pressure: A Self-Determination Theory Perspective' in Woon Chia Liu, John Chee Keng Wang and Richard M Ryan (eds), *Building Autonomous Learners: Perspectives from Research and Practice Using Self-Determination Theory* (Springer, 2016) 9–29, 10; Edward L Deci, Anja H Olafsen and Richard M Ryan, 'Self-Determination Theory in Work Organizations: The State of a Science' (2017) 4 *Annual Review of Organizational Psychology and Organizational Behaviour* 19.

36 See for example, Roscoe Pound, *Lawyers from Antiquity to Modern Times* (West Publishing Co, 1953); Robert J Bonner, *Lawyers and Litigants in Ancient Athens: The Genesis of the Legal Profession* (Benjamin Blom, 1927); John A Crook, *Law and Life of Ancient Rome* (Cornell University Press, 1967); James A Brundage, 'The Rise of the Professional Jurist in the Thirteenth Century' (1994) 20 *Syracuse Journal of International Law and Commerce* 185; John Hamilton Baker, *An Introduction to British Legal History* (Butterworths, 3rd ed, 1990); R Blain Andrus, *Lawyer: A Brief 5,000 Year History* (ABA Book Publishing, 2009).

37 Edward D Re, 'The Profession of the Law' (2000) 15(2) *Journal of Civil Rights and Economic Development* 109, 110.

possessing technical expertise and knowledge, members of a profession publicly declare and represent accountable and ethical practice in their discipline in the service of others. A 'profession' can be differentiated from an 'industry' or 'trade' because a profession is driven by more complex contributions to society than simply providing profitable services driven by market ideology.[38] As Justice Kiefel of the Australian High Court has said: 'Practising lawyers do not just run a business, selling their skills and services to clients in return for fees. The practice of law is a profession and this sets it apart from other, commercial, enterprises'.[39] The practice of law is therefore a profit-making business influenced by market forces, which also involves the provision of ethical and altruistic services concerning liberal democratic rights, advocacy for the vulnerable and upholding the rule of law.[40]

Inevitably, a level of tension arises between these motivations. Such tensions, particularly in the contemporary neoliberal global society, may constitute a significant source of stress for legal professionals. Legal ethics for example, have particularly been brought into question giving rise to claims that the legal profession is in crisis.[41] Further, the obligation to put the interests of others before a lawyer's own (possibly financial) interests is another source of tension. For example, a lawyer may offer the choice of a simple solution to their client's problem or a much more expensive solution which offers only marginal advantages (but is much more profitable to the lawyer). In what terms is that advice offered? What if the temptation to stress the expensive alternative is not simply to maximise personal income, but to maintain a job in a practice where the lawyer is employed and has fee-earning goals to meet? For lawyers working in law firms there will be real pressure to generate income based on budgets to achieve a certain number of billable hours, usually achieved by recording work in six-minute increments.[42] The issue of income generation may be a high-stakes issue. At a time when public funding of legal services has been reduced in many jurisdictions, working efficiently with an eye to the clock may be a matter of survival for many firms,

38 See, for example, Bernard Barber, *The Logic and Limits of Trust* (Rutgers University Press, 1983) 108. For a seminal discussion of contemporary 'market ideology' in the US context see Leonard Silk and David Vogel, *Ethics and Profits: The Crisis of Confidence in American Business* (Simon and Schuster, 1976).

39 Susan Kiefel, 'Ethics and the Profession of the Lawyer' (2010) Address to the Queensland Law Society: The Vincents' 48th Annual Symposium, Canberra, High Court of Australia, 26 March, 1 <www.hcourt.gov.au/assets/publications/speeches/current-justices/kiefelj/kiefelj-2010-03-26.pdf> accessed 7 May 2019.

40 Joanne Bagust, 'The Legal Profession and the Business of Law' (2013) 35 *Sydney Law Review* 27, 27–28 referring to Marion Crain, 'The Transformation of the Professional Workforce' (2004) 79 *Chicago-Kent Law Review* 543.

41 Anthony T Kronman, *The Lost Lawyer: Failing Ideals of the Legal Profession* (Belknap Press, 1995).

42 See for example, Susan S Fortney, 'Soul for Sale: An Empirical Study of Associate Satisfaction, Law Firm Culture, and the Effects of Billable Hour Requirements' (2000) 69 *University of Missouri-Kansas City Law Review* 239; Sharon Toker, 'The Economic Evaluation of Time Can Cause Stress' (2018) 4(1) *Academy of Management Discoveries* 101.

particularly small firms. For example, in the UK the Legal Aid, Sentencing and Punishment of Offenders Act 2012 and cuts to local authority funding 'has taken some £100 million annually out of the advice economy'.[43] In large corporate law firms, the sheer value of the subject matter of the lawyer's work adds its own stress. These firms' premises give an impression of great wealth, but competition for this work is fierce.

Competitive pressures have been increased by changes in the regulation of legal services and the development of information and communication technology.[44] Much of the work that was previously exclusive to lawyers may now be undertaken by others or by businesses established by non-lawyers. Much routine work may now be done by paralegals with limited qualifications or outsourced to developing economies where labour costs are lower.[45] The development of something approaching artificial intelligence means that much work currently undertaken by professional lawyers may come to be undertaken by computers. The increase in competitive pressures is likely to continue.

The nature of the pressures on individual lawyers is bound to differ depending on their practice context. The demands on corporate commercial lawyers to work long hours are legendary in terms of a negative impact on the possibility of work/life balance.[46] Lawyers working with clients accused of crimes, who have lost their employment, their housing, their benefits or their right to stay in the country, or who seek protection from domestic violence or incarceration because of mental health problems, face very different stressors in the form of vicarious trauma.[47] What is true of all of them is that they face a serious risk of burnout.

It is evident therefore that, in countries like England and Wales and Australia, the practice of law has changed in significant ways and the stressors of practice are significant. Some of these changes are reflected across the world as a result of neoliberalism, the globalisation of commerce and the accessibility that the use of the internet brings. The next sections discuss in more detail, using the lens of SDT, the potential ways in which these changes can negatively impact the

43 Low Commission, 'Getting it Right in Social Welfare Law' (2015) 95 <www.lag.org.uk/about-us/policy/the-low-commission-200551> accessed 7 May 2019.

44 Richard Susskind, *The End of Lawyers: Rethinking the Nature of Legal Services* (Oxford University Press, 2010); Richard Susskind and Daniel Susskind, *The Future of the Professions: How Technology Will Transform the Work of Human Experts* (Oxford University Press, 2015).

45 See for example, Alison M Kadzik, 'The Current Trend to Outsource Legal Work Abroad and the Ethical Issues Related to Such Practices' (2006) 19 *Georgetown Journal of Legal Ethics* 731.

46 In a 2013 survey, 75% of UK solicitors in the commercial field said workload was the main source of stress: Richard Collier (n 3). Comparably, see: Directorate-General for Internal Policies, *Occupational Health Concerns: Stress-Related and Psychological Problems Associated with Work* (Policy Department Economic and Scientific Policy (A), 2013) <www.europarl.europa.eu/RegData/etudes/etudes/join/2013/507455/IPOL-EMPL_ET(2013)507455_EN.pdf> accessed 7 May 2019.

47 Marjorie A Silver, Sanford Portnoy and Jean Koh Peters, 'Stress, Burnout, Vicarious Trauma, and Other Emotional Realities in the Lawyer/Client Relationship' (2004) 19 *Touro Law Review* 847.

well-being of lawyers as part of the argument that the legal profession should adopt a stronger focus on self-care as a part of a positive professional identity.

The stressor of the power of the client

A significant body of research has considered the shift of power from the legal profession to the purchaser of legal services.[48] In this context it would be inaccurate to describe most purchasers of legal services as consumers because the majority comprise commercial organisations including organisations with an in-house lawyer or legal team. The Law Society estimates that the UK Legal Services market was worth around £30 billion in 2017.[49]

Much has also been written about the globalisation of legal practice,[50] and the impact upon large city-based commercial law firms where the corporate client wields great influence as a result of the potential profits that accompany instruction.[51] In such a high-stakes relationship there is a loss of bargaining power for lawyers who must constantly look over their shoulder at competitor firms who are keen to win the client's business. According to the 2018 LexisNexis Bellwether report, there is the view amongst members of the UK legal profession that 'clients currently have an unparalleled ability to shop around', and lawyers are concerned that if the costs of legal services are driven down, then the profession will be compromised.[52]

As Sommerlad has said, 'clients' power is such that it has taken precedence over lawyers' duty to the law and to the administration of justice'.[53] This shift of

48 See for example, Raymond H Brescia, 'Uber for Lawyers: The Transformative Potential of a Sharing Economy Approach to the Delivery of Legal Services' (2016) 64 *Buffalo Law Review* 745.

49 The Law Society of England and Wales, *Legal Services Sector Forecasts 2017–2025* (Law Society of England and Wales, 31 October 2017) <www.lawsociety.org.uk/support-services/research-trends/legal-services-sector-forecasts> accessed 7 May 2019.

50 See, e.g. John Flood, *Legal Education in the Global Context: Challenges from Globalization, Technology and Changes in Government Regulation* (Report for the Legal Services Board, 2011) <www.legalservicesboard.org.uk/news_publications/latest_news/pdf/lsb_legal_education_report_flood.pdf> accessed 7 May 2019, citing Laurel Terry, 'The Future Regulation of the Legal Profession: The Impact of Treating the Legal Profession as "Service Providers"' (2008) *Journal of the Professional Lawyer* 189; James R Faulconbridge et al., 'Legal Education, Globalisation, and the Cultures of Professional Practice' (2009) 22(4) *Georgetown Journal of Legal Ethics* 1335.

51 See also Lisa Webley, 'Legal Professional De(Re)Regulation, Equality, and Inclusion, and the Contested Space of Professionalism within the Legal Market in England and Wales' (2014) 83 *Fordham Law Review* 2349.

52 Jon Whittle, *The Culture Clash* (Bellwether Discussion Paper LexisNexis UK, 2018) <www.lexisnexis.co.uk/pdf/LexisNexis_Bellwether_Report_2018_The_Culture_Clash.pdf> accessed 7 May 2019.

53 Hilary Sommerlad, 'The New "Professionalism" in England and Wales: Talent, Diversity, and a Legal Precariat' in Spencer Headworth et al. (eds), *Diversity in Practice: Race, Gender, and Class in Legal and Professional Careers* (Cambridge University Press, 2016) 226–260, 250–251.

power and competitive pressure for financial gain could result in individual lawyers prioritising extrinsic goals and values with the consequent loss of autonomy, ethical decision-making and personal well-being. Sommerlad argues further that the position of the Legal Aid lawyer is no better thanks to the 'strict cost pressures' they are under,[54] providing an example of a different lack of professional autonomy resulting from working in a restricted funding environment.

Junior Lawyers Division (JLD) resilience and well-being survey 2017/2018

The JLD in the UK has 70,000 members. It represents legal practice course (LPC) students (including paralegals who have undertaken their LPC), trainee solicitors and solicitors with up to five years' post qualification experience (PQE). The JLD conducted a Resilience and Well-being Survey of its members in 2017 and in 2018 which reported increased levels of stress. Of those reporting work-related stress, the same proportion of respondents reported either severe or extreme levels of stress in 2018 as in 2017 (26%). Of qualified solicitors with 0–5 years PQE who responded to the survey, 29.2% reported experiencing high levels of stress. This is higher than the 19% of Practising Certificate holders reporting severe or extreme levels of stress across the wider solicitor profession.[55] The most significant causes of stress reported in the survey included: high workload, client demands, lack of support, ineffective management, lack of control and billable hours targets.[56] We note, however, that the proportion of participants completing the survey is relatively low, although growing, being 214 responses in 2017 and 959 responses in 2018.

In 2018, in answer to the question asking if participants had experienced any of the following as a result of stress in the last month, 42.3% had experienced problems with family life or relationships, 41.9% considered taking time off but didn't, 40.4% nearly made a mistake that would not have happened otherwise, 34.4% looked for another job, 31.6% made a mistake, but only 12.8% took time off.

Research evidence suggests that when lawyers are experiencing excessive stress, they are more likely to make mistakes,[57] and these may include ethical transgressions. The reported experiences of stress in legal work are telling when analysed from the perspective of SDT.[58] The proportion of respondents (70%) who either nearly made or actually made a mistake as a response to stress suggests a level of anxiety about reduced competence. SDT makes it clear that all human beings need to feel that they are good at what they do or at least that they can become

54 Ibid 250.

55 Kayleigh Leonie, *JLD Resilience and Well-Being Survey Report* (The Law Society, April 2018) <http://communities.lawsociety.org.uk/Uploads/p/d/i/jld-resilience-and-wellbeing-survey-report-2018.pdf> accessed 7 May 2019.

56 Ibid 10.

57 For evidence of the concern in relation to stress and error at work see Leonie (n 55).

58 Ibid 12.

so, and this feeling is considerably undermined if the workload and working environment fail to provide sufficient time and support for the competent completion of work tasks.[59] Indeed, the survey results explicitly indicate that the majority of participants would like more support at work. Further, it appears possible from the data to conclude that junior lawyers are not developing sufficient relationships of trust at work with more senior colleagues (relatedness) and are unlikely to be experiencing autonomy support at work.

The stressor of changes in public opinion about the profession

According to Sommerlad, 'one of the most significant changes to the legal profession has been the fragmentation of its close-knit collegial character – the product of its self-governing professional association, its organisation into partnerships and the apprenticeship system'.[60]

For example, in the UK, the Legal Services market has been liberalised largely as a result of the Clementi Review of the profession.[61] This Review resulted in the enactment of the *Legal Services Act 2007* which aims to give consumers of legal services more choice. However, a possible unanticipated negative consequence of these developments, and of both the regulation of the profession by the statutorily established Legal Services Board (LSB), as well as the introduction of Alternative Business Structures (ABS) as regulated entities through which legal services can be offered, is that the legal profession has lost another of its defining features – self-regulation – and this potentially adversely impacts the experience of autonomy in professional legal practice.

Further, these developments have served to create confusion amongst consumers of legal services which has potentially led to a decline in the public's view of the trustworthiness of lawyers. The Legal Services Board has reported that 'over the last six years trust in lawyers has declined, going from 47% in 2011 to 42% in 2016'.[62] Levels of trust increased slightly in 2017 to 45% but as a profession lawyers fall 'significantly behind doctors and teachers'.[63] A lack of trust in the profession may be fuelled by reports of unethical behaviour by solicitors such as was included in the recent House of Commons Women and Equalities Committee

59 Sommerlad (n 53).

60 Ibid 229.

61 David Clementi, 'Review of the Regulatory Framework for Legal Services in England and Wales' (Final Report of Department for Constitutional Affairs, 2004) 10–11 <www.avocats paris.org/Presence_Internationale/Droit_homme/PDF/Rapport_Clementi.pdf> accessed 7 May 2019.

62 Fiona Lewis and Ian Neale, 'The Legal Service Board Consumer Panel 2016 Research Tracker Report' (2016) 14 <www.legalservicesconsumerpanel.org.uk/publications/research_and_reports/documents/Howconsumersarechoosing.pdf> accessed 7 May 2019.

63 Legal Services Board Consumer Panel, 'Tracker Survey 2017 Briefing note: How Consumers Are Choosing Legal Services' (2017) <www.legalservicesconsumerpanel.org.uk/publications/research_and_reports/documents/How_consumers_are_choosing_Final_2017.pdf> accessed 7 May 2019.

Report on Sexual Harassment in the Workplace.[64] Further, Stephen Vaughan and Emma Oakley's research into the ethicality of city lawyers has found apathy in city law firms and a lack of ethical leadership.[65]

These issues have possible implications for lawyer well-being when examined through the lens of the basic need for relatedness. According to Krieger, 'the truly professional lawyer will be competent in legal skills, but beyond that she will feel closely connected to others in her community because she respects and is respected by them'.[66] If the view of the lawyer as a trusted member of the local community is brought into question and the professional role of the lawyer in society is considered to be compromised, practitioners offering legal services potentially become just another profit-seeking business, and this has possible deleterious consequences for the possibility of a positive professional legal identity and the well-being of lawyers.

The stressor of technology

Richard Susskind has long argued that if the legal profession is to be sustainable into the future and if lawyers are to continue to enable access to justice there is a need to embrace the opportunities and challenges that new technology brings and law schools should bring this material into their curriculum.[67] Yet whilst the demands upon legal professionals have changed with technological developments and new business models, legal education has not adapted to include attention to matters such as understanding how to run a business, strategy, marketing, reading balance sheets, analysing data, use of statistics or project management. Thus, new lawyers are entering the profession with some basic competence needs unfulfilled.

Conclusion

Our key argument in this chapter is that the changing nature of the legal profession and the stressors legal professionals experience in contemporary practice contexts potentially negatively influence the well-being of individual lawyers by reducing satisfaction of SDT's identified basic needs – autonomy, competence and

64 House of Commons, Women and Equalities Committee, 'Sexual Harrassment in the Workplace' (Firth Report of Session 2017–19) <https://publications.parliament.uk/pa/cm201719/cmselect/cmwomeq/725/725.pdf> accessed 7 May 2019.

65 Steven Vaughan and Emma Oakley, '"Gorilla Exceptions" and the Ethically Apathetic Corporate Lawyer' (2016) 19(1) *Legal Ethics* 50.

66 Lawrence S Krieger, 'The Inseparability of Professionalism and Personal Satisfaction: Perspectives on Values, Integrity and Happiness' (2004) 11 *Clinical Law Review* 425, 430.

67 Susskind (n 44). See also John Flood, 'Professions and Professional Service Firms in a Global Context: Reframing Narratives' in Mike Saks and Daniel Muzio (eds), *Professions and Professional Service Firms: Private and Public Sector Enterprises in the Global Economy* (Routledge, 2018) 26, 43–45.

relatedness.[68] According to Krieger, satisfying the three basic needs of SDT is likely to increase professionalism and ethical behaviour.[69] For these reasons self-care for lawyers that enables fulfilment of the three basic needs is a professional virtue.

However, it is important to note also that many of the sources of inappropriate stress, and the means of effectively addressing them, lie in the hands of the legal sectors' employers and regulators. In the non-commercial sector, governments bear the responsibility of funding high-quality legal services. Basic psychological needs theory suggests that organisations and regulators are most significant in enabling competence, autonomy and relatedness.[70] As Christine Parker has reminded us, the system itself is broken and it is critical that the profession is attuned to the risk that the issue will be individualised, imposing responsibility solely on individual lawyers for their own well-being.[71]

The ethical responsibilities here are complex. Individual lawyers have a level of responsibility for their own professional development and mental well-being and enacting self-care strategies to promote their autonomy, competence and relatedness. However, it is quite unreasonable for them to be expected to do this effectively in an inimical culture and environment. We suggest that it is important to look critically at the stressors discussed herein and recognise that some are a function of the way in which legal practice is organised, structured and managed. We need, therefore, to challenge structural, political and cultural elements of the profession that exacerbate the stressors, and we need to hold the leaders of the profession responsible for appropriate action. It might be over-optimistic to expect to change the neoliberal assumptions that the globalised commercial economy has adopted, but this should not prevent us from continuing to challenge them and draw attention to the problems they create.

Nevertheless, while work on the structural professional issues remains a work-in-progress, lawyers themselves can be informed by SDT to enact self-care strategies. This is important because any reduction in the well-being of individual lawyers has far-reaching implications for the legal profession and its reputation and sustainability into the future, and consequently for society at large. A fully functioning society needs a strong legal profession to support the rule of law. Lawyers therefore need to feel empowered to respond to these challenges in order to maintain a positive professional identity, and self-care strategies that support the basic needs of autonomy, competence and relatedness should be included in the education of lawyers both at law school and through continuing professional development and life-long learning.

68 For an overview of the many surveys on lawyers' satisfaction with their legal careers, see Jerry M Organ, 'What Do We Know About the Satisfaction/Dissatisfaction of Lawyers? A Meta-Analysis of Research on Lawyer Satisfaction and Well-Being' (2011) 8(2) *University of St Thomas Law Journal* 225.

69 Krieger (n 4) 188.

70 Sheldon and Krieger (n 4) 582–584.

71 Christine Parker, 'The "Moral Panic" Over Psychological Wellbeing in the Legal Profession: A Personal or Political Ethical Response?' (2014) 37(3) *UNSW Law Journal* 1103, 1136. See also Claire Carroll, 'Wellbeing Discourse: Alert Not Alarmed' (2019) 29(1) *Legal Education Review* 1.

3 Values

The flip side of the well-being coin

Vivien Holmes

Introduction

Both ancient philosophers and modern psychologists assure us that our happiness and our values are inextricably linked: true happiness (eudaimonia)[1] comes 'not from mere pursuit of pleasure, but from living in accordance with [values] that create a sense of meaning, connection and self'.[2] In this chapter, I treat subjective well-being (well-being)[3] and happiness as expressions of this state of thriving (eudaimonia), and explore this 'inextricable' relationship between well-being, values and legal ethics.[4]

In exploring this relationship, I am interested in the implications for law students and lawyers, law schools and legal workplaces. While I write from an Australian perspective, international research shows that the more we enact, rather than just subscribe to, certain values, the greater will be our well-being.[5] Further, the psychological factors that influence whether lawyers experience well-being also influence their ethical decision-making and level of professionalism.[6] We know

1 A classical Greek word (associated with Aristotle) commonly translated to mean 'happiness', 'living a complete human life', or 'the realisation of human potential': Richard M Ryan, Veronica Huta and Edward L Deci, 'Living Well: A Self-Determination Theory Perspective on Eudaimonia' (2008) 9 *Journal of Happiness Studies* 139; Carol D Ryff and Burton H Singer, 'Know Thyself and Become What You Are: A Eudaimonic Approach to Psychological Well-Being' (2008) 9 *Journal of Happiness Studies* 13.

2 Kathryn E Williams, Joseph Ciarrochi and Patrick CL Heaven, 'Relationships Between Valued Action and Wellbeing Across the Transition from High School to Early Adulthood' (2015) 10 *The Journal of Positive Psychology* 127, 127.

3 Subjective well-being (SWB) comprises an affective component (the net balance between a person's positive and negative affect) and a cognitive component (a person's level of life satisfaction): ibid 132.

4 While values are personal/individual standards that guide our behaviour and our judgement of what is important in life (https://en.oxforddictionaries.com/definition/value), I use the term 'ethics' to denote a generally accepted set of moral principles and 'legal ethics' to mean the principles and standards governing the professional actions of lawyers.

5 Kennon M Sheldon and Lawrence S Krieger, 'Walking the Talk: Value Importance, Value Enactment, and Well-Being' (2014) 38 *Motivation and Emotion* 609.

6 Lawrence S Krieger, 'The Inseparability of Professionalism and Personal Satisfaction: Perspectives on Values, Integrity and Happiness' (2004) 11 *Clinical Law Review* 425.

that law school curricula affect student well-being[7]; law schools likewise play a critical role in supporting (or inhibiting) the development of professional values and in teaching skills to enable students and future lawyers to live out those values.[8] Alongside this, law schools can facilitate (or inhibit) the development in students of a positive professional identity; that is, a positive conception of the legal profession and its role in society, and a positive conception of their own role within the profession.[9] After law school, workplace culture can profoundly influence our well-being, while also influencing whether we are able to express/enact our professional values.[10] Evidence suggests that effective regulation can encourage legal practices to improve their ethical cultures,[11] which in turn could improve well-being and underpin positive professional identities in lawyers.

Values enactment and well-being

There is a complex relationship between well-being, values and 'valued action' ('successful enactment of values in daily life').[12] Valued action has been associated with lower psychological distress, greater life fulfilment, improved 'psychological quality of life' and better physical health.[13] It also seems that simply reflecting on personal values can keep 'neuroendocrine and psychological responses to stress at low levels'.[14] Not surprisingly, when values are *enacted*, rather than just endorsed, the benefits to well-being appear to be greater. In a study by Sheldon and Krieger, participants were questioned about the extent to which they acted on their values, as well as the importance to them of those values.[15] The authors were interested in whether 'walking' one's values (i.e. enacting them) has a more powerful effect on well-being than just 'talking' (merely endorsing) one's values. They found the walking measure to be 'the more reliable or robust predictor

7 Molly Townes O'Brien, Stephen Tang and Kath Hall, 'Changing Our Thinking: Empirical Research on Law Student Wellbeing, Thinking Styles and the Law Curriculum' (2011) *Legal Education Review* 149.

8 Vivien Holmes, '"Giving Voice to Values": Enhancing Students' Capacity to Cope with Ethical Challenges in Legal Practice' (2015) 18 *Legal Ethics* 115.

9 Rachael Field, James Duffy and Anna Huggins, 'Supporting Transition to Law School and Student Well-Being: The Role of Professional Legal Identity' (2013) 4 *The International Journal of the First Year in Higher Education* 15.

10 Tony Foley et al., 'Helping Junior Lawyers Thrive' (2015) 89 *Law Institute Journal* 44.

11 Sundeep Aulakh and Joan Loughrey, 'Regulating Law Firms from the Inside: The Role of Compliance Officers for Legal Practice in England and Wales' (2017) 45(2) *Journal of Law and Society* 254.

12 Williams, Ciarrochi and Heaven (n 2) 128.

13 Ines Trindade et al., 'Clarity of Personal Values and Committed Action: Development of a Shorter Engaged Living Scale' (2016) 38 *Journal of Psychopathology and Behavioral Assessment* 258, 259. 'Engaged living', which the authors define as 'the evaluation and performance of valued life activities' (268), is akin to valued action.

14 J David Creswell et al., 'Affirmation of Personal Values Buffers Neuroendocrine and Psychological Stress Responses' (2005) 16 *Psychological Science* 846.

15 Sheldon and Krieger (n 5) 611.

of wellbeing',[16] and concluded that 'happiness is more strongly associated with *doing* the "right" thing than just *saying* the right things are important'.[17] Their study shows that consistency between the values we hold and the way we behave is good for our mental health, 'or at least symptomatic of an integrated state of functioning which is related to mental health'.[18]

Does holding and acting on certain values lead to greater well-being, or does well-being enable valued action? A study by Williams and colleagues specifically focussed on the question of whether values are antecedent to well-being or whether well-being is antecedent to values.[19] Their research examined the relationship between subjective well-being (SWB) and values amongst a group of young people transitioning from high school to adult life, studying the participants when they were in year 12 (last year of secondary education Australia) and a year later. It is worth noting that many young people in this age group enter university,[20] and a not insignificant number of those experience a decrease in well-being.[21] The study findings suggest an indirect relationship between well-being and values: young people who experience positive emotions (a component of SWB) are more able to engage in life's challenges and opportunities and thus build high life satisfaction (that is, they compare their lives favourably with their subjective ideal of a 'good life'). In turn, young people who experience high life satisfaction are more likely to 'engage in valued activity and succeed in living according to their values as they move beyond high school'.[22] The study thus suggests that if young people are to develop 'the sense of meaning and direction that values provide',[23] they need to feel satisfied with their lives.[24]

16 Ibid 617.
17 Ibid.
18 Ibid.
19 Williams, Ciarrochi and Heaven (n 2) 136.
20 The study participants included young people who were university students and others who were employed full-time, seeking work or in vocational training: ibid 138.
21 Wendy Larcombe et al., 'Prevalence and Socio-Demographic Correlates of Psychological Distress Among Students at an Australian University' (2016) 41 *Studies in Higher Education* 1074.
22 Williams, Ciarrochi and Heaven (n 2) 136.
23 Ibid.
24 This is an important finding, given recent research which has found correlations between the amount of time young people spend in front of screens (particularly the smart phone) and decreasing levels of life satisfaction and happiness, along with increased levels of loneliness and symptoms of depression: Jean Twenge, *IGen: Why Today's Super-Connected Kids Are Growing Up Less Rebellious, More Tolerant, Less Happy – and Completely Unprepared for Adulthood – and What That Means for the Rest of Us* (Simon and Schuster, 2017). While Twenge's study is of US young people, a recent Australian study also reports an increase in mental health problems in young people, with young women being twice as likely as young men to meet the criteria for having a probable serious mental illness: Mission Australia and Black Dog Institute, 'Youth Mental Health Report. Youth Survey 2012–2016' (2016) <www.missionaustralia.com.au/publications/research/young-people> accessed 7 May 2019.

While Williams and colleagues' study suggests that well-being is a precursor to valued action, the authors note that most previous research suggests that values are antecedent to well-being.[25] Correlational analyses in Williams' study did indicate that 'the higher importance a young person placed on their values overall, and the more they succeeded in enacting their values, the greater their life satisfaction and positive emotion'.[26] That is, success in acting on one's values was found to be correlated with increased SWB: 'emerging adults who place more importance on their values . . . and increasingly enacted their values experienced more happiness'.[27] As the authors note, this is in line with earlier research showing that 'commitment to personally relevant values and goals is important for a successful transition to adulthood'[28] and supports the view that well-being can be a 'side benefit associated with valued action'.[29] It is worth asking here whether law schools are encouraging or facilitating the development in students of 'personally relevant values and goals' and/or providing opportunities for them to acquire skills related to valued action. I explore this question later in the chapter.

Another perspective on the relationship between values and well-being is that it is iterative. Action on values improves happiness 'in the moment', but future happiness depends on continued action in line with one's values.[30] This perspective is consistent with a positive psychology perspective: valued action leads to moments of happiness which 'help build lasting personal resources such as resilience which will, in turn, promote further valued action'.[31] Whatever the exact relationship between values, valued action and well-being, it is clear that they remain 'inextricably linked' and we do well to remember we cannot address well-being without addressing values.

Which values?

If we are more likely to be well and happy when we enact our values (or, to enact our values when we are well and happy), does it matter what those values are? Yes. As noted in the introduction, well-being/happiness comes 'not from mere pursuit of pleasure, but from living in accordance with [values] that create a sense of meaning, connection and self'.[32] The relationship between psychological needs and values helps explain this. According to Self-Determination Theory (SDT), if we are to live a satisfying life (i.e. to be happy and experience well-being), several psychological needs must be met: our needs for autonomy, competence and

25 Williams, Ciarrochi and Heaven (n 2) 136.
26 Ibid 136–137.
27 Ibid 137.
28 Ibid.
29 Ibid.
30 Ibid.
31 Ibid.
32 Ibid 127.

relatedness.[33] When our need for autonomy is met, we feel that we are able to live in a way that reflects our true self. If our competence need is met, we feel capable of mastering tasks and meeting challenges. And when we feel relatedness to others, we feel closely connected to the important people in our lives.[34] We are more likely to have these needs met if we hold to certain values: self-understanding, good relationships with others, helping others and building community.[35] These values are 'pro-social' values which underpin behaviour of benefit to others or society as a whole.

Further, our values underscore our motivations,[36] and our motivations influence our well-being.[37] For example, if we are intrinsically motivated to succeed as a lawyer, because we genuinely enjoy and value our work and find it fulfilling, we are much more likely to experience satisfaction and well-being than if we are primarily motivated by money, status or the need to impress others.[38] If we primarily focus on extrinsic values such as wealth or power, we can undermine our well-being,[39] because we are not prioritising activities that meet our psychological needs.

Values, well-being and professionalism

The psychological factors that influence whether we are mentally healthy and happy also influence our ethical decision-making, our professional identity and thus our level of professionalism. While some consider legal ethics as simply avoiding the behaviour proscribed by professional conduct rules, ethical professionalism extends beyond mere compliance with rules.[40] Krieger's work has elucidated

33 Lawrence S Krieger, 'The Most Ethical of People, the Least Ethical of People: Proposing Self-Determination Theory to Measure Professional Character Formation' (2011) 8 *University of St Thomas Law Journal* 168, 170.

34 Ibid 171.

35 Ibid 171, 172–173.

36 Yuval Feldman, 'The Complexity of Disentangling Intrinsic and Extrinsic Compliance Motivations: Theoretical and Empirical Insights from the Behavioural Analysis of Law' (2011) 35 *Washington University Journal of Law & Policy* 11, 12. As Feldman writes, 'Extrinsic motivation is linked to actions that are driven by external commands or incentives. Conversely, intrinsic motivation is found when the behaviour is chosen from within the individual, usually out of a sense of moral or civic duty' (12).

37 Tim Kasser and Richard M Ryan, 'Further Examining the American Dream: Differential Correlates of Intrinsic and Extrinsic Goals' (1996) 3 *Personality and Social Psychology Bulletin* 280; Tim Kasser, 'Materialistic Values and Goals' (2016) 67 *Annual Review of Psychology* 489.

38 Lawrence S Krieger and Kennon M Sheldon, 'What Makes Lawyers Happy? A Data Driven Prescription to Redefine Professional Success' (2014) 83 *The George Washington Law Review* 554.

39 Krieger (n 6) 429; Krieger (n 33) 178–181; Krieger and Sheldon (n 38).

40 Vivien Holmes et al., 'Practising Professionalism: Observations from an Empirical Study of New Australian Lawyers' (2012) 15 *Legal Ethics* 29. Some scholars argue that the traditional notions of professionalism no longer hold. See, for example Paula Baron and Lillian Corbin, 'The Unprofessional Professional: Do Lawyers Need Rules?' (2017) 20 *Legal Ethics* 155, 167.

the strong links between SDT's psychological needs and professionalism: a professional (someone with a positive professional identity) exhibits integrity (which is connected to autonomy), competence and service, and displays interpersonal skills when relating to colleagues and clients (relatedness to others).[41] It is fairly easy to see correlations between these characteristics of a professional and the factors discussed previously that contribute to our thriving.

These connections are emphasised in Krieger and Sheldon's report of their research into lawyers practising in four US states.[42] That research found that the satisfaction of basic psychological needs and internal motivation were very strong predictors of lawyer happiness (defined as subjective well-being and life satisfaction). Prestige, high incomes and other external benefits do not 'compensate a lawyer who has not secured autonomy, integrity meaningful/close relationships, and interest and meaning in her work'.[43] Thus, public service lawyers reported stronger well-being and life satisfaction than did lawyers in prestigious, well-paid jobs. The authors observed that the survey:

> did not seek to measure professionalism or ethics, but it did measure psychological factors that are virtually certain to be important sources of ethical and professional behaviour for lawyers . . . These factors also include the strongest predictors of well-being in our subjects, suggesting that one powerful approach to raising the level of professional behaviour among lawyers is to teach law students and lawyers to maximise their own happiness.[44]

If we adopt Krieger and Sheldon's suggestion that we can improve professionalism and ethical conduct by teaching law students and lawyers to be happier, we would be well advised to assist students and lawyers to develop and enact pro-social/professional values, because the enactment of such values contributes to happiness. Law schools play an important role here, which is discussed in the next section.

Values education and well-being

Educational research points to a strong nexus between values education, academic achievement and student well-being. While much of this research pertains to primary and secondary school students, it offers important insights for tertiary education. In the *International Research Handbook on Values Education*

41 Krieger (n 33).
42 Krieger and Sheldon (n 38).
43 Ibid 623.
44 Ibid. As my colleague Stephen Tang commented in conversation with me, Krieger and Sheldon's terminology of 'maximising happiness' runs the risk of turning happiness into an economic commodity (something that can be quantified and essentially bought/sold/traded), where the quantity ('maximise') is its value. Such discourse about well-being could subtly flip intrinsic motivations into extrinsic motivations (happiness as just another thing to obtain) and minimise the role of values.

and Student Wellbeing, Lovat explains the genesis of the modern values education movement:

> In 1994, a Carnegie Corporation Taskforce on Student Achievement drew on new research in the neurosciences to show that effective learning requires a response that is as much about affect and social dynamics as about cognition. In so doing, it re-defined the notion of learning to include matters of communicative competence, empathic character, self-reflection, and self knowing as being as central to intellectual development as the recall of facts and figures. [Today] a values approach to learning is seen to be an indispensable artefact to any learning environment if student wellbeing, including academic success, is to be maximized.[45]

The values in 'values education' are wide in their scope, including social and community engagement (i.e. pro-social values).[46] Likewise, the concept of 'well-being' is understood to include '[m]oral seriousness', through which young people 'address the major issues which confront society (environmental sustainability, career choices, relationships, racism etc) and acquire personal integrity'.[47]

Notably, the values education movement acknowledges that schools must enact the values they aim to teach, including social/community engagement, democratic decision-making processes and respectful relationships.[48] Importantly, values education is not a separate, add-on program. While add-on programs have a place (which can be an important place) they should be seen 'in the wider context of the many different elements entailed in personal and communal well-being, and thus the many ways in which values are embodied, transferred and developed through the wider curriculum and pedagogy'.[49] Pring contrasts this approach with a 'business' approach to education, with its narrow definition of success and use of management-speak to constrain educational vision and offerings.[50]

Similar themes have been raised in relation to education in law school. The Carnegie Foundation's report, *Educating Lawyers*,[51] noted that the 'moral development of professionals requires a holistic approach to the educational experience'.[52] This approach needs to be a 'highly self-conscious, reflexive one',[53] because law schools 'cannot help but affect' students' values, ethical perspectives

45 Terence Lovat, Neville Clement and Ron Toomey (eds), *International Research Handbook on Values Education and Student Wellbeing* (Springer, 2010) 1.
46 Richard Pring, 'Introduction' in Lovat, Clement and Toomey, ibid xx.
47 Ibid xxiii.
48 Ibid xxi.
49 Ibid xx.
50 Ibid xx–xxi.
51 William M Sullivan et al., *Educating Lawyers: Preparation for the Practice of Law* (Jossey-Bass, 2007), referred to as the *Carnegie Report.*
52 Ibid 31.
53 Ibid 32.

and emergent professional identities: law schools 'constitute a powerful moral apprenticeship, whether or not this is intentional'.[54]

Legal ethics literature contains a strong thread of research calling for a holistic approach to ethics education, including deep discussion of professional values, the role of the legal profession in society, the importance of public service (including upholding the rule of law) and emphasis on the development of students' positive professional identities.[55] The point worth emphasising here is that the insights from this literature flesh out our understanding of how law schools can promote well-being: well-being promotion cannot be divorced from promoting and teaching professional values, including encouraging students to look beyond their own (sometimes privileged) sphere to their contribution to the wider community, and providing opportunities for students to make such contributions.[56] Of course, law schools themselves must 'walk the talk' on professional values, including engagement in justice endeavours.

Remembering the importance of values *enactment* to well-being, it is worth noting another contribution to well-being from legal ethics literature: a recent focus on behavioural ethics. Scholarship in behavioural legal ethics contributes to our understanding of ethical decision-making[57] and, importantly, ethical action, including how we might help students develop skills to act in accordance with their values when confronted with ethical challenges. In particular, the Giving Voice to Values (GVV) pedagogy developed by Gentile[58] has been shown to

54 Ibid 139.

55 See, for example, Julian Webb, 'Developing Ethical Lawyers: Can Legal Education Enhance Access to Justice' (1999) 33 *Law Teacher* 284; Julian Webb, 'Being a Lawyer/Being a Human Being' (2002) 5 *Legal Ethics* 130; Christine Parker and Adrian Evans, *Inside Lawyers Ethics* (Cambridge University Press, 2nd ed, 2013); Alice Woolley, 'Intuition and Theory in Legal Ethics Teaching' (2011) 9 *University of St Thomas Law Journal* 285; Neil Hamilton and Verna Monson, 'Legal Education's Ethical Challenge: Empirical Research on How Most Effectively to Foster Each Student's Professional Formation (Professionalism)' (2011) 9 *University of St Thomas Law Journal* 325; Nigel Duncan, 'Addressing Emotions in Preparing Ethical Lawyers' in Paul Maharg and Caroline Maughan (eds), *Affect and Legal Education: Emotion in the Learning and Teaching the Law* (Ashgate Publishing Group, 2011). A textbook that deftly brings well-being, ethics and professionalism together is Rachael Field, James Duffy and Anna Huggins, *Lawyering and Positive Professional Identities* (LexisNexis Butterworths, 2014). See also Chapters 4, 5, 7, 9 and 11 of this work.

56 Clinical courses are important examples of such opportunities: Donald Nicolson, 'Legal Education, Ethics and Access to Justice: Forging Warriors for Justice in a Neo-Liberal World' (2015) *International Journal of the Legal Profession* 1; Donald Nicolson, '"Education, Education, Education": Legal, Moral and Clinical' (2008) 42 *Law Teacher* 145. As are other experiential and student activism projects, such as Molly Townes O'Brien, 'Connecting Law Student Wellbeing to Social Justice, Problem-Solving and Human Emotions' (2014) 14 *QUT Law Review* 52, 57–60. See also, Chapters 9, 10 and 11 of this work.

57 Robert A Prentice, 'Teaching Behavioral Ethics' (2014) 31 *Journal of Legal Studies Education* 325; Robert A Prentice, 'Behavioral Ethics: Can It Help Lawyers (and Others) Be Their Best Selves?' (2015) 29 *Notre Dame Journal of Law, Ethics & Public Policy* 35.

58 Mary C Gentile, *Giving Voice to Values. How to Speak Your Mind When You Know What's Right* (Yale University Press, 2010).

assist students to prepare for ethically challenging situations, such as the situation of being asked by a superior to do something unethical.[59] The GVV approach focusses on helping students/junior lawyers to find the right words for talking with colleagues about values, and to offer their own perspectives on ethical issues. This in turn gives them a sense of agency, 'a significant counter to the feeling that they are just passive recipients of prevailing norms'.[60] The GVV pedagogy highlights the importance of values and ethics in professional life and encourages students to reflect on what sort of professional they wish to be;[61] it encourages the development of positive professional identities.

Law school values and well-being in a hypercompetitive world

In suggesting that law schools need to combine a focus on well-being with a more explicit focus on values, I acknowledge the competitive environment within which modern law schools operate and the hypercompetitive world of practice, to which some graduates aspire and whose modus operandi cannot help but influence legal practice in general. Thornton's research on Australian law schools warns that, in response to competition policy, market pressures and a pervading neoliberal agenda, many law schools have adopted a more commercial focus, privileging subjects relevant to business over critique and social justice, rather than 'aiming to produce critical thinkers who can contribute constructively to the pressing issues of our time'.[62] Likewise, it is worth noting changes to admission requirements in England: candidates will be required to do a 'Solicitors Qualifying Exam', current indications being that this exam will assess knowledge of business law and practice but not, for example, family, consumer or employment law.[63] While I note that business and commercial law have a key role to play in addressing 'the pressing issues of our time',[64] I agree with Thornton that uncritical acceptance of a commercial mindset corrodes a law school's proper role and ethos. Coper explains that ethos as

> inspiring commitment not only to the rule of law and the deep and enduring values of our western democratic legal tradition, but also of imagining the future and thus working for the continuous improvement of the law and operation of the legal system.[65]

59 Holmes (n 8).
60 Ibid 129.
61 Ibid 136.
62 Margaret Thornton, '"Selling the Dream": Law School Branding and the Illusion of Choice' (2013) 23 *Legal Education Review* 249, 270. See also Margaret Thornton, 'The Law School, the Market and the New Knowledge Economy' (2007) 17 *Legal Education Review* 1.
63 Solicitors Regulation Authority 'Assessment Specification for SQE Stage 1 Pilot' <www.sra.org.uk/sra/policy/sqe/pilot/sqe-assessment-specification.page> accessed 7 May 2019.
64 Thornton, '"Selling the Dream"' (n 62), 270.
65 Michael Coper, 'What Makes a "Good" Law School?' (2017) 91 *Australian Law Journal* 628, 631.

The *Carnegie Report* acknowledges the influence of a highly competitive economic environment on legal practice and on the ideals of the profession,[66] but stresses that it is precisely because of these pressures that legal educators need to take very seriously their role in the development of students' professional values: '[l]aw schools can help the profession become smarter and more reflective about strengthening its slipping legitimacy by finding new ways to advance its enduring commitments'.[67]

Part of the pressure on Australian law schools to adopt a more business-focused curriculum is the pervasive view that elite corporate firms 'represent the most desirable destinations for [many] law graduates'.[68] Likewise in the USA, 'power track' careers (highly paid, large firm work) seem to be held in high esteem by law schools and law students.[69] The *Carnegie Report* argues that, without conscious attention to this issue by law schools, the 'power track' values of compensation, advancement, prestige and status 'are likely to trump concern for other dimensions of job satisfaction' such as collegiality, intrinsic interest of the work and social value of the work, setting students up 'for dissatisfaction and soul searching in their early practice lives'.[70] This warning is borne out by Krieger and Sheldon's findings, discussed earlier, about the relative happiness and well-being of 'prestige' lawyers and service lawyers. Their findings emphasise that a 'systematic effort' is required 'to recast perceptions of "success" in law school and the profession'[71] by changing the institutional focus on 'power track' values to a focus on 'support, collaboration, interest and personal purpose'.[72] The *Carnegie Report* likewise calls for 'serious curricular attention' to the mixed messages students receive about professional identity and purpose, noting that failure by law schools to pay such attention is a failure 'to provide the kind of open-eyed preparation needed for today's complicated professional world'.[73]

This message is reinforced by Moorhead's cross-jurisdictional research of the ethical identity of law students, which gathered data on the 'ethicality' of UK and US law students via measures of moral outlook, values and (professional) identity.[74] Moorhead's results suggest that 'the pull of the legal profession may have more of an effect on ethical identity than any socialising effects from the push

66 Sullivan et al. (n 52) 126.
67 Ibid 128.
68 Thornton (n 62) 260.
69 Sullivan et al. (n 52) 138.
70 Ibid.
71 Krieger and Sheldon (n 38) 624.
72 Ibid.
73 Sullivan et al. (n 52) 138. It is also a failure to prepare the future profession for its vital role in upholding the rule of law in a world facing monumental environmental, social and economic challenges: Vivien Holmes and Simon Rice, 'Our Common Future: The Imperative for Contextual Ethics in a Connected World' in Francesca Bartlett, Reid Mortensen and Kieran Tranter (eds), *Alternative Perspectives on Lawyers and Legal Ethics: Reimagining the Profession* (Routledge, 2010).
74 Richard Moorhead et al., 'The Ethical Identity of Law Students' (2016) 23 *International Journal of the Legal Profession* 235, 238.

of legal education'.[75] More specifically, while the study found that the ethical identity of students is strongly influenced by the 'innate characteristics' of students (especially gender), it also found that career intentions influence ethicality. Notably, students intending to practise business law (as compared to government law or working for individual/private clients) 'had ethical identities . . . associated with a somewhat greater susceptibility to unethical behaviour'.[76] This finding prompted Moorhead and colleagues to suggest that 'law schools may need to look harder at how they prepare their students for legal practice . . . and firms should consider how they signal their own ethical identities'.[77]

Ethics and well-being in the workplace: Ethical climate

Since the legal workplace can influence ethical identity from afar (i.e. while students are still at law school), it is no surprise that it has a profound impact once students become lawyers. And since enactment of values is related to well-being, it is also no surprise that well-being suffers when the workplace environment precludes or inhibits valued action. Insights into whether a workplace enables ethical behaviour can be gained by surveying the ethical climate of the workplace; 'ethical climate' being employee perceptions of how the members of an organisation 'typically make decisions concerning "events, practices, and procedures" requiring ethical criteria'.[78]

Together with colleagues Tang, Foley and Rowe, I have researched new lawyers' perceptions of the 'ethical climate' of Australian legal workplaces.[79] Such perceptions are likely to influence the perceiver's own decision-making on issues with ethical import.[80] Our research found that respondents' perceptions of the ethical climate of their workplaces could be readily measured on three independent dimensions, with participants perceiving their workplace climate as containing *more* or *less* of each one of these dimensions:[81]

- **Power and Self-Interest:** the extent to which power, control and instrumental outcomes are more important and valued, compared with normative

75 Ibid 256. The study did find that some educational offerings, such as ethics courses and clinical programs, appear to be associated with greater ethicality (ibid 258).

76 Ibid 250. This could perhaps be partially explained by a shift from intrinsic/justice to extrinsic/profit motivations during law school. See Molly Townes O'Brien and Stephen Tang, 'Stop Struggling for the Struggle's Sake: Make It Meaningful' Paper presented at the *International First Year in Higher Education* Conference, 7–10 July 2013, Wellington.

77 Moorhead et al. (n 74) 258.

78 John D Cullen, Bart Victor and James W Bronson, 'The Ethical Climate Questionnaire: An Assessment of Its Development and Validity' (1993) 73 *Psychological Reports* 667, 669.

79 Forthcoming.

80 Jennifer J Kish-Gephart, David A Harrison and Linda Klebe Treviño, 'Bad Apples, Bad Cases, and Bad Barrels: Meta-Analytic Evidence About Sources of Unethical Decisions at Work' (2010) 95 *Journal of Applied Psychology* 1.

81 These dimensions are very similar to those identified by Kish-Gephart and colleagues in their meta-analysis of research into sources of unethical decisions at work as the most significant dimensions of ethical work climate for predicting (un)ethical behaviour: ibid.

principles such as honesty, ethicality or relational values and a corresponding preparedness to break rules to obtain benefit when necessary.

- **Integrity and Responsibility:** the extent to which there is a sensitivity to behaving ethically and adhering to formal ethical rules, and an inclination to be compliant, conscious and accountable to prescriptive requirements.
- **Ethic of Care:** the extent to which people in the workplace express empathy and understanding for each other and strive to develop positive and respectful relationships with others as an attentive professional.

Our findings are reported in detail elsewhere,[82] but of particular note here is that higher perceptions of an ethical climate of 'power and self-interest' were predictive of a greater intensity or frequency of symptoms associated with depression. Conversely, workplace ethical climates reported as having a higher integrity/responsibility dimension were significantly negatively associated with depression and anxiety symptoms. The 'ethic of care' dimension was negatively associated with depression, stress and anxiety symptoms. In other words, workplaces perceived to have stronger integrity and ethic of care dimensions are likely to have fewer employees experiencing concerning levels of depression, stress and/or anxiety symptoms.

Another pertinent finding from this research relates to job satisfaction: our findings suggest that job satisfaction correlates with both perceptions of ethical culture and the meeting of psychological needs through that culture. Workplace cultures perceived to be high in the integrity and ethic of care climate dimensions were correlated with higher job satisfaction than those high in the 'power and self-interest' dimension. These findings are consistent with Kish-Gephart and colleagues' observations that higher job satisfaction is related to a lower level of unethical behaviour in organisations.[83]

This research strongly supports the view that well-being cannot be reduced simply to an individual's personal experiences, but is just as likely to be determined by the culture of the organisation in which they work, and specifically the values embedded in that culture. Our results are in line with the work of other scholars who have drawn attention to the impact of organisational structures and cultures on well-being, and the danger of seeing well-being as solely an individual responsibility.[84] Our results also support Krieger and Sheldon's findings that external benefits do not 'adequately compensate a lawyer who does not regularly experience autonomy, integrity, close relationships and interest and meaning in her work'.[85]

82 Vivien Holmes, Tony Foley and Margie Rowe, 'Australian Legal Practice: Ethical Climate and Ethical Climate Change' in Ron Levy et al. (eds), *New Directions for Law in Australia: Essays in Contemporary Law Reform* (ANU Press, 2017).

83 Kish-Gephart, Harrison and Treviño (n 80) 12.

84 Paula Baron, 'Sleight of Hand: Lawyer Distress and the Attribution of Responsibility' (2014) 23 *Griffith Law Review* 261; Christine Parker, 'The "Moral Panic" Over Psychological Wellbeing in the Legal Profession: A Personal or Political Ethical Response?' (2014) 37 *UNSW Law Journal* 1103.

85 Krieger and Sheldon (n 38) 623.

Ethics and well-being in the workplace: Hypercompetition

It is in employers' interests to take heed of the research discussed in this chapter, since the psychological well-being of employees is likely to 'improve productivity, morale and retention' of employees.[86] The likelihood of some employers heeding this message is perhaps somewhat slim. Scholars such as Bagust,[87] Thornton,[88] and Collier[89] have drawn attention to the hypercompetitive cultures prevailing in (some areas of) private legal practice, including the elite global firms in which many law students aspire to work. Such cultures exhibit practices and attitudes (including 24/7 commitment, gendered conceptions of success; workplace bullying) that are inimical to well-being[90] and also to many professional values, such as collegiality and public service.[91] Collier suggests that, within these cultures, any new emphasis on well-being (mindfulness sessions, in-house gyms, discussion of work/life balance) is a 'catch all' concept 'deployed . . . to maximise productivity, manage risk . . . and help create wealth and competitive advantage'.[92] As Chan notes in her study of Australian lawyers' well-being, within such cultures, 'individual resilience is not a sustainable solution'.[93]

It may be, as Chan suggests, that continued exposure of the effects of highly competitive and stressful forms of legal practice, the continued attrition from such practice, and the emergence of alternative forms of practice will bring about change in the legal profession.[94] Reports by the Law Council of Australia (NARS report)[95] and the International Bar Association[96] are part of such exposure, both reports highlighting that discrimination against, and sexual harassment of, women continues to be a significant problem in the legal profession. Echoing the scholars discussed previously, the IBA report notes the effects of 24/7 culture and gendered conceptions of the 'ideal lawyer':

> The ever-increasing demands of billable hours, the use of technology-enabling work to intrude on lawyers' time outside of work and the continued

86 Ibid 625.

87 Joanne Bagust, 'The Legal Profession and the Business of Law' (2013) 35 *Sydney Law Review* 27.

88 Margaret Thornton, 'Hypercompetitiveness or a Balanced Life? Gendered Discourses in the Globalisation of Australian Law Firms' (2014) 17 *Legal Ethics* 153.

89 Richard Collier, 'Wellbeing in the Legal Profession: Reflections on Recent Developments (or, What Do We Talk about When We Talk about Wellbeing?)' (2016) 23 *International Journal of the Legal Profession* 41.

90 Ibid 52.

91 Paula D Baron and Lillian C Corbin, 'Ethics Begins at Home' (2016) 19(2) *Legal Ethics* 281.

92 Collier (n 89) 51–52.

93 Janet Chan, 'Conceptualising Legal Culture and Lawyering Stress' (2014) 21 *International Journal of the Legal Profession* 213, 228.

94 Ibid 229.

95 Law Council of Australia, 'National Attrition and Re-Engagement Study (NARS) Report' (Law Council of Australia) <https://www.lawcouncil.asn.au/docs/a8bae9a1-9830-e711-80d2.../NARS%20Report.pdf> accessed 7 May 2019.

96 Jane Ellis and Ashleigh Buckett, *Women in Commercial Legal Practice* (IBA Legal Policy & Research Unit, 2017).

> expectation that the 'ideal legal worker' must commit him or herself 'unconditionally' to work is used to call into question women's (among others) commitment to their careers.[97]

It is unlikely, however, that exposure is enough. It may be that regulation has a role to play. Proactive regulation has been used to target areas of ethical concern in the past: in the Australian state of New South Wales, regulation focussing on the 'ethical infrastructure' of legal practices was shown to be effective in improving firm management and supervision, resulting in fewer client complaints.[98] Compliance Officers, required under UK legislation, have been described as playing 'a critical role . . . in protecting and promoting professional values'.[99] Baron and Corbin argue in favour of specific rules relating to values, suggesting that the profession no longer has a shared understanding of professionalism, the norms of which are in any case 'rapidly being superseded by'[100] the norms of consumerism. Looking more broadly, others have suggested reform of discrimination/workplace/human rights regulatory systems.[101]

Conclusion

In an early published draft of their article, Krieger and Sheldon verge on leaving responsibility for well-being with the individual by concluding that '[t]he factors found in this study to bear most strongly on personal well-being are all matters of individual choice'.[102] Their published paper concludes with more nuance. For the reasons discussed in this chapter, I take issue with this strong emphasis on individual choice in the field of well-being. But, in some senses, Krieger and Sheldon are correct to highlight choice, because, as they say, our 'choices ultimately determine the morale and functional quality of institutions and organizations, and the tenor of the legal profession'.[103] One of our choices is where we target our energies in promoting well-being in law school and the profession. In this chapter, I have argued that we cannot divorce well-being from values and ethics. If law schools are serious about student well-being, they need to consciously promote

97 Ibid 5.

98 Christine Parker, Tahlia Gordon and Steve Mark, 'Regulating Law Firm Management: An Empirical Assessment of an Innovation in Regulation of the Legal Profession in New South Wales' (2010) 37 *Journal of Law and Society* 466; Susan Fortney and Tahlia Gordon, 'Adopting Law Firm Management Systems to Survive and Thrive: A Study of the Australian Approach to Management-Based Regulation' (2012) 10 *University of St Thomas Law Journal* 152.

99 Aulakh and Loughrey (n 11) 28.

100 Baron and Corbin (n 40) 172.

101 Margaret Thornton, *Sex Discrimination in Uncertain Times* (ANU Press, 2010). Such regulation must be informed by research in behavioural ethics: Yuval Feldman, *The Law of Good People: Challenging States' Ability to Regulate Human Behaviour* (Cambridge University Press, 2018).

102 Draft article, initially published on SSRN, on file with author.

103 Ibid.

and model pro-social, professional values and support students to develop positive professional identities. Employers concerned for staff well-being will consider the ethical climate of their practices and implement changes where appropriate. Regulators concerned about mental ill-health in the profession can target regulation to effect positive ethical change.

The legal profession's primary duty is to uphold the rule of law. In a world facing enormous political, social and environmental challenges, that duty has never been more important. To fulfil their responsibilities, lawyers need to be well, which means being deeply connected to values.

4 Well-being and a positive professional identity in the legal profession

A snapshot of the UK Bar

Rachel Spearing and Rachael Field

Introduction

The legal profession in the US, the UK and Australia has become increasingly aware that significant numbers of lawyers are experiencing concerningly high levels of psychological distress.[1] This is a serious issue relevant to the future sustainability of the profession. A profession in distress is ill-equipped to cope with the challenges of uncertainty and disruption that are now endemic in the contemporary world of work.[2] It is also an issue that pertains to the efficacy of legal practice, as there is evidence linking stress, anxiety and depression with impaired professional judgement.[3]

1 This is empirically well-established as evidenced in a significant body of scholarship too large to cite in its entirety here. See, for example, the scholarship of the accompanying chapters of this book as well as the works included in Rachael Field, James Duffy and Colin James (eds), *Promoting Law Student and Lawyer Well-Being in Australia and Beyond* (Routledge, 2016). See also recent works such as: Filippa Anzalone, 'Lawyer and Law Student Well-Being' (2018) 22(4) *AALL Spectrum* 44; Natalie K Skead, Shane L Rogers and Jerome Doraisamy, 'Looking Beyond the Mirror: Psychological Distress; Disordered Eating, Weight and Shape Concerns; and Maladaptive Eating Habits in Lawyers and Law Students' (2018) 61 *International Journal of Law and Psychiatry* 90.

2 Richard Susskind, *The End of Lawyers? Rethinking the Nature of Legal Services* (Oxford University Press, 2008, rev ed, 2010); Richard Susskind, *Tomorrow's Lawyers: An Introduction to Your Future* (Oxford University Press, 2013); Richard Susskind and Daniel Susskind, *The Future of the Professions: How Technology Will Transform the Work of Human Experts* (Oxford University Press, 2015).

3 See for example, John F Harkness Jr, 'Lawyers Helping Lawyers: A Message of Hope' (1999) 73 *Florida Bar Journal* 10. This article reported that over half the grievances filed against lawyers have addiction or mental disorder as a significant contributing factor. In 2009, John Briton, the Legal Services Commissioner for Queensland, made the claim in an address to the Queensland Bar that one-third of the unprofessional conduct and professional misconduct matters heard by the Commission involved psychological ill-health: John Briton, 'Lawyers, Emotional Distress and Regulation' Address to the Bar Association of Queensland 2009 Annual Conference <www.lsc.qld.gov.au/__data/assets/pdf_file/0006/106197/lawyers-emotional-distress-and-regulation.pdf> accessed 7 May 2019. See also, Office of the NSW Legal Services Commissioner, 'Substance Abuse and Mental Health Issues in the Legal Profession: An Issues Paper' (NSW Legal Services Commissioner, 2007); Michael Appleby, 'Annual Mental Health Lecture: A Good Lawyer is a Well Lawyer' (2016) 242 *Ethos: Official Publication of the Law Society of the Australian Capital Territory* 16; Paula Baron, 'The

In the UK, the Bar Council supported a well-being study in 2014 to which 2456 barristers responded.[4] A third of the respondents indicated that they were disengaged at work, reports of rumination and self-critical perfectionism were at notable levels, and the respondents recognised significant pressure coming from personal expectations of high standards and the pursuit of excellence and perfection.[5] In relation to the experience of negative stress, the report identified that the main source of pressure was 'associated with work',[6] with two thirds of respondents indicating that their current levels of stress impacted on their work. The results also reflected significant levels of distress that possibly indicated emotional exhaustion.[7] Further, more than half of the respondents reported 'that they do not enjoy refreshing, good quality sleep and only a minority reported that they were able to take breaks throughout the day'.[8] In relation to solicitors, the UK Law Society's recent health and well-being survey 'found that almost all practising certificate holders (95%) have negative stress in their working lives, with 16% reporting that they had experienced "severe" or "extreme" levels of stress'.[9] The empirical research on the experience of high levels of psychological distress in the profession is mirrored by studies of experiences of legal education indicating that elevated levels of psychological distress (including depression, anxiety and substance abuse) are also prevalent amongst law students.[10]

There are many possible responses to the psychological distress phenomenon in the legal profession. For example, Bar Associations and Law Societies around the world have created well-being related continuing professional development opportunities; member assistance services offer around the clock confidential counselling; expanded risk-management strategies have been put in place and resource portals including advice referrals have been established.[11] Gibson argues

---

Elephant in The Room? Lawyer Wellbeing and the Impact of Unethical Behaviours' (2015) 41(1) *Australian Feminist Law Journal* 87.

4 Rachel Spearing and Positive Group, *Wellbeing at the Bar: A Resilience Framework Assessment (RFA)* (Bar Council, 2015) <www.barcouncil.org.uk/media/348371/wellbeing_at_the_bar_report_april_2015__final_.pdf> accessed 7 May 2019.

5 Ibid 3–4.

6 Ibid 4.

7 Ibid.

8 Spearing and Positive Group (n 4).

9 Monidipa Fouzder, 'Mental Health Taskforce for Legal Professionals' (2016) *The Law Society Gazette* <www.lawgazette.co.uk/news/mental-health-taskforce-for-legal-professionals/5055285.fullarticle> accessed 7 May 2019.

10 No specific studies with law students have yet been done in the UK, however the issue is well established in Australia and the US. See for example Field, Duffy and James (n 1). See also Jerome M Organ, David B Jaffe and Katherine M Bender, 'Suffering in Silence: The Survey of Law Student Well-Being and the Reluctance of Law Students to Seek Help for Substance Use and Mental Health Concerns' (2016) 66 *The Journal of Legal Education* 116.

11 Frances Gibson, 'Psychiatric Disability and the Practising Lawyer in Australia' (2012) 20 *Journal of Law and Medicine* 391, 393. See also Christopher Kendall, *Report on Psychological Distress and Depression in the Legal Profession* (Law Society of Western Australia, 2011) <https://www.lawsocietywa.asn.au/wp-content/uploads/2015/08/Report-on-psychological-distress-and-depression-in-the-legal-profession.pdf> accessed 7 May 2019. See also, for example, Law Institute of Victoria, 'Fighting a Common Enemy' (2010) 84(10) *Law Institute*

that issues of mental health can be well-managed if 'legal workplaces are structured to ensure a person is given support'.[12] Such support could include: 'good mentoring and management, education programs for staff, a supportive environment where people are able to reveal illness without fearing stigmatising or discrimination, and appropriate working hours and leave arrangements'.[13] Some of the enacted initiatives in the UK include the 'I am the Bar' campaign of the UK Bar, the Inner Temple's 'Pegasus Access Diversity Scheme (PADS)', and the Law Society's 'Diversity in the Workplace' initiative. Richard Collier refers to organisational efforts within particular UK law firms to promote well-being, with several firms establishing 'dedicated wellbeing programmes for staff'.[14] He notes the focus of the UK charity LawCare on providing services 'to help lawyers, their immediate families and their staff to deal with issues such as stress, depression, addiction, eating disorders and related emotional difficulties'.[15] Ensuring that the legal academy is included as part of the solution to this problem also has positive potential. For example, well-being, self-care and self-regulation skills and strategies could be explicitly taught and embedded in the law curriculum from the first year of law school.[16]

This chapter argues that another possible strategy to promote and support lawyer well-being is the inculcation and endorsement of a positive professional identity across the legal profession, beginning at law school. This hypothesis is based on positive psychology and its meta-theory – Self-Determination Theory.[17] The chapter first considers the nature of a professional identity, and how a legal professional identity might manifest itself. The results of a small-scale survey of a

---

Journal 6; Colin James, 'Lawyer Dissatisfaction, Emotional Intelligence and Clinical Legal Education' (2008) 18 *Legal Education Review* 123.

12 Gibson (n 11) 394.

13 Ibid 394. See also Colin James, 'Resilient Lawyers: Maximising Well-Being in Legal Education and Practice' in Field, Duffy and James (n 1); Colin James, 'Lawyers' Wellbeing and Professional Legal Education' (2008) 42(1) *The Law Teacher* 85.

14 Richard Collier, '"Love Law, Love Life": Neoliberalism, Wellbeing and Gender in the Legal Profession – The Case of Law School' (2014) 17(2) *Legal Ethics* 202, 207.

15 See for example, LawCare, 'Supporting the Legal Community' *Home Page,* 2019, <www.lawcare.org.uk> accessed 7 May 2019.

16 Rachael Field, Report on an Australian Learning and Teaching Council (ALTC) Fellowship: *Stimulating Strategic Change in Legal Education to Address High Levels of Psychological Distress in Law Students* (ALTC, 2014) <https://altf.org/fellowships/stimulating-strategic-change-in-legal-education-to-address-high-levels-of-psychological-distress-in-law-students/> accessed 7 May 2019.

17 See generally, Richard Ryan and Edward Deci, 'Self-Determination Theory and the Facilitation of Intrinsic Motivation, Social Development and Well-being' (2000) 55(1) *American Psychologist* 68; Richard Ryan and Edward Deci, 'Overview of Self-Determination Theory: An Organismic Dialectical Perspective' in Edward Deci and Richard Ryan (eds), *Handbook of Self Determination Research* (University of Rochester Press, 2002); Richard Ryan and Edward Deci, 'Self-Determination Theory and the Role of Basic Psychological Needs in Personality and the Organization of Behaviour' in Oliver John, Richard Robins and Lawrence Pervin (eds), *Handbook of Personality: Theory and Research* (Guilford Press, 3rd ed, 2008) 654.

self-selecting sample of barristers conducted at the General Council of the Bar Conference in London in October 2015 is then presented. The intention of the survey was to test the hypothesis in a preliminary way with members of the UK Bar that inculcating a sense of professional identity in lawyers is important for the well-being of barristers, and that legal education has a role to play in establishing the foundations for such an identity from the time lawyers are law students.

Before continuing, it is worth noting Christine Parker's concern that a focus on the phenomenon of psychological distress in individual lawyers, and an emphasis on supporting lawyers to develop strategies to be psychologically well, risks domesticating, depoliticising and defusing 'profound ethical and socio-political questions' associated with how the legal profession is being negatively impacted by neoliberal forces.[18] Parker has asserted that there is 'a danger that the wellbeing discourse will be co-opted by powerful interests that seek to confine change to the individual and not the collective social, economic and political levels'.[19] We agree that structural and cultural issues are contributing to the experience of psychological distress across a range of professions in contemporary times. It is a matter for leadership within the legal profession that these issues are acknowledged, confronted and addressed. However, we also believe that lawyers as human beings deserve the support of their profession and colleagues in building capacity, both individually and collectively, to cope with the challenges of the neoliberalist legal work environment. This is not with an intention to increase the individual productivity or profitability of lawyers, but rather to enable a life well-lived, and so that lawyers are in a position to defend and protect the place of the rule of law in society, and of lawyering, as a professional practice for the public good.[20] Our position supports the prioritisation in the legal profession of psychological health over economic productivity and we add our voice to the call for public policy and public education to emphasise this focus.

Positive professional identities for lawyers[21]

It is difficult to articulate the concept of 'professional identity' definitively. There is no single, precise meaning for the term, because, as Hall, Townes O'Brien and

18 Christine Parker, 'The "Moral Panic" Over Psychological Wellbeing in the Legal Profession: A Personal or Political Ethical Response?' (2014) 37(3) *UNSW Law Journal* 1103, 1105.

19 Ibid 1105.

20 See on the issue of neoliberal influences on the profession for example, Margaret Thornton, 'Squeezing the Life Out of Lawyers: Legal Practice in the Market Embrace' (2016) 25(4) *Griffith Law Review* 471; John Flood, 'Megalawyering in the Global Order: The Cultural, Social and Economic Transformation of Global Legal Practice' (1996) 3 *International Journal of the Legal Profession* 169; David Barnhizer, 'Profession Deleted: Using Market and Liability Forces to Regulate the Very Ordinary Business of Law Practice for Profit' (2003) 17 *Georgetown Journal of Legal Ethics* 203.

21 See generally Rachael Field, James Duffy and Anna Huggins, *Lawyering and Positive Professional Identities* (Lexis Nexis, 2014); Susan L Brooks, 'Fostering Wholehearted Lawyers:

Tang have noted, 'professional identity is not a static concept'.[22] Rather, a professional may have multiple identities because it is a 'relational phenomenon',[23] a complex mix of expectations and perceptions that individuals have in the context of their professional self-concept.[24] As Ibarra says, a professional identity includes a 'constellation of attributes, beliefs, values, motives and experiences' by which we define ourselves in our professional lives.[25]

A professional identity is how we understand what it means to be *in* and *of* a profession. The concept of a legal professional identity is therefore a broad church, with much room for diverse manifestations at an individualised level for lawyers working across all the various arms of the profession. Descriptions of a professional identity from the literature include: 'certain attitudes and habits of heart and mind that are thought critical to the practice and culture of the profession';[26] a sense of 'professional self-consciousness and constructive introspection, and an attitude of respect and responsibility to others';[27] a sense of individual agency, internal beliefs and standards;[28] contextual relationality, belonging to a professional community of practice and connection with fellow members of the profession;[29] a broader sense of understanding one's professional role as a lawyer 'relative to all of the stakeholders in the legal system, including clients, courts, opposing parties and counsel, the firm, and even the legal system itself (or society as a whole)';[30] and 'the framework that a lawyer uses to make decisions'.[31]

White et al. have identified three key generic elements that together make up a 'professional identity' as a concept.[32] First, *personal identity*, including factors

---

Practical Guidance for Supporting Law Students' Professional Identity Formation' (2018) 14 The *University of St Thomas Law Journal* 412.

22 Kath Hall, Molly Townes O'Brien and Stephen Tang, 'Developing a Professional Identity in Law School: A View from Australia' (2010) 4 *Phoenix Law Review* 19, 30.

23 Douwe Beijaard, Paulien Meijer and Nico Verloop, 'Reconsidering Research on Teachers' Professional Identity' (2004) 20 *Teaching and Teacher Education* 107.

24 Sheldon Stryker and Peter Burke, 'The Past, Present and Future of an Identity Theory' (2000) 63(4) *Social Psychology Quarterly* 284, 286.

25 Herminia Ibarra, 'Provisional Selves: Experimenting with Image and Identity in Professional Adaptation' (1999) 44(4) *Administrative Science Quarterly* 764.

26 Barry Sullivan and Ellen Podgor, 'Respect, Responsibility, and the Virtue of Introspection: An Essay on Professionalism in the Law School Environment' (2001) 15 *Notre Dame Journal of Law, Ethics and Public Policy* 117, 118.

27 Ibid 119.

28 Benjamin V Madison and Larry O Natt Gantt, 'The Emperor Has No Clothes, But Does Anyone Really Care? How Law Schools are Failing to Develop Students' Professional Identity and Practical Judgment' (2015) 17(2) *Regent University Law Review* 339.

29 Ibid. See also Martin J Katz, 'Teaching Professional Identity in Law School' (2013) 42 *The Colorado Lawyer* 45.

30 Ibid.

31 Scott E Fruehwald, 'Developing Law Students' Professional Identities' (2015) 37 *University of La Verne Law Review* 1, 2.

32 Mary T White et al., 'Perceptions of Factors Contributing to Professional Identity Development and Specialty Choice: A Survey of Third- and Fourth-Year Medical Students' (2011) 17(1) *Annals of Behavioral Science and Medical Education* 18.

such as one's personal history, life experiences, personality, feelings, goals and values. Second, *role identity*, which is made up of professional functions, activities and responsibilities specific to individual professions. Third, *social identity*, which refers to the values and goals to which the profession collectively commits within a societal context.

The personal identity that lawyers bring to their professional identity formation is of course unique to each individual, and their particular context. However, the *role* and *social* identities for lawyers, as members of a community of expert professional practice, have synergies across the various arms of the profession, notwithstanding that the various lawyering roles involve different aspects of practice and diverse ways of contributing to the law as a professional endeavour.

As Mills noted in 1943, every discipline has a 'professional ideology';[33] namely, 'a system of ideas and ideals',[34] 'that reflects beliefs and interests' and 'underlies action'.[35] The professional ideology of law that informs the role and social identities of members of the legal profession provides lawyers with a sense of professional meaning and purpose.[36] This ideology is bound up with being part of a 'noble profession',[37] a profession with altruistic values and objectives of public service in terms of upholding the rule of law,[38] seeking to promote and achieve justice in a liberal democratic society, and helping people with complex transactional and dispute resolution issues with sophisticated technical knowledge, skills and expertise.[39]

Upholding the rule of law is a particularly central and bonding value element of the social identity of the legal profession. As a political and legal ideal in liberal democracies the rule of law provides a foundational framework for civic systems of law and government to achieve social stability, 'peace, freedom and decency', and the protection of individual and collective rights and freedoms.[40] Contributing to upholding this important principle means that the role of a lawyer is much

33 Charles Wright Mills, 'The Professional Ideology of Social Pathologists' (1943) 49 *American Journal of Sociology* 165.

34 Oxford English Dictionary online: <www.oxforddictionaries.com/definition/english/ideology> accessed 7 May 2019.

35 Collins English Dictionary online: <www.collinsdictionary.com/dictionary/english/ideology> accessed 7 May 2019.

36 Frank M Loewenberg, 'Professional Ideology, Middle Range Theories and Knowledge Building for Social Work Practice' (1984) 14 *British Journal of Social Work* 309, 320.

37 References are made to a 'noble profession' in Michael Kirby, 'Billable Hours in a Noble Calling' (1996) 21 *Alternative Law Journal* 257; Warren K Winkler, 'Civil Justice Reform – The Toronto Experience' (2007) 39(1) *Ottawa Law Review* 99.

38 Geoffrey de Q Walker, 'Rule of Law and the Democratic World Order' in Suri Ratnapala and Gabriel A Moens (eds), *Jurisprudence of Liberty* (LexisNexis, 2nd ed, 2010).

39 See for example, Laurence Boulle and Rachael Field, *Dispute Resolution in Australia: Law and Practice* (LexisNexis, 2017) Ch 1. See also Chapter 2 of this book.

40 Gerard Brennan, 'The Role of the Legal Profession in the Rule of Law' Address at the Supreme Court, Brisbane 31 August 2007, 1 <www.nswbar.asn.au/circulars/brennan.pdf> accessed 7 May 2019.

more than a money-making enterprise,[41] rather it is informed by intrinsic and altruistic motivations grounded in service to the community. As Justice Kiefel of the Australian High Court has said: 'Practising lawyers do not just run a business, selling their skills and services to clients in return for fees. The practice of law is a profession and this sets it apart from other, commercial, enterprises'.[42] The role and social identities of lawyers therefore include contributing to maintaining political inclusion, protecting the citizenry against arbitrary action, ensuring relative equality among citizens and defending liberty and autonomy within a context of democratic responsibility and accountability.[43] Lawyers support liberty, provide a voice to the vulnerable, and enable social, political and economic participation.[44] The role of lawyers in putting this social identity into practice involves high levels of competence and skill in giving legal advice, and providing legal representation and advocacy.

Our hypothesis that a positive professional identity has a role to play in promoting lawyer well-being is supported by positive psychology.[45] Positive psychology is a relatively recent addition to the discipline of psychology that focusses on promoting what goes psychologically right with people. In this way, it departs from the traditional concern of psychology which has been to address what has gone psychologically wrong with people.[46] As Martin Seligman, one of the founders of positive psychology has said: 'psychology is not just the study of weakness and damage; it is also the study of strength and virtue. Treatment is not just fixing what is broken; it is nurturing what is best within us'.[47]

Positive psychology is preventative and future focussed. It aims to help people create their own conditions for increased psychological well-being, and to harness their strengths and virtues so as to nurture what is best within themselves. The development of a positive professional identity is, we believe, an important strategy in promoting strength and virtue and what is best within lawyers, and it

41 For a seminal discussion of contemporary 'market ideology' in the US context see Leonard Silk and David Vogel, *Ethics and Profits: The Crisis of Confidence in American Business* (Simon and Schuster, 1976).

42 Susan Kiefel, 'Ethics and the Profession of the Lawyer' Address to the Queensland Law Society: The Vincents' 48th Annual Symposium, Canberra, High Court of Australia, 26 March 2010, 1 <www.hcourt.gov.au/assets/publications/speeches/current-justices/kiefelj/kiefelj-2010-03-26.pdf> accessed 7 May 2019.

43 See for example, Charles Tilley, *Democracy* (Cambridge University Press, 2007).

44 Mary Parker Follett, 'Constructive Conflict' in Pauline Graham (ed), *Mary Parker Follett: Prophet of Management: A Celebration of Writings from the 1920s* (Harvard Business School Press, 1996) 67.

45 See generally William C Compton and Edward Hoffman, *Positive Psychology: The Science of Happiness and Flourishing* (Cengage Learning, 2nd ed, 2013). See also Martin E Seligman and Mihaly Csikszentmihalyi, 'Positive Psychology: An Introduction' (2000) 55(1) *American Psychologist* 5.

46 See for example, William C Compton, *An Introduction to Positive Psychology* (Wadsworth Publishing, 2005).

47 Martin Seligman quoted in Compton and Hoffman (n 45) 1. See also, Martin E Seligman, *Authentic Happiness* (Free Press, 2002) x.

is important to ensuring that lawyers flourish through the experience of authentic and fulfilling professional endeavours, and have the psychological resources to cope with the stressors and challenges of legal professional practice.

Seligman articulated the PERMA framework in his influential book *Flourish*.[48] It resonates with and makes accessible much of the complexity of Self-Determination Theory,[49] a key meta-theory of positive psychology that helps us to understand how psychological well-being can best be supported. The letters of PERMA each stand for one of five elements in support of well-being: positive emotion, engagement, positive relationships, meaning and accomplishment. While PERMA has been criticised for its limited focus 'on well-being outcomes rather than the inputs and processes that lead to well-being', and for failing to 'inform people of the processes involved in cultivating well-being',[50] it is nevertheless, of the existing positive psychology frameworks, one that can be used effectively for the purpose of explaining why a positive professional identity can be said to support lawyer well-being.

First, positive emotion (P) refers to hedonic feelings of happiness, including peace, gratitude, satisfaction, pleasure, inspiration, hope, curiosity and love, as well as joy, interest and contentment.[51] Positive emotion has received particular attention in the positive psychology field.[52] Huppert and So, for example, have found that positive emotion is central to flourishing,[53] a finding that is supported

48 Martin Seligman, *Flourish: A Visionary New Understanding of Happiness and Well-being* (Free Press, 2011). See also Felicia A Huppert, Nick Baylis and Barry Keverne, *The Science of Well-Being* (Oxford University Press, 2005); Felicia A Huppert and Cary L Cooper, *Wellbeing: A Complete Reference Guide, Volume VI: Interventions and Policies to Enhance Wellbeing* (John Wiley & Sons, 2014).

49 See the references in (n 17). See also, Maarten Vansteenkiste, Christopher P Niemiec and Bart Soenens, 'The Development of the Five Mini-Theories of Self-Determination Theory: An Historical Overview, Emerging Trends, and Future Directions' in Timothy C Urdan and Stuart A Karabenick (eds), *The Decade Ahead: Theoretical Perspectives on Motivation and Achievement* (Emerald Group Publishing Limited, 2010) 105, 131; Kennon Sheldon, Geoffrey Williams and Thomas Joiner, *Self-Determination Theory in the Clinic: Motivating Physical and Mental Health* (Yale University Press, 2003).

50 Reuben D Rusk and Lea Waters, 'A Psycho-Social System Approach to Well-Being: Empirically Deriving the Five Domains of Positive Functioning' (2015) 10(2) *The Journal of Positive Psychology* 141, 142.

51 Barbara L Fredrickson, 'The Broaden-and-Build Theory of Positive Emotions: Philosophical Transactions – The Royal Society of London Series B Biological Sciences' (2004) *The Royal Society* 1367. See also Margaret L Kern, Lea E Waters, Alejandro Adler and Mathew A White, 'A Multidimensional Approach to Measuring Well-Being in Students: Application of the PERMA Framework' (2015) 10(3) *The Journal of Positive Psychology* 262.

52 Sonja Lyubomirsky, Laura King and Ed Diener, 'The Benefits of Frequent Positive Affect: Does Happiness Lead to Success?' (2005) 131 *Psychological Bulletin* 803; Nathaniel M Lambert, Frank D Fincham and Tyler F Stillman, 'Gratitude and Depressive Symptoms: The Role of Positive Reframing and Positive Emotion' (2012) 26 *Cognition and Emotion* 615; Rusk and Waters (n 50).

53 Felicia Huppert and Timothy So, 'Flourishing Across Europe: Application of a New Conceptual Framework for Defining Well-Being' (2013) 110 *Social Indicators Research* 837.

by other research.[54] Fredrickson has identified that experiencing positive emotions begets and cultivates further experiences of positive emotion in an 'upward spiral'.[55] Further, positive emotions increase well-being because they positively influence social, cognitive and physical functioning.[56] Harnessing the notion of a professional identity can assist lawyers in experiencing positive emotion in many ways, for example, through feelings of personal efficacy (personal identity) as well as a sense of competence and expertise (role identity) and drawing on the public service of law, the identity of the legal profession as a 'helping profession', and the contribution of lawyers to upholding the rule of law, promoting justice and defending rights and liberties (social identity).

Second, a sense of engagement (E) is also known to support psychological well-being. There are many definitions of engagement including psychological interest, behavioural involvement and concentration/focus.[57] Engagement is said to refer to 'psychological connection to activities (for example, feeling absorbed and engaged in life)'.[58] Engagement creates strong feelings of being interested and alert. In positive psychology theory, a true and deep sense of engagement is referred to as 'flow'. Flow is associated with peak performance. Jackson, for example, has written of how 'flow' can be harnessed to optimise the performance of elite athletes.[59] Lawyers too can harness the notion of engagement, or flow, to optimise their performance and success. A positive professional identity offers an important context for nurturing the interest and engagement of lawyers. In particular, the role and social identities of lawyering offer constructive ways to ensure engagement. Assisting clients through the provision of expert legal advice, representation and advocacy is relational, purposeful and positive, making it possible for lawyers to achieve interest and maintain engagement (role identity). Contributing to the broader goals of the protection of individual rights and the pursuit of justice and liberal values also offers incentive for engagement in the professional pursuits of lawyering (social identity).

Third, experiencing positive relationships (R) is critical to well-being because humans are essentially social beings and so feel nourished by 'feeling socially integrated, cared about and supported by others, and satisfied with one's social connections'.[60] Positive relationships are ones that are caring, valuable, worthwhile and mutually rewarding.[61] They are sustaining because they provide a sense of purpose and meaning by offering security and reassurance in difficult times, and shared joy in good times.[62] There is a growing body of evidence finding that positive relationships are associated with many other benefits such as affirmative

54 Kern et al. (n 51). See also Lyubomirsky, King and Diener (n 52).
55 Fredrickson (n 51) 1373.
56 Ibid. See also Chapter 8 of this book.
57 Kern et al. (n 51) 263.
58 Ibid 263.
59 Susan A Jackson and Mihaly Csikszentmihaly, *Flow in Sports* (Human Kinetics, 1999).
60 Kern et al. (n 51) 263.
61 Ibid 266.
62 Ibid.

emotions, work success and improved health.[63] Relationships are certainly important to our personal identities, but relationships in professional contexts also matter. Legal practice often involves long hours and significant time spent with colleagues and clients. A positive sense of professional identity has significant potential to support collegial and positive relationships within the profession. For example, a positive personal identity can support generosity towards others as well as capacity for empathy and compassion; a positive role identity in terms of feelings of shared competence and expertise can support respect and collegiality; and a commitment to the shared values of lawyering (social identity) can create bonds and connections of a higher order.

Fourth, meaning (M) refers to 'believing that one's life is valuable and feeling connected to something greater than oneself'.[64] For Seligman, serving interests beyond one's own individual concerns creates a 'Meaningful Life',[65] a sense of purpose and meaning in life that contributes to well-being. Consistent with the preceding discussion, it is clear that the role and social identities of lawyers provide some profound ways of identifying and embedding a deep sense of meaning and purpose; both in relation to providing assistance and advocacy to individual clients, as well as more broadly in terms of the social service contribution of upholding the rule of law.

Finally, accomplishment (A) involves 'making progress toward goals, feeling capable to do daily activities, and having a sense of achievement'.[66] Accomplishment supports a sense of competence and strengthens self-belief. These are important elements of well-being for lawyers, particularly for their sense of role identity – an insight which the survey of UK barristers discussed in the next section emphasises.

Survey of UK barristers' perceptions of professional identity and well-being

We believe there is a strong theoretical foundation for the hypothesis that inculcating a positive professional identity can be an effective strategy to promote and support lawyer well-being. However, the legal profession has not necessarily traditionally explicitly recognised, discussed or promoted a positive professional identity, nor is it something addressed overtly at law school through the curriculum.

In 2015, at the Bar Council's Annual Conference, we conducted a small-scale exploratory survey of barristers who attended the Wellbeing at the Bar Workshop. The purpose of the study was to explore barrister's perceptions of the importance

63 Ryan T Howell, Margaret L Kern and Sonja Lyubomirsky, 'Health Benefits: Meta-Analytically Determining the Impact of Wellbeing on Objective Health Outcomes' (2007) 1(1) *Health Psychology Review* 83. See also Shelley E Taylor, 'Social Support: A Review' in Howard S Friedman (ed), *The Oxford Handbook of Health Psychology* (Oxford University Press, 2011) 189.

64 Kern et al. (n 51) 263.

65 Seligman (n 48) 13.

66 Kern et al. (n 51) 263.

of inculcating a sense of professional identity for the well-being of the profession. Twenty-one barristers of the thirty-two who attended the Workshop completed the voluntary and anonymous survey, for which ethics approval had been obtained from the University of Portsmouth (FEC Ref No: E359).

Survey methodology

The survey aimed to explore barristers' perceptions of a professional identity and to build a preliminary understanding of common themes in their perception of this phenomenon to inform further research. It was not our intention to obtain any quantitative statistical data for proving these perceptions, or to make any generalisable claims. For this reason, we were drawn to a phenomenographical conceptual framework for the study, although we acknowledge that the survey method adopted did not allow for the exploration of perceptions through in-depth interviews, which is a common attribute of this method.[67]

Phenomonography is a qualitative, interpretivist research methodology, that explores the different ways in which people understand the same concept or phenomenon (in this instance the nature of a legal professional identity for barristers in the UK).[68] Phenomonography was first established as a methodology for education research in the late 1970s,[69] but is now used extensively in diverse disciplines; for example it has been used to explore the concept of 'price' in economics and of 'motion' in physics.[70] As a research and analysis methodology it is anchored in the notion that individuals experience the world differently because experience is always partial. Thus, different ways of understanding a concept are impacted by which aspects or features of the concept are noticed, and not noticed, in terms of how people are aware of the concept.

67 Jörgen Sandbergh, 'Are Phenomenographic Results Reliable?' (1997) 16(2) *Higher Education Research & Development* 203. For some critical perspectives on phenomenography and its theory see for example, John TE Richardson, 'The Concepts and Methods of Phenomenographic Research' (1999) 69(1) *Review of Educational Research* 53; Graham Webb, 'Deconstructing Deep and Surface: Towards a Critique of Phenomenography' (1997) 33(2) *Higher Education* 195.

68 See for example, John A Bowden and Eleanor Walsh (eds), *Phenomenography* (RMIT, 2000); Gerlese Åkerlind, 'Variation and Commonality in Phenomenographic Research Methods' (2005) 24(4) *Higher Education Research & Development* 321; Ference Marton, 'Phenomenography – Describing Conceptions of the World Around Us' (1981) 10 *Instructional Science* 177; Ference Marton, 'Phenomenography – A Research Approach Investigating Different Understandings of Reality' (1986) 21(2) *Journal of Thought* 28; Lennart Svensson, 'Theoretical Foundations of Phenomenography' (1997) 16(2) *Higher Education Research & Development* 159.

69 See for example, Michal Prosser and Keith Trigwell, 'Using Phenomenography in the Design of Programs for Teachers in Higher Education' (1997) 16(1) *Higher Education Research & Development* 41.

70 Ming-fai Pang and Ference Marton, 'Learning Theory as Teaching Resource: Enhancing Students' Understanding of Economic Concepts' (2005) 33(2) *Instructional Science* 159; Eleanor Walsh et al., 'Physics Students' Understanding of Relative Speed: A Phenomenographic Study' (1993) 30(9) *Journal of Research in Science Teaching* 1133.

The survey included open and closed questions. The narratives found in the survey data of open questions are a snapshot of a small sample of self-selecting barristers. Qualitative methods accommodate small sample sizes because the aim is not to prove theory but rather to explore phenomena and perceptions. A sample size of more than twenty participants is a standard-to-large sample size for a thematic, phenomenographical analysis and when analysed alongside some of the pertinent literature, the responses provide some illuminating preliminary insights which can inform the development of our further research in this area. The narratives for the open questions were thematically coded by each of the researchers independently and then cross-checked for consistency and the accuracy of coding and theme identification.

Survey results

In terms of the closed questions: responses to the question, 'do you personally think you have a sense of professional identity as a barrister?': sixteen respondents said yes, two said no and three did not respond. Those who did not respond commented: 'Sometimes', 'never thought about it' and '?'. One respondent who answered yes added: 'I know that I project or emphasise certain characteristics that I perceive to be desirable as a barrister – even if they don't come naturally'. One respondent who replied 'no' added: 'Just one ID'.

In response to the question 'do you think having a positive professional identity is associated with good mental health and well-being for barristers?': thirteen respondents answered yes, four said no and four did not tick 'yes' or 'no' but responded with the following free text responses: 'Not sure', 'Never thought about it', 'Don't know', 'Doubled-edged. Danger that we become defined by it'. Of the respondents who answered 'yes', four commented further that not having a positive professional identity can lead to the experience of stress.

In relation to the question as to whether legal education has a role in starting to inculcate a legal professional identity in law students: sixteen respondents said yes and zero respondents said no, however five respondents did not respond by circling 'yes' or 'no', instead offering free text responses such as 'possibly', 'it would depend', and 'not sure'.

In terms of the open questions: responses to the question 'What do you understand the term "professional identity" to mean for barristers?' elicited four key themes. First, about one quarter of respondents were unable to say what a professional identity means for barristers. Responses included: 'Never heard of it', 'Not sure', 'Don't know what this means' and 'Don't know'. Second, respondents identified professional conduct as a core element of a professional identity for barristers. This theme was the largest theme with responses clearly focussed on the *act* of being a barrister and *role identity* – repeated phrasing in answers encompassed words such as 'conduct', 'act', 'behave', and 'be', with references made to 'knowledge', 'advocacy' and 'standards'. Responses included: 'How you behave as a professional', 'Conducting yourself in a professional manner', 'Knowing how to behave in your professional life', 'Your role as a barrister and a certain public persona about how you carry yourself and behave', 'A knowledge of law which is better than that of most people, together with a determined approach to ensure the highest standards of professional work, even at your personal cost', and 'That blend of skill and ability which allows one to practice advocacy effectively'. The third theme related to being professional in 'your day job' and 'separating yourself from your work'. Responses included for example, 'Who you are in your day job rather than at home', 'Knowing you can step out of your day job as a barrister', 'A perception of self that is specific to one's professional "mask" and life as opposed to the "mask" or life within other aspects of one's life – professional identity can be very different'.

Responses to the question asking respondents to describe the elements of a positive professional identity for barristers focussed predominantly on role and personal identity factors. There was no identification of an element of a positive professional identity that could be considered within the theme of a social identity (that is the values and goals of lawyering within a societal context). Role identity factors were the most commonly mentioned with the ideas of competence, ability, intelligence and positive, accurate and thorough performance frequently listed. Good preparation, organisation skills and independence were also considered important along with a good client manner, client care and empathy and – more generally – being well mannered, polite and demonstrating professional behaviour and ethical standards.

In relation to personal identity, confidence was one of the most mentioned characteristics followed by being hardworking, in control, and respected. Honesty and integrity were often listed along with a 'determination to do what is right rather than convenient'. One response however recognised a need (in line with a theme identified previously) to 'separate yourself from the material you work with, (putting) a barrier between work and life' (that is a barrier between personal and role identities).

The final question asked: 'in what ways could law schools teach law students to develop a professional identity that would prepare them well for legal practice?' The responses were grouped broadly into three themes: case preparation, ethical development and continuing professional development of careers. Eight responses either stated 'don't know' or were left blank.

Discussion

White et al.'s three key generic elements of 'professional identity' discussed earlier – *personal identity*, *role identity* and *social identity* – provide a useful framework for analysing how the participant barristers in this study perceive the term. First, it is notable that many respondents confidently attested to having a sense of professional identity as a barrister and many associated it with good mental health, but about a quarter of the participants were unsure about defining what that might mean. Therefore, while there is a certain instinctive, innate appreciation for the concept and its potential, there is a concomitant uncertainty about it.

Participants in the study who were able to define the term more concretely provided responses that were predominantly very fixed on the notion of role identity. 'Professional conduct' as a core element of a professional identity for barristers constituted the largest theme, but a strong sense of the need to keep role and personal identities separate to some extent also came through. In terms of the process of identifying the elements of a professional identity, responses retained a strong focus on role identity although a number of aspects of a personal identity were also mentioned. Interestingly, there was no identification of elements of a social identity. Role performance through the operational activities and skills of being a barrister – in particular, for example ability, intelligence, competence, preparation – was highlighted over professional values such as access to justice and the rule of law. This we found surprising as the preceding discussion of positive psychology theory suggests that the social identity value factors perhaps have some of the strongest potential to support lawyer well-being and are being missed.

Further, although personal identity factors were listed as elements of a professional identity, some responses reflected the need to place a dividing barrier between one's personal self and one's professional self as a potential survival mechanism: 'separating yourself from work'. Most worrying was the mention of 'putting a mask on' – that a professional identity involves being someone other than one's authentic self. This is a matter for further investigation, particularly in relation to assisting those from non-traditional backgrounds who may feel they have to 'fit the mould' and assume a particular professional identity as a barrister which may subsequently lead to a loss of sense of self, a lack of authenticity and an increase in the stressors within practice.

Respondents mostly agreed that there is a possible role for inculcating a positive professional identity in legal education but understandably lacked confidence in what this might look like. It is difficult to know how to teach something that one struggles to define. White et al.'s framework offers a way to encourage law students to draw upon their own personal values, as well as finding meaning through role expertise and the place of lawyers within society (upholding the rule of law, providing access to justice). Subjects such as Law and Society, Dispute Resolution and Ethics offer significant opportunities to explore identity issues. However, the teaching of the concept should also be scaffolded throughout the degree and students should consistently be exposed to exploring it through the core compulsory curriculum. Once in the profession the way in which a lawyer's professional identity continues to evolve not only requires lawyers to self-regulate as independent and life-long learners and to be self-motivated to progress their development, it also requires leadership from senior members of the profession in addressing structural and cultural issues that work against the possibility of professional identity formation.

Future research

The insights of the barristers who participated in this study motivate us to explore the notion of a positive professional identity and its relationship to lawyer well-being through future and more detailed research in the UK and Australia. In particular, we aim to investigate in further depth four key themes that our analysis has found sit implicitly within the relevant theory as well as our study's data set. First, the importance of authenticity and being one's true self as a lawyer; practising in an area where there is a connection of interest and engagement, finding true meaning and purpose in role and social identities and enacting genuine beliefs and values. Second, the importance of connectedness; being active about addressing isolation through seeking out mentors, taking the initiative to engage and build collegial professional relationships and networks. Third, the importance of actively building a sense of professional confidence and competence. Fourth, the importance of appreciating the societal contribution of lawyering through a social identity that acknowledges the profession as a 'helping profession' and lawyers as advocates for clients and their interests across a range of dispute resolution and transactional contexts.

Conclusion

In 2007, the US *Carnegie Report* made clear the importance of professional identity to the efficacy of legal practice, referring to it as one of the profession's key apprenticeships.[71] Pratt et al. have also noted that a focus on professional identity is opportune and timely.[72] Further analysis of a positive professional identity for lawyers is important as the profession at large, and on an international scale, is grappling with understanding what it means to be a modern lawyer, and how best to support well-being within the profession. In a transitional time of professional disruption, ideals must be reconceptualised and rearticulated, evolution and change must be accepted, and an integrated holistic and whole concept of what it means to be in and of the legal profession must be developed.

The framework adopted for the preceding discussion of how a positive professional identity for lawyers might be conceived and constructed included three elements: personal, role and social identity. Using positive psychology and Martin Seligman's concept of PERMA, we argued that this framework has potential to support lawyer well-being because it assists lawyers to connect 'what they do' with 'who they are'.[73] Lawyers with a positive professional identity are more likely to be agile, resilient, responsive and reflective professionals; and will be more likely to manage the challenges and stressors of contemporary legal practice and flourish in their professional legal role.

This chapter also presented a small-scale qualitative study of UK barristers' perceptions of a professional identity and its relationship to well-being, along with the potential role legal education may have in inculcating a professional identity.

71 William M Sullivan et al., *Educating Lawyers: Preparation for the Profession of Law* (John Wiley & Sons, 2007) Ch 4.

72 Michael G Pratt, Kevin W Rockmann and Jeffrey B Kaufmann, 'Constructing Professional Identity: The Role of Work and Identity Learning Cycles in the Customization of Identity Among Medical Residents' (2006) 49(2) *Academy of Management Journal* 235.

73 Jan Jacobowitz, 'Cultivating Professional Identity and Creating Community: A Tale of Two Innovations' (2013) 36 *University of Arkansas at Little Rock Law Review* 319.

This study suggested a strong emphasis in the participant barristers' minds on role identity, somewhat to the detriment of personal and social identities. Our future research will continue to explore the phenomenon of a professional legal identity in more detail, including issues such as authenticity, connectedness, confidence and competence and the importance of the social values and goals of the legal profession.

5 Determined to be professional, ethical and well

Anneka Ferguson and Stephen Tang

Introduction

It is a truth universally acknowledged[1] that a student in possession of a law degree is in search of a job. However, does that degree allow them to enter the profession as competent, well and ethical professionals with skills and attitudes to survive and succeed in the legal profession? Has the law degree equipped graduates to serve their clients and the community as expected?[2]

Increasingly, the other truth to be acknowledged is that legal education is undermining the well-being of many (though not all) law graduates. In Australia, many law graduates will either leave the profession in their first five years[3] or experience mental distress at levels that are likely to be detrimental both personally and professionally.[4] Nonetheless, this chapter suggests that legal education need not be harmful through an examination of the potential for self-determination theory (SDT) and a values-informed curriculum to explain both the nature of, and provide a solution to, the problem.

This discussion will be informed by an examination of the results of an empirical study of several student cohorts within the Graduate Diploma of Legal Practice

1 With apologies to Jane Austen for hijacking the first line of "Pride and Prejudice" for the purposes of a quirky opening line in a chapter.

2 See for example, in Australia: Kath Hall, Molly Townes O'Brien and Stephen Tang, 'Developing a Professional Identity in Law School: A View from Australia' (2010) 4 *Phoenix Law Review* 20; Kath Hall, 'Do We Really Want to Know? Recognizing the Importance of Student Psychological Well-Being in Australian Law Schools' (2009) 9 *Queensland University of Technology Law and Justice Journal* 1; in the USA: Roy Stuckey et al, *Best Practices for Legal Education* (Clinical Legal Education Association, 2007); William Sullivan et al, *A Vision and Road Map: Educating Lawyers – Preparation for the Profession of Law* (Jossey-Bass, 2007); and in the UK: Jane Creaton, 'Modernizing the Courts and the Legal Profession' (2003) 9 *Contemporary Politics* 115; Avrom Sherr, 'Legal Education, Legal Competence and Little Bo Peep' (1998) 32 *Law Teacher* 37.

3 Elisabeth Hetterich, 'Promotion and Succession Management and Associated Retention Issues in Australian Law Firms' (2012) <https://eprints.qut.edu.au/54735/1/Elisabeth_Hetterich_Thesis.pdf> accessed 7 May 2019.

4 For example, Norm Kelk et al., *Courting the Blues: Attitudes Towards Depression in Australian Law Students and Legal Practitioners* (BMRI, 2009).

(GDLP) at the Australian National University School of Legal Practice (formerly ANU Legal Workshop) which:

- Demonstrates that symptoms of distress and the corresponding negative effects on the basic psychological needs of autonomy, competence and relatedness observed in previous studies can be stabilised or reversed; and
- Analyses curriculum features that potentially contributed to these positive results and, in the process, appear to build a stronger sense of professional identity.

Well-being in legal education

Law student well-being and psychological distress has been researched in the US for at least four decades.[5] This research indicates that the problem is common and has been persistent across a variety of tertiary institutions over time. Causal explanations provided include the innate nature of law students,[6] an emphasis on thinking like a lawyer,[7] the substantial workload stress and crippling authoritarianism cultures in law schools,[8] and misuse of the Socratic method.[9]

The discussion only gained significant momentum in Australia after the 2009 *Courting the Blues* report, which resoundingly indicated that significant issues of law student and lawyer psychological distress were just as prevalent in Australia.[10] Subsequently, there has been a rise in empirical examinations seeking explanations for this psychological distress. Accordingly, we know that in Australia:

- Law students do not come to law school in psychological distress but it increases worryingly over the first year;[11]
- Law students' perfectionism does not explain increases in anxiety and depressive symptoms (although may contribute to stress);[12] and

5 For example, Andrew Benjamin et al., 'The Role of Legal Education in Producing Psychological Distress among Law Students and Lawyers' (1986) *American Bar Foundation Research Journal* 225.

6 Matthew Dammeyer and Narina Nunez, 'Anxiety and Depression Among Law Students: Current Knowledge and Future Directions' (1999) 23 *Law & Human Behavior* 55.

7 Peter Teachout, 'Uneasy Burden: What It Really Means to Learn to Think Like a Lawyer' (1996) 47 *Mercer Law Review* 543; Stephen Wizner, 'Is Learning To "Think Like a Lawyer" Enough?' (1998) 17(1) *Yale Law & Policy Review* 583.

8 Stephen Halpern, 'On the Politics and Pathology of Legal Education' (1982) *Journal of Legal Studies Education* 32, 383.

9 Elizabeth Mertz, *The Language of Law School: Learning to 'Think Like A Lawyer'* (Oxford University Press, 2007).

10 Kelk et al. (n 4).

11 Molly Townes O'Brien, Stephen Tang and Kath Hall, 'Changing Our Thinking: Empirical Research on Law Student Wellbeing, Thinking Styles and the Law Curriculum' (2011) 21 *Legal Education Review* 149.

12 Wendy Larcombe and Katherine Fethers, 'Schooling the Blues? An Investigation of Factors Associated with Psychological Distress Among Law Students' (2013) 36 *University of New South Wales Law Journal* 390.

- Improved course satisfaction does not predict reduced psychological distress symptoms.[13]

Thus, without a satisfactory explanation for the distress observed at law school and in the profession, it was necessary for both our research (discussed in this chapter) and the research of others to shift to examining the impact of law school on student's self-determination and values.

Self-determination theory

Ryan and Deci began developing SDT in the 1980s, with its most recent formulation expressed in their comprehensive 2017 publication.[14] SDT states that '[h]uman beings can be proactive or engaged, or alternatively passive and alienated largely as a function of the social conditions in which they develop and function'.[15] In SDT, the three innate psychological needs that facilitate motivation, assimilation of information, behavioural regulation and well-being are:

- **Competence** – the knowledge that you can deal with your environment;
- **Autonomy** – a sense that you can control your direction and choices; and
- **Relatedness** – knowing that you have a meaningful connection with others.[16]

As an organismic theory of motivation, a deficit in one of these psychological needs motivates discrepancy reduction efforts. For example, a lack of connection – i.e. relatedness – can motivate people to try to create connections, yet having a satisfactory connection doesn't motivate a person to try to get more.[17]

Krieger and Sheldon's studies of US law students and lawyers suggest, as per Ryan and Deci, that negative outcomes in well-being/professionalism in students/lawyers may be associated with undermined SDT needs in law school and practice.[18] The first study of two different law school cohorts suggested that 'the law school experience was associated with troubling increases in extrinsic values

13 Wendy Larcombe et al., 'Does an Improved Experience of Law School Protect Students Against Depression, Anxiety and Stress? An Empirical Study of Wellbeing and the Law School Experience of LLB and JD Students' (2013) 35 *Sydney Law Review* 407.

14 Richard Ryan and Edward Deci, *Self Determination Theory: Basic Psychological Needs in Motivation, Development and Wellness* (Guilford Press, 2017).

15 Richard Ryan and Edward Deci, 'Self Determination Theory and the Facilitation of Intrinsic Motivation, Social Development, and Well-Being' (2000) 55(1) *American Psychologist* 68.

16 Ibid. For further discussion of SDT in the wellness for law context see also, for example, Chapter 2 of this book.

17 Kennon Sheldon et al., 'A Two Process View of Facebook Use and Relatedness Need-Satisfaction: Disconnection Drives Use, and Connection Rewards It' (2011) 100(4) *Journal of Personality and Social Psychology* 766.

18 Kennon Sheldon and Lawrence S Krieger, 'Does Legal Education Have Undermining Effects on Law Students? Evaluating Changes in Motivation, Values and Wellbeing' (2004) 22(2) *Behavioral Sciences & the Law* 261.

and declines in self-determined motivation'.[19] A second study compared the SDT, educational and well-being outcomes of the law student cohorts of a traditional (i.e. emphasising theoretical scholarship) and a less-traditional law school (i.e. focused on faculty with more teaching and lawyering experience and practical skills training). This study confirmed that broad negative effects occurred throughout the three years of law school, including increasing student distress and decreasing internal motivation for legal work. It also showed that these negative effects were correlated with decreased satisfaction of SDT needs. The data also suggested that more thorough faculty autonomy-support in the non-traditional law school accounted for positive differences in need satisfaction when compared to the more traditional law school.[20]

When Krieger and Sheldon examined SDT, well-being and career success of lawyers, they concluded that 'the psychological factors seen to erode during law school are the very factors most important for the wellbeing of lawyers' and that 'the factors most emphasised in law schools – grades, honors and potential career income, have nil to modest bearing on lawyer wellbeing'.[21] This work moved the discussion on law student/lawyer well-being from describing the problem to setting legal educators the challenge of constructing a law school curriculum and environment that supports rather than undermines self-determination.

Huxley-Binns and Ferris considered this when creating a curriculum for legal theory/jurisprudence.[22] They particularly paid attention to the volition of law students – i.e. that they have chosen to study law – whilst also recognising that the full range of human motivation exists. For example, whilst motivation is ideally intrinsic, few students are truly intrinsically motivated. Thus, any curriculum design must recognise the importance of relatedness in engaging and transitioning extrinsically motivated to intrinsically motivated learners.

These different types of motivation could also be considered in terms of the student values as drivers; to examine what is important to each and how extrinsic or intrinsic values impact on motivation. Accordingly, while competence, autonomy and relatedness explain the 'what' of a human's basic psychological needs, your values provide the 'why'. Interestingly, Townes O'Brien and Tang's survey of first year students (beginning and end) about their expectations/experiences of law school showed that extrinsic motivations such as 'Personal success' and 'Professional prestige' increased significantly over just the first year of study; whereas intrinsic motivations such as 'making a difference' and 'intellectual curiosity'

19 Ibid 283.

20 Kennon Sheldon and Lawrence S Krieger, 'Understanding the Negative Effects of Legal Education on Law Students: A Longitudinal Study' (2007) 33(6) *Personality and Social Psychology Bulletin* 883.

21 Lawrence S Krieger and Kennon Sheldon, 'What Makes Lawyers Happy? A Data-Driven Prescription to Redefine Professional Success' (2015) 83 *The George Washington Law Review* 554, 560.

22 Rebecca Huxley-Binns and Graeme Ferris, 'Putting Theory into Practice: Designing a Curriculum According to Self-Determination Theory' (2013) 19(3) *International Journal of Pedagogy and Curriculum* 1, 5.

significantly decreased.[23] Our research, uniquely positioned at another liminal point in students' legal careers (between undergraduate study and admission to practice) can provide another perspective on values and students' well-being.

Research context

In 2009–2010, the ANU School of Legal Practice (ANUSLP) re-invented their GDLP curriculum in accordance with best practice research on providing simulated, integrated, collaborative and professional legal education.[24] In Australia, the GDLP is the practical legal training requirement upon completion of a LLB or JD for law graduates to be eligible for admission to practice. The GDLP competencies are set and accredited by the Law Admissions Consultative Committee.[25] However, these requirements only dictate the GDLP content and not the pedagogy. Accordingly, the ANUSLP was able to combine the core competencies of the GDLP curriculum into an 18-week online integrated learning environment entitled the Professional Practice Core (PPC). Significant features of this environment were a heavy emphasis on supported teamwork, the demonstration of professionally ethical behaviour, real world 'messy' simulations, extensive mentoring and resubmitting client-focused work to legal practitioner teachers until a competent standard was reached. These innovations challenged the status quo of legal education as a series of face-to-face but depersonalised, individualistic subjects pursued through readings, lectures, seminars and moderated exams.

Although these innovations were not explicitly aimed at addressing SDT needs, questions were raised as to whether the curriculum adjustments were providing a positive impact on student well-being, professionalism and collaborative proficiency despite an increased workload, focus on teamwork and competency-based assessment standards. And thus, in 2012 we embarked on an ambitious empirical research project to evaluate the impacts of the PPC pedagogy.

Initial research results

The initial iterations of this empirical research in 2012 indicated that, in stark contrast to high levels of psychological distress consistently found in both US and Australian studies, the ANUSLP GDLP students entered the 18-week PPC course with levels of psychological distress (depression, anxiety and stress

23 Molly Townes O'Brien and Stephen Tang, 'Stop Struggling for the Struggle's Sake: Make It Meaningful' (Conference paper presented at the International First Year in Higher Education Conference, 7–10 July 2013, Wellington) 1.

24 For details of the curriculum changes see Anneka Ferguson and Elizabeth Lee, 'Desperately Seeking . . . Relevant Assessment? A Case Study on the Potential for Using Online Simulated Group Based Learning to Create Sustainable Assessment Practices' (2012) 22(1) *Legal Education Review* 121; Anneka Ferguson, 'Creating Practice-Ready, Professional and Well Law Graduates' (2015) 8(2) *Journal of Learning Design* 22.

25 See <www.lawcouncil.asn.au/resources/law-admissions-consultative-committee/documents-about-present-admission-policies> accessed 7 May 2019.

symptoms) at or lower than community peers. Moreover, these levels of distress did not change over the course. Despite the intensity of the PPC and the different pedagogy, students remained psychologically healthy.[26]

Thus, in 2013 we began to explicitly explore whether it was progress in SDT factors that explained the positive psychological results. Then, in Winter 2013, we introduced the concept of 'valued-living' as contained in Acceptance and Commitment Therapy (ACT) in order to specifically examine the relationship between values and positive psychological functioning.[27]

As such, this chapter analyses the data in relation to the hypotheses that from the beginning of the PPC until the end of the PPC:

- There would be no significant change in levels of psychological distress as measured on the Depression Anxiety Stress Scale (DASS-21) (Hypothesis 1);
- Corresponding to the lack of change in the DASS-21 there would be no significant change in subjective well-being, as measured on the Satisfaction With Life Scale (SWLS) (Hypothesis 2);
- Students will report increases in autonomy, competence and relatedness as measured on the Basic Psychological Needs Scale (BPNS) (Hypothesis 3);
- Students will report increases in progress towards values and decreases in obstruction of values, as measured on the Valuing Questionnaire (VQ-8) (Hypothesis 4).

And, that:

- Higher levels in autonomy, competence and relatedness predict lower rates of psychological distress as measured on the DASS-21 (Hypothesis 5); and
- Lower levels of obstruction of values and higher levels of progress towards values predict lower rates of distress as measured on the DASS-21 (Hypothesis 6).

Methodology

Survey participants

We conducted quantitative online surveys of students at the beginning and end of the Summer/Winter 2012/2013 PPC cohorts.[28]

All PPC students were invited to complete the survey as part of their course induction. However, research participation was voluntary and subject to informed consent, and was clearly not a course requirement. Students were provided with

26 Stephen Tang and Anneka Ferguson, 'The Possibility of Wellbeing: Preliminary Results from Surveys of Australian Professional Legal Education Students' (2014) 14(1) *QUT Law Review* 27.

27 Matthew Smout, Matthew Davies, Alison Christie and Nicholas Burns, 'Evaluating Acceptance and Commitment Therapy: Development of the Valuing Questionnaire (VQ)' (2014) 3(3) *The Journal of Applied Behavioral Science* 164.

28 Beginning = first two weeks of PPC. End = final two weeks of PPC.

Table 5.1 Sample sizes and retention rates for each survey cohort

Cohort	*Start n*	*End n*	*Retention %*
1. Pilot (Summer 2012)	53	49	92.5
2. Winter 2012	338	245	72.5
3. Summer 2013	496	300	60.4
4. Winter 2013	355	275	77.5
Total	**1222**	**869**	**mean** = 75.7

Table 5.2 Measures and topics included in each survey cohort

Measure	*Sum 2012*	*Win 2012*	*Sum 2013*	*Win 2013*
Demographics, employment location/ hours	x	x	x	x
<u>PART 1</u>				
LLB/JD institution/assessment experiences	x	x		
PPC Experiences/Expectations	x	x	x	x
Law student/legal professional identity	x	x	x	x
Values and working styles		x	x	x
Subjective professionalism indicators	x	x	x	x
Professional knowns/unknowns	x	x	x	x
Career preferences	x	x	x	x
<u>PART 2</u>				
Depression Anxiety Stress Scale (DASS-21)	x	x	x	x
Satisfaction With Life Scale (SWLS)	x	x	x	
Basic Psychological Needs Scale (BPNS)			x	x
Valuing Questionnaire (VQ)				x

the opportunity to opt-in for contact with an independent psychologist if their level of psychological distress was concerning. Ethics approval was received.[29]

The sample size of each cohort is shown in Table 5.1. The Summer 2012 cohort was a small pilot study used to evaluate the measures and procedure. The sample size from Winter 2012 onwards was pleasing and accounted for at least 60% of enrolled students in the beginning-of-PPC survey.[30]

Part 1 of the survey comprised self-report, multiple-choice questions presented on Likert scales. Participants were shown statements to which they responded, usually on a five-point scale between 'Strongly Disagree' and 'Strongly Agree'. Exceptions to this are outlined in Table 5.2.

29 ANU HREC Protocol No.2011/698 – no special conditions attached.
30 See Tang and Ferguson (n 26).

Part 2 of the survey used published and validated self-report scales (see Table 5.2 and following discussion). Responses were coded/summed following the directions of the original instrument to yield an index of the relevant psychological construct.

This chapter focuses on the Part 2 survey, as the Part 1 questions on educational outcomes have been discussed elsewhere.[31]

Depression Anxiety Stress Scale (DASS-21)

The 21-item version of the DASS[32] was used as the measure of psychological distress in all four studies as it has good validity and psychometric properties demonstrated across a number of studies including in Australian samples of younger adults.[33]

The DASS-21 addresses three aspects of psychological distress (depression, anxiety and stress) in separate seven-item subscales. Participants rate symptoms to the extent that they were experienced over the past week on a four-point scale, ranging from 'did not apply to me at all' to 'applied to me very much/most of the time'. DASS-21 subscale totals can then be transformed into five severity categories (normal, mild, moderate, severe and extremely severe)[34] referring to the intensity or frequency of symptoms. As it is wholly inappropriate to make clinical diagnoses based on the DASS-21 alone,[35] these categories are used only as an overall indication of the level of distress. However, scores in the moderate category and above generally indicate a level of psychological distress that likely causes some impairment in the person's life, relationships and daily activities.

Satisfaction With Life Scale (SWLS)

In all but the Winter 2013 survey, the 5-item SWLS was included as a positive measure of subjective well-being.[36] The SWLS was scored on a 7-point Likert scale. The SWLS provides an overall indicator of participant's judgments about life satisfaction, although it does not yield much information about the sources or limits of these beliefs. Subjective self-reports of life satisfaction are, however, not necessarily indicative of well-being-congruent behaviours or relationships.

31 Ibid.
32 Sydney H Lovibond and Peter F Lovibond, *Manual for the Depression Anxiety Stress Scales* (Psychology Foundation, 2nd ed, 1995).
33 See, for example, John Crawford et al., 'Percentile Norms and Accompanying Interval Estimates from an Australian General Adult Population Sample for Self-Report Mood Scales' (2011) 46 *Australian Psychologist* 3.
34 Lovibond and Lovibond (n 32) 26. The DASS manual has very little to say about the application and interpretation of the severity categories.
35 Ibid.
36 Ed Diener et al., 'The Satisfaction with Life Scale' (1985) 49 *Journal of Personality Assessment* 71.

Basic Psychological Needs Scale (BPNS)

The Basic Psychological Needs Scale (BPNS), which emerged from SDT research, was included in the 2013 Summer/Winter surveys.[37] The BPNS attempts to measure levels of perceived autonomy, relatedness and competence in a 21-item instrument, divided into three subscales for each of the psychological needs.[38] Items provide subjective evaluation by participants of how their SDT needs are being generally met or impaired. While the psychometric evidence for the measurement of SDT need satisfaction is still accumulating and not entirely settled,[39] the BPNS represented the best-available measure at the time.

Valuing Questionnaire (VQ)

The VQ measures the extent to which a person is actively living according to their personal values.[40] Such 'valued living' is a central concept in the research and practice of Acceptance and Commitment Therapy (ACT). In this therapeutic approach, the enactment of personal values is one ingredient of psychological flexibility as the basis of well-being rather than the absence of distress. As the PPC developed a unique emphasis on the importance of identifying/voicing personal values as part of legal professional practice we included this measure to investigate values as a parallel/integral correlate to SDT.

We included a pre-publication version of the 8-item short form Valuing Questionnaire (VQ-8) in the Winter 2013 survey to measure participants' perceptions of their valued living and relationships to psychological distress and other contextual predictors. The VQ-8 contains two subscales relating to *progress* (enactment of personally important values) and *obstruction* (the disruption of valued living through avoidance of unwanted experience or distraction).

Results

Hypothesis 1 – Psychological distress

DASS-21 scores on each subscale were highly and positively skewed, reflecting the overall low level of symptoms as expected in a non-clinical sample. DASS-21 scores were analysed as counts, using a generalised linear model,[41] controlling for participant age, gender and PPC cohort.

37 Ryan and Deci (n 14).

38 Marylène Gagné, 'The Role of Autonomy Support and Autonomy Orientation in Prosocial Behavior Engagement' (2003) 27 *Motivation and Emotion* 199.

39 Mary Johnston and Sara Finney, 'Measuring Basic Needs Satisfaction: Evaluating Previous Research and Conducting New Psychometric Evaluations of the BNPS General Scale' (2010) 35 *Contemporary Educational Psychology* 280.

40 Smout et al. (n 27).

41 A negative binomial model with log link was used to account for skewness on the DASS-21 subscale scores.

Table 5.3 Proportion of PPC students in the moderate or above category on each DASS-21 subscale across all cohorts

DASS-21 Subscale	*% Moderate and above*		*% Change*
	Start of PPC	*End of PPC*	
Depression	10.9	14.0	3.1*
Anxiety	15.9	17.1	1.2
Stress	13.2	20.1	6.9***
Average	*13.3*	*17.1*	*4.1*

* $p < .05$; *** $p < .001$.

On the depression subscale, there was a small but statistically significant overall increase from the start of the course (M = 2.66)[42] to the end of the course (M = 3.27).[43] No change was observed in anxiety subscale scores from PPC beginning to end (M = 2.18 vs. M = 2.38). A small increase on the stress scale was observed between the two time points (M = 4.73 vs. M = 5.75). There was, however, also significant variability in average scores between cohorts, possibly reflecting differences in the curricular content and course experience. In particular, the Winter 2013 cohort had higher average depression scores compared with earlier cohorts, reconciling these findings with our earlier reports.[44]

Although Hypothesis 1 was not supported, the magnitude of the change on the depression and stress scales was small, with an average increase of half to one point on a 21-point subscale. This change may be better represented by examining the DASS-21 category scores, particularly the proportion of participants in the moderate and above range of each subscale. The results across all cohorts (Table 5.3) show a statistically significant, but low level, change in stress and depression but not anxiety. By contrast, other Australian studies commonly report that approximately one-third of law students or lawyers have elevated levels of psychological distress. The PPC student levels were lower by up to half. Notwithstanding the increase in depression and stress scores detected, PPC participants in these cohorts had significantly lower levels of distress – i.e. were far more stable – than observed in other studies of law students and lawyers.

Hypothesis 2 – Subjective well-being

Data for this analysis excluded the Winter 2013 cohort, which did not include the SWLS. The distribution of the SWLS was sufficiently normal, so a linear model was used accounting for the same variables as described earlier. Supporting Hypothesis 2, there was no change in SWLS scores across the PPC (M = 23.80 vs. M = 23.68).

42 Adjusted marginal means.
43 All significant *ps* < .001 in this section.
44 Tang and Ferguson (n 26).

Scores at both time points were in the high-average range,[45] indicating that students reported a reasonably high level of subjective well-being, unaffected by the course.

The correlations between the SWLS and DASS-21 subscales were only mildly moderately negative in strength (Depression: $r_s = -.389$; Anxiety: $r_s = -.231$; Stress: $r_s = -.227$).[46] This confirmed that subjective well-being cannot be considered as the inverse of psychological distress.

The lack of change in the SWLS over the PPC should be considered with the small increase in DASS-21 depression and stress scores. Taken together, these results suggest that some distress-related changes in behaviours or thinking occurred, but not to an extent that they reduced overall high subjective perceptions of well-being.

Hypothesis 3 – Basic psychological needs

These analyses were based only on the two 2013 PPC cohorts, with a corresponding reduction in sample size. The three subscales of the BPNS were analysed separately with the same set of predictor variables.

Contrary to hypotheses, there was no change in reported autonomy over the PPC ($M = 3.56$ at both time points).[47] Consistent with hypotheses, however, there were statistically significant but small increases in the satisfaction of competence ($M = 3.49$ vs. $M = 3.58$)[48] and relatedness needs ($M = 3.94$ vs. $M = 4.00$).[49] Differences between cohorts on baseline levels of psychological need satisfaction may have also clouded the effects observed.

Hypothesis 4 – Values progress and obstruction

The VQ-8 was only included in the Winter 2013 cohort and has the smallest sample size. In a linear model, there was a small but significant increase in students' reported progress towards their values from the start to the end of the PPC ($M = 15.02$ vs. $M = 15.69$).[50] With no change in the already relatively low levels of values obstruction across the duration of the PPC ($M = 8.13$ vs. $M = 8.66$), these results support VQ's underlying theory that progress towards, and obstruction of, values are not completely intertwined.

Hypothesis 5 – Basic psychological needs and distress/subjective well-being

The next analyses examined the extent to which the three SDT dimensions would explain levels of psychological distress as measured on the DASS-21. The BPNS factors were therefore added as covariates to the model in Hypothesis 1.

45 Diener et al. (n 36).
46 Using Spearman's *rho* given the non-normal DASS-21 scores. All *ps* < .001.
47 BPNS scores are reported based on item means rather than subscale totals, since there is an uneven number of items across subscales.
48 $p < .001$.
49 $p = .015$.
50 $p = .045$.

All three BPNS subscales were negatively associated with the DASS-21 depression subscale. Autonomy was the strongest predictor of lower depression scores ($B = -.431$), with smaller negative effects of competence ($B = -.121$) and relatedness ($B = -.157$).[51] There was still a difference between the start and end of the course ($B = .237$), indicating that basic psychological need satisfaction did not fully account for changes in depression scores over the course.

By contrast, on the DASS-21 anxiety subscale, higher levels of autonomy ($B = -.343$), and to a much lesser extent relatedness ($B = -.101$), predicted lower levels of anxiety symptoms. There was no effect of competence ($B = -.060$); nor were there any differences between the start and end of the course when accounting for the influence of basic psychological needs. Similarly, levels of perceived autonomy ($B = -.235$) and relatedness ($B = -.079$), but not competence ($B = .004$), were predictive of DASS-21 stress scores. As with the depression subscale, there was still a small increase in stress scores over the PPC even after accounting for satisfaction of psychological needs ($B = .177$).

This pattern of results was mirrored when the SWLS total score was used instead as the dependent variable. Autonomy was by far the strongest predictor of higher subjective well-being ($B = 2.832$), with a small effect of relatedness ($B = .994$), and no significant effect of competence ($B = .194$). As was the case when the SWLS was examined on its own, there were no differences from the start to the end of the course ($B = .028$).

On the whole, levels of psychological distress and well-being could be partially explained by the extent to which students felt that their basic psychological needs were being met. The level of perceived autonomy was the most important influence on both positive and negative dimensions of well-being, even though levels of autonomy did not appear to be affected by the PPC itself. There was also little impact of competence apart from a very small effect on depression scores.[52]

Hypothesis 6 – Basic psychological needs, valuing and distress

Finally, both the VQ-8 and BPNS were added to the model to predict the DASS-21 scores. Obstruction of values was significantly predictive of higher levels of psychological distress on all three DASS-21 subscales (depression: $B = .397$, anxiety: $B = .337$, stress: $B = .226$).[53] However, progress towards values was only weakly and negatively associated with lower depression scores ($B = -.188$),[54] and not anxiety and stress scores. Autonomy remained a significant predictor of lower levels of distress on the depression and anxiety subscales (depression: $B = -.195$, anxiety: $B = -.223$)[55] but not the stress subscale ($B = -.108$). Other than a small

51 All significant $ps < .01$ in this section.

52 Compare with Tony Foley et al., 'Helping Junior Lawyers Thrive' (2015) 89(9) *Law Institute Journal* 44.

53 All $ps < .001$.

54 $p = .001$.

55 $ps < .003$.

association between relatedness and depression ($B = -.149$),[56] no other BPNS scales remained as significant predictors of psychological distress.

Any changes in psychological distress which could be attributed to the difference between the end and start of the course were now better accounted for by the combination of VQ-8 and BPNS. Values obstruction emerged as a consistent predictor of psychological distress over and above the SDT factors. However, these findings require further exploration and corroboration given the small sample size of this analysis.

Discussion

Self-determination theory

Hypothesis 5's results were similar to Krieger and Sheldon's finding of a negative relationship between increasing law students' meeting of the basic psychological needs of autonomy, competence and relatedness and decreases in psychological distress. That is, if the legal education environment improves these SDT factors, there will be less psychological distress as a result. In particular, our results support the emphasis that Krieger and Sheldon place on autonomy support for reducing psychological distress.[57] For example, in Hypothesis 5 whilst reported feelings of competence provided some insulation against depressive symptomology, it is not the insulating factor against anxiety and stress symptomology that autonomy and relatedness are. And, whilst subjective well-being is not the inverse of psychological distress (per Hypothesis 2 results) the strongest predictors of subjective well-being were subjective autonomy and relatedness and not competence. These results support us to question what legal education should be reinforcing in order to ensure better well-being outcomes. That is, is the emphasis on competence through exam results misplaced when autonomy and relatedness are important for professional well-being?

Where our data differ from Krieger and Sheldon is that within the 2013 PPCs our students (Hypothesis 3), though starting from pretty sound levels of SDT factors at the start of the course, still experienced statistically significant increases in reported competence and relatedness from the beginning to the end of their course. In addition, even though there was no significant increase in reported autonomy, students were already starting from a high point on this autonomy subscale and certainly did not experience a decrease. Thus, these findings are the reverse of the patterns of decreasing SDT need satisfaction observed in Krieger and Sheldon's studies and, consistent with their observations, are likely as a result of the supported autonomy features of the curriculum (discussed in more depth in the 'Impact of results' section).

Furthermore, the lower levels of autonomy satisfaction in Winter 2013 students should be further examined to determine what autonomy triggers were removed

56 $p = .009$.
57 Krieger and Sheldon (n 21).

for this cohort. Observationally, the Winter 2013 curriculum, when compared to the Summer 2013 course had an increased emphasis on students recording time through a quasi-time billing system, and there was increased administrative rather than learning-based workload in some parts of the course. These factors may account for the lower levels of autonomy observed. Such an interpretation warns future curriculum developers to ensure workload is meaningful and suggests that the known negative psychological impact of time billing in legal practice[58] should not be replicated in legal education.

Values

Whilst our survey design did not elicit the nature of the values that our students were pursuing, the Hypothesis 6 results strongly support the idea that if a student subjectively reports no feeling of values obstruction, they also experience lower levels of psychological distress. Separately, if students indicate they felt they were making values progress, it was predictive of lower depressive symptomology. In terms of curriculum evaluation, Winter 2013 PPC students reported a significant increase in values progress from the start to the end of the course and no change in their fairly low starting levels of obstruction (Hypothesis 4). This is particularly intriguing given the lower autonomy levels in this cohort. But it could possibly be attributed to the introduced emphasis on identifying and reflecting on personal and professional values through both the practice management component of the course and the practice of the Giving Voice to Values curriculum.[59]

Impact of results

Excitingly, this research suggests that it is possible to provide a value-positive and supportive legal education experience to assist the development of an ethical professional identity without increasing psychological distress. So, what is it about the curriculum and pedagogy of the PPC that encourages these stable or positive results?

Consistent with Krieger and Sheldon's findings of the different results achieved between the non-traditional (practical legal skills focus) and traditional law schools, that the PPC is practical legal training must factor in the positive results achieved. However, given the different pedagogies used under the banner of 'practical legal skills training' the analysis of why a positive-values and SDT environment occurred in this study must go further than this.

The PPC, as a simulated and collaborative legal environment based on meeting client needs rather than traditional exam structures, changed many of the dynamics prevalent in traditional legal education. Firstly, the student-teacher relationship was changed as the client, rather than the teacher, became the focus

58 Adele Bergin and Nerina Jimmieson, 'Australian Lawyer Well-Being: Workplace Demands, Resources and the Impact of Time-billing Targets' (2014) 21(3) *Psychiatry, Psychology and Law* 427.

59 See, for example, Ferguson, "Creating . . ." (n 24).

of student efforts. The hierarchical teacher/tutor roles were replaced with mentoring relationships. Mentors provided quick feedback and guidance to support students' autonomy to professionally develop and seek their own competence. Critical to this changing dynamic is that assessment was integrated into the transaction (not as separate examinations) as a function of meeting the client's needs; and mentor feedback was geared towards helping students to re-edit their work to achieve competence.[60] Teacher and student thus became mentor and mentee, and this autonomy-supportive environment provided students with intrinsic motivation to 'do their best' for their client and themselves rather than aiming towards an arbitrary and extrinsically motivated numerical grade.

This approach also may have the benefit of improving the professional outcomes in legal education. As one of us previously reported, the positive findings from our study in relation to SDT and values are also associated with students' reported increases in professionalism and professional identity. They indicate that there is a positive relationship between students' concepts of what they know and will know upon admission to practice.[61]

Another dynamic that changed was the relationship between students. There is no bell-curve moderation of exam grades and it is open for every student to achieve competence or higher, without reference to anyone else's achievements. The individual competition and often debilitating obsession with grades evident within other legal education is therefore intentionally removed. Combined with the supported teamwork environment through which the students completed most formative transactional work and the employment of practicing lawyers as mentors, the PPC provided the environment for students to build relatedness with each other and the profession. In line with Huxley-Binns and Ferris' assertions that building community can encourage intrinsic motivation in those who may not come to the program intrinsically motivated, it would seem that teamwork is a fundamental component of the success in building relatedness through the course.

Finally, given the PPC's 'messy' integrated learning environment, the power of the practice management component in supporting SDT and values cannot be underestimated. For example, this component:

- **Supported autonomy** through practice mentoring of individuals/teams by legal practitioners;
- **Encouraged competency development** for the next steps in students' careers – i.e. beyond the academy – through explicit examinations of how to recognise, feel comfortable with/competently address the uncertainties of practice, as well as how to learn from mistakes;
- **Developed relatedness** through discovering and leveraging the diversity of experiences and skills within the team to meet a client's needs and through genuine connections with legal practitioners; and

60 Ferguson and Lee (n 24).
61 Ferguson, 'Creating . . .' (n 24).

- Explicitly provided students with the ability to ethically **enact their values** through concrete examples and practice.[62]

Conclusion

As with any research conducted in a non-experimental environment, there is a risk that the results are not due to students' interactions with the PPC or the factors we have identified. However, given that these results were achieved within 18 weeks and that the PPC was a primary component of the student experience during this time, it is likely to have contributed to the results.

We encourage legal educators and legal education researchers to consider the conclusion that can be drawn from our research. Specifically, our results suggest that it is possible to reverse the well-documented trends of declining well-being and motivation seen in law students. This is achieved not through aesthetic and transient interventions at the surface level of well-being, but through intentional and innovative curriculum developments. These changes return the focus of the learning environment from competence to autonomously supporting students to build a sense of being able to make progress towards their own values and professional identity, and to do so within a community that affords them meaningful relatedness.

62 Ibid.

6 The information gap

A comparative study of the paradigms shaping perceptions of career success for law undergraduates and professional legal training students in Australia and the latent implications of non-professional legal career opportunities for law graduates in England

Barry Yau, David Catanzariti and Joanne Atkinson

Introduction

This chapter identifies an information gap existing in Australian law schools and for law graduates in the UK, particularly England. We examine a lack of knowledge within Australian law school communities of the range and breadth of career opportunities available to students. We also consider the latent attitudes of some English law firms towards graduates who are recruited into paralegal roles instead of sought-after training contracts, creating a knowledge gap about the limited opportunities to gain professional qualification in the future.

The research draws on qualitative data obtained in Australia and England, two jurisdictions which traditionally share a similar route to professional legal qualification. This chapter will explore the application of Bourdieu's theory to our research. In Australia, Bourdieu assumes a greater significance because the number of top-tier firms has remained largely constant over many decades,[1] whilst Australian law schools have increased six fold from 1960 to 2018.[2] In England, there is a similar oversupply of graduates relative to the number of legal professional roles available. The number of training contracts available overall has remained relatively stable, but over the past decade, the number of paralegals

1 Ashley Pinnington and John Gray, 'The Global Restructuring of Legal Services Work? A Study of the Internationalisation of Australian Law Firms' (2007) 14(2) *International Journal of the Legal Profession* 148, 154.

2 Herbert Kritzer, 'Law Schools and the Continuing Growth of the Legal Profession' (2013) 3(3) *Oñati Socio-Legal Series* 450, 455; Council of Australian Law Deans, 'Studying Law in Australia' <https://cald.asn.au/slia/> accessed 7 May 2019. At the time of writing, Australia has 38 university law schools, and two non-university law schools offering accredited law qualifications.

in law firms has increased exponentially. The term paralegal is not regulated, but refers to a non-admitted person who may undertake a multitude of roles from purely administrative functions to fully fledged caseload management.[3] Estimates of the number of paralegals working in the UK (including 'graduate lawyer paralegals' (GLPs)) vary from 60,000–300,000, while the number of new training contracts registered each year for the last three years has remained at around 5,000.[4] Consequently, many graduates who miss out on training contracts end up accepting non-professional GLP positions, we believe, in the hope of gaining a future training contract with the same employer. This is perhaps surprising for readers from Australia where paralegal roles are often viewed as internships completed alongside undergraduate study.

The Australian study researched the relationship between the information gap and student well-being, recognising the disproportionate influence of larger top-tier law firms on students' perceptions of success and belonging, and the dearth of alternative career information. The English study reports on examining the information gap from a law firm perspective, particularly analysing the perceptions of decision makers in mid-tier law firms of the job roles and career pathways available to tomorrow's graduates. While there is an extensive body of research looking at the recruitment practices of top-tier or large City law firms in England – the 'top-tier' firms which so frequently come to represent success in the minds of many students – the attitudes of smaller firms, where many graduates will find employment and may attain satisfaction and fulfilment, is under-explored in the literature. The English study specifically explored the perceptions of mid-tier law firms of the emerging distinction between those graduates selected for training contracts and who are therefore able to complete their professional qualification to become a solicitor, and those who are offered GLP roles, often on a long-term basis.

We acknowledge that the English and Australian studies interrogate different constituencies in the graduate recruitment relationship, representing a limitation of our comparative analysis.

The information gap and well-being

The 'information gap'[5] in Australian law schools emerged as a key and recurrent theme in the Australian study.[6] We contend the information gap has wrought a paucity of information within the law school student community about the

3 Michael Proffitt (ed), *Oxford English Dictionary* (Oxford University Press, 2018); Richard Simmons, 'Hug Your Paralegal' (2016) 31 *The Lawyer* 18.

4 The Law Society, 'Early Trends' <www.lawsociety.org.uk/law-careers/becoming-a-solicitor/entry-trends/> accessed 7 May 2019.

5 A term coined by an LLB participant.

6 The overall research objective analysed attitudes of law students and early career commercial lawyers towards studying and practising commercial law. Ethics approval was granted 24 December 2013 (ANU HREC Protocol: 2013/717). The commercial law focus stems from commercial/corporate law being the most common legal area practised by entry-level lawyers in Australia: Maxine Evers et al., 'Looking to the Past to Plan for the Future: A Decade of Practical Legal Training' (2002) 45 *The Law Teacher* 18, 27.

breadth of opportunities in legal practice and other careers, and potentially impacts the well-being[7] of law students and early career commercial lawyers.

In England the information gap relates to the lack of transparency in the recruitment marketplace about the criteria law firms are using to select trainee solicitors and GLPs. The evidence suggests that, although some firms recruit from their own paralegal pool, the attitude of many law firms is that they will not consider GLPs when recruiting for solicitor training contracts, and thus the profession in England is becoming increasingly stratified.

The Australian research identifies a probable correlation between the information gap and the undermining of perceived levels of 'autonomy, self-esteem and a sense of competence' that well-being requires,[8] particularly as an individual's identity develops while seeking success through, for instance, securing meaningful employment in a competitive job market.[9] It is contended that the GLPs in England will also experience similar feelings when they identify their limited prospects of success in obtaining a future training contract with their current employer. This research is supported by findings of Krieger in the US which set out how students and lawyers measure the paradigms of success:

> Assuming that the legal 'success' paradigm is, indeed, largely defined by grades, external recognition, and money or position, these inherently competitive goals, values, and motives will promote tension and insecurity and will minimize satisfaction and wellbeing in the lives of many law students and lawyers.[10]

Bourdieu's tools

While certain research themes have arisen relating to Self-Determination Theory, we formed the view that Bourdieu's theoretical tools postulated the appropriate theoretical lens to analyse the qualitative data in the Australian and English studies. Bourdieu's theory is apt as it helps us make sense of the paradigm in which power is exerted by significant agents and the information they impart in the legal community, and their influence on the well-being of law students seeking career success.

7 Despite no 'consensus definition' of well-being, a key common element is 'positive features such as the quality of a job or happiness with one's life': Andrew Clarke, 'Developing a KPI for Measuring Staff Wellbeing: Implications for Australian Law' (2017) 7 *Victoria University Law & Justice Journal* 22, 25; Paul Schulte and Harri Vainio, 'Well-Being at Work – Overview and Perspective' (2010) *Scandinavian Journal of Work, Environment & Health* 422, 423.

8 Wendy Larcombe et al., 'Does an Improved Experience of Law School Protect Students Against Depression, Anxiety and Stress? An Empirical Study of Wellbeing and the Law School Experience of LLB and JD Students' (2013) 35 *Sydney Law Review* 407.

9 Melissa Coade, 'Counting the So-Called 'Glut' of Law Grads' *Lawyers Weekly*, 25 November 2016.

10 Lawrence S Krieger, 'Institutional Denial About the Dark Side of Law School, and Fresh Empirical Guidance for Constructively Breaking the Silence' (2002) 52 *Journal of Legal Education* 112, 122.

Bourdieu provides a framework to illuminate how themes relevant to the information gap have contributed to undermining competence, autonomy and relatedness within the Australian law school student body. Whilst in England further research is required to establish the experience amongst the emerging group of GLPs, Bourdieu's theory provides a valuable insight on how well-being could be impacted upon becoming aware of the potential consequences of joining the GLP track.

Bourdieu's 'field', a 'space of conflict and competition' (e.g. the Australian law school community/English mid-tier law firms), conserves or transforms the structure of relations of forces constituting the field.[11] Emerging from behaviour and practises exhibited by agents in the field – the game itself – is 'doxa', being 'tacit, unexamined, taken-for-granted presuppositions' (e.g. achieving high distinction grades and a willingness to work very long hours in legal practice in Australia/England).[12] Akin to the rules of a game, doxa is 'self-evidently worth knowing and doing', and organises the field's action.[13] Bourdieu's 'habitus' – the feel for the game[14] – is a pattern of dispositions, practices and inculcated values recognised by individuals as a requirement to play.[15] This arises from dispositions (e.g. values, tastes) inculcated through family, community, educational institutions and social structures (e.g. the law, legal profession, academia).[16] It adapts itself to the field[17] where powerful agents (e.g. law firms)[18] utilise their capital (e.g. symbolic, social, economic) to designate and determine the capital's value (e.g. law school reputation, attitudes to commercial law, academic grades) that participants (law students and graduates) need to secure the attention of law firms[19] and achieve success ordained by such firms.[20] Power in the field creates

11 Pierre Bourdieu, 'Journalistic Field' in Rodney Benson and Eric Neveu (eds), *Bourdieu and the Journalistic Field* (Polity Press, 2005) 30.

12 Hilary Sommerlad, 'Researching and Theorizing the Processes of Professional Identity Formation' (2007) 34(2) *Journal of Law and Society* 190, 194.

13 Kristoffer Greaves, 'Re-Imagining Practical Legal Training Practitioners – Soldiers for "Vocationalism", or Double Agents?' (2014) 7(1–2) *Journal of the Australasian Law Teachers Association* 101.

14 Lisa Adkins, 'Reflexivity: Freedom or Habit of Gender?' (2003) 20(6) *Theory, Culture & Society* 21, 24.

15 Pinnington and Gray (n 1) 154; Andrew Cook, James Faulconbridge and Daniel Muzio, 'London's Legal Elite: Recruitment Through Cultural Capital and the Reproduction of Social Exclusivity in City Professional Service Fields' (2012) 44 *Environment and Planning A* 1744, 1748.

16 Greaves (n 13).

17 Alice Sullivan, 'Bourdieu and Education: How Useful is Bourdieu's Theory for Researchers?' (2002) 38(2) *The Netherlands' Journal of Social Sciences* 144.

18 Australian top-tier commercial law firms are informally termed the 'Big Six' (equivalent to the UK's 'Magic Circle'). Our participants regularly cited the 'Big Six' as shorthand for top-tier firms.

19 Jen Webb, Tony Schirato and Geoff Danaher, *Understanding Bourdieu* (Allen & Unwin, 2002) 24.

20 Pierre Bourdieu, *Distinction: A Social Critique of the Judgment of Taste* (Harvard University Press, 1984) 122; Fiona Kay and John Hagan, 'Raising the Bar: The Gender Stratification of Law-Firm Capital' (1998) 63(5) *American Sociological Review* 728, 732.

dispositions and expectations leading to 'reproduction' of symbolic dominance. This replicates 'conditions of oppression' of the dominated, who being intolerant of, or struggling with, these conditions become 'resigned or fatalistic'.[21] Bourdieu claims those dominated (e.g. law students wishing to pursue a commercial law career but not gaining a top-tier graduate placement in Australia/English law, or graduates who apply for and miss out on a training contract but accept a position as a GLP), are complicit as victims of 'symbolic violence',[22] perceiving their oppression (e.g. feelings of inferiority) as 'the natural order of things'.[23]

Between the mid-2000s and the early 2010s, the literature indicates an increase in the application of Bourdieu's concepts to inform studies of social and power structures in legal education and practice in countries such as Canada, Australia, the US and England. The literature illustrates Bourdieu's 'thinking tools'[24] were utilised to research the transformation of Canadian law students' identities in a social space sponsored by major law firms,[25] links between social background and student admission to Oxford University,[26] social class influence on US legal education[27] and professional identity formation in Legal Practice Course (LPC) students at a 'new' UK university and local (high-street) law firm lawyers.[28] Researchers also applied Bourdieu's tools to study the extent to which major Australian law firms are coerced and influenced by the political, economic and symbolic power of US and UK firms,[29] the recruitment processes reproducing elites and elite cultures within London City law firms,[30] and the prospects of females seeking Canadian law firm partnerships.[31]

It is posited that an exponentially large number of Australian law students are potentially influenced by the top-tier firms dominating the field. Our data underscores the implications on the professional identity and well-being of law students and graduate commercial lawyers feeling marginalised by their information gap experience. In England we contend this experience has two tiers. The first is the disappointment of law graduates failing to secure a training contract in a hugely competitive market and opting instead to take a position as a GLP. The second is realising the existence of the information gap in relation to the low likelihood

21 Pierre Bourdieu, *Pascalian Meditations* (Stanford University Press, 2000) 217.
22 Pierre Bourdieu and Loic Wacquant, *An Invitation to Reflexive Sociology* (University of Chicago Press, 1992) 167.
23 Webb (n 19) 25.
24 Loic Wacquant, 'Towards a Reflexive Sociology: A Workshop with Pierre Bourdieu' (1989) 7(1) *Sociological Theory* 26, 50.
25 Desmond Manderson and Sarah Turner, 'Coffee House: Habitus and Performance Among Law Students' (2006) 31(3) *Law & Social Inquiry* 649.
26 Anna Zimdars, Alice Sullivan and Anthony Heathl, 'Elite Higher Education Admissions in the Arts and Sciences: Is Cultural Capital the Key?' (2009) 43 *Sociology* 648.
27 Lucille Jewell, 'Bourdieu and American Legal Education: How Law Schools Reproduce Social Stratification and Class Hierarchy' (2008) 56 *Buffalo Law Review* 1155.
28 Sommerlad (n 12) 190.
29 Pinnington and Gray (n 1) 148.
30 Cook et al. (n 15).
31 Kay and Hagan (n 20).

of securing a future training contract in the firm as a consequence of accepting a GLP role. As the situation evolves, we have identified that further investigation is required in the future to collect qualitative data from GLPs for analysis through the lens of Bourdieu's theory.

Method

For the Australian study, invitations were posted on social media and by email in 2014–15[32] to prospective participants from three categories: LLB and JD students[33] at the Australian National University (ANU) and the University of Canberra,[34] ANU PLT students, and early career commercial lawyers[35] practising in Canberra. Participants volunteered for a semi-structured interview or focus group comprising participants from their category. The researchers moderated six focus groups (two for each category) in the second half of 2014 and held 24 semi-structured interviews over 2014–15; all were audio-recorded and transcribed.[36] Participants responded to questions and talking points including identifying attitudes to studying and practising commercial law, lawyers' experiences and reflections of commercial practice and well-being perspectives.[37] The research investigators independently reviewed the transcripts and follow-up questionnaire responses identifying elements to categorise into themes and connections, to develop a consensus-based coding scheme for data interpretation.[38] The investigators then used the scissor-and-sort method to code phrases, sentences and participant exchanges relevant to the categorical themes.

In England the University of Portsmouth conducted a qualitative study in 2017 to explore emerging graduate roles and career pathways not revealed by existing data.[39] The study looked exclusively at the views of mid-tier law firms and did not seek to explore in-house opportunities, careers at the Bar, in the public sector or in other branches of the legal profession, or in legal education. The study was conducted via semi-structured face-to-face interviews with partners and HR directors in purposively selected mid-tier law firms in London and South East England. Participants were identified as decision makers in graduate

32 Sent to prospective volunteers referred by third parties interested in our research.

33 All LLB/JD participants had already completed the Corporations Law subject.

34 Both universities are located in Canberra.

35 Practising five years or less as a commercial lawyer.

36 All focus groups (4–6 participants) were at ANU. Fourteen interviews were conducted via Skype, ten were conducted in person: seven LLB, eight ANU PLT, and nine lawyers participated.

37 In 2015, follow-up questionnaires were sent to participants to gather further responses about well-being, as these were supplementary to the original questions. Approximately half of these participants responded to this questionnaire.

38 Jamie Harding, *Qualitative Data Analysis from Start to Finish* (Sage, 2013); Lia Litosseliti, *Using Focus Groups in Research* (A&C Black, 2003).

39 Ethical approval was granted January 2017 by the University of Portsmouth Business and Law Ethics Committee Ref E432.

recruitment and invited to participate via email. Take-up was low; more than 50 potential participants were approached, yielding seven positive responses. The low participation rate is disappointing because it represents a limitation in the generalisability of the study's findings. However it might be surmised that the low take-up indicates low engagement with the current debate about the future of the profession among mid-tier firms. This is borne out by some participants' responses to questions about the new Solicitors Qualifying Exam (SQE) ('We are just waiting to see what happens') and solicitor apprenticeships ('Not on our radar at all') for example. This may go some way toward explaining the disproportionate influence of top-tier, large and City-based law firms on students' perceptions of success, echoing the Australian study results.

Data analysis and themes

For legal educators, the study of the Australian and English legal environments is highly significant as a means of seeking to close the information gap and consider how to prepare graduates more effectively for success.[40] We explored the values specific to the doxa and habitus within the fields of power[41] by conducting a thematic analysis of participants' responses. The analysis seeks meaning in the participants' responses by applying Bourdieu's tools, appreciating that whilst a participant's responses could be snapshots not necessarily representing their whole experience, they provide the basis of our emerging themes.

Dominance

In Australia the strong consensus of the participant early career commercial lawyers highlighted the theme of top-tier firms dominating the law school space at the expense of others. 'There was never a night for anything other than top-tier commercial law firms' remarked lawyer Martha[42] reflecting on her law school's careers and clerkship[43] nights. Dinah observed top-tier firms 'sponsor everything'. Naomi found the rarity of 'non-commercial firms' (e.g. family law firms) at her law students' society (LSS) information sessions 'pretty limiting' because top-tier firms mostly dominated. Martha recalled her clerkship information nights lacked firms 'below' top-tiers, and no events 'spinning the benefits' of working as a lawyer for mid-tier/boutique firms, government or NGO. An exchange between

40 Questions have been raised in, *inter alia*, Ewan Ingleby and Caroline Gibby, 'Law and Ethics: Problematizing the Role of the Foundation Degree and Paralegal Education in English Post-Compulsory Education' (2016) 21(1/2) *Research in Post-Compulsory Education* 151.

41 Zander Navarro, 'In Search of a Cultural Interpretation of Power: The Contribution of Pierre Bourdieu' (2006) 37(6) *Institute of Development Studies Bulletin* 11.

42 Names anonymized.

43 Top-tier and other large commercial firms typically recruit LLB/JD students in their penultimate year of study to undertake a 2–3 month 'clerkship', from which these firms predominantly recruit their graduate lawyers. References to 'clerkships' by participants were usually associated with top-tier firm internships.

LLB participants (both former LSS committee members) appeared to explain one way top-tier firms utilise economic capital to send a powerfully repetitious message to students in the law school field. Phoebe could only remember firms that 'spent money through the LSS – seeing their names on signs and attending clerkship evenings', thinking 'these are the firms I can work for'. Only as Phoebe's studies progressed did she learn of other opportunities. Phoebe noted big firms became 'premium sponsors' through giving the LSS money for naming rights and headlining clerkship evenings – 'LSS career event of the year'. Joanna inferred the LSS committee sometimes drew a 'certain type of person' aiming for top-tier careers and 'assume everyone else is as well', perpetuating top-tier firm dominance in the field.

In the past, entry into the legal profession in England was largely controlled by regulatory bodies acting as 'gatekeepers',[44] restricting access to the profession to those demonstrating a prescribed level of performance in professional examinations. When the Solicitors Regulation Authority disbanded its joint academic stage board in 2013 (relinquishing oversight of the law degree and LPC), the effect was to place law firms in the gatekeeping role, with the ability to determine how many and which candidates progress to professional qualification.[45] The resulting shift of power to a new elite[46] in law firms and companies has in Bourdieu's terms narrowed the field of power considerably.[47] The decision-making process around recruitment and selection is now played out in private.[48] This development has the potential to create significant challenges for law graduates trying to make sense of the expectations (the habitus) relating to law firm recruitment practices. Additionally, the introduction of the new SQE in England is likely to generate more alternative routes into the profession beyond the two-tier approach of training contracts or GLPs.[49] Currently, these alternative routes are under-explored in the literature. As the profession becomes more stratified, there is a real risk that law firms at all levels will deploy their capital (social, economic and symbolic) to attract a small homogeneous group of graduates to training contracts, leaving candidates without the requisite resources of social or cultural capital to pursue alternative routes such as GLPs. In other words, those candidates already enjoying the advantage of belonging to an elite (whether via

44 Patricia Leighton, 'The LLB as a Liberal Degree? A Re-Assessment from an Historical Perspective' (2015) 22(1) *International Journal of the Legal Profession* 87.

45 Melissa Hardee, 'Central Exam Idea Does Not Add Up' *Law Society Gazette* (London, 29 February 2016).

46 Mathieu Hilgers and Eric Mangez (eds), *Bourdieu's Theory of Social Fields: Concepts and Applications* (Routledge, 2015).

47 Andrew Francis and Hilary Sommerlad, 'Access to Legal Work Experience and its Role in the (Re)production of Legal Professional Identity' (2009) 16(1) *International Journal of the Legal Profession* 63.

48 Louise Ashley et al., *A Qualitative Evaluation of Non-Educational Barriers to the Elite Professions* (Social Mobility and Child Poverty Commission, June 2015) 9.

49 Solicitors Regulation Authority, https://www.sra.org.uk/sra/policy/sqe.page accessed 7 May 2019.

their university, contacts or their ability to 'fit' into an elite environment) are further rewarded while others, who may be better suited to the role, risk remaining as GLPs.

Grades, very long hours, value of training contracts

In the Australian study, two LLB participants expressed confidence about the doxa by understanding the value of their own capital in aiming for careers in top-tier firms. Luke shared the perception and awareness amongst his peers that a 'commercial focus' in the LLB is necessary for top-tier firm entry, and Joshua recognised the importance of mathematical skills. Timothy, a global firm lawyer, recounted 'The quickest way to cull clerkship applicants is to look at the grades'. This confirmed LLB student Joanna's presupposition that top-tier clerkship evenings 'target the top five-ten percent of students academically'. A consistent thread in interviews of LLB and PLT students was the assumption that top-tier firms demand very long and maybe unrealistic hours: 'they work you around the clock' (Amos, LLB student), 'insane hours, working until 11pm' (Eunice, LLB student), '80 hour weeks, 90 hour weeks' (Samuel, LLB student), 'start early in the morning, finish late at night, go in on weekends' (Esther, PLT student). Eunice and Samuel acknowledged their statements were based on 'horror stories' or rumours 'heard in law school'. We assert that anecdotes of long hours and high distinction grades have capital for top-tier firms as it shapes and even acculturates their version of a model top-tier lawyer in Australia.

The practices by which mid-tier law firms recruit individuals for training contracts represents the doxa in the English study. The practices encompass benchmarks to select applicant law graduates for training contracts, and often to recruit those not deemed suitable for training contracts as GLPs. As the role of trainee solicitor is completely separate and distinct from that of paralegal, the application process is also completely separate – it is certainly not the case that unsuccessful applicants for training contracts would be offered a paralegal role as a consolation. However, with the recruitment window for training contracts typically opening much earlier than that for GLPs, students keen to secure a training contract understand the necessity of applying for training contracts during their undergraduate years and may only begin to look at paralegal positions if they experience numerous rejections.

Most participants in the English research foresaw an increase in recruitment of GLPs and other administrative support roles over the coming years, while trainee solicitor recruitment was forecast to remain stable or even decline.[50] This reflects the evolution of the law firm model from one where a solicitor managed every aspect of a client matter to one where routine tasks are now managed by

50 Amanda Hamilton, 'In an Ever-Changing Legal Landscape, Paralegals Are the Way Forward' (2014) 48(1) *The Law Teacher* 104.

non-professionals, so that fewer solicitors lead ever-growing teams of paralegals.[51] This latter model is particularly prevalent in administration- and process-heavy areas of practice such as residential conveyancing. The perceived status of the GLP is lower than that of a trainee solicitor even though their workloads may be very similar.

Shock, awe and anxiety

In the Australian research, PLT participant Tamar's comment, 'The whole clerkship thing. Never really understood it', encapsulates the struggle of some students in understanding and adopting the habitus. Our data highlights some coherent resistance – even loathing – to the habitus, the feel for the 'clerkship game'. Martha described top-tier marketing as a 'shock and awe campaign', 'bombarding' and 'spamming' students with the prestigious decree 'this is what you're going to be when you're a commercial lawyer, these are all the benefits you'll have'. Naomi thought it 'a bit offensive' how 'impressionable' the firms thought students were, highlighting firms' aggressiveness in deploying capital. Lawyer Deborah cynically associated these firms' free distribution of promotional items at careers days with their message 'oh gosh, great to work there'. Yet Timothy, who secured a top-tier clerkship, stated that he viewed these objects as 'cool', impressed these firms wield economic capital to 'brand and advertise' themselves – he aspired to be part of that. The distribution of notepads, pens and USB sticks conveys an elite top-tier corporate branding and symbolises the assertion of the top-tiers' dominance in the field. When combined with the top-tiers' generous financial sponsorship of the LSS, this appears to influence some students in the field to accept that a top-tier career represents the principal pathway to success.

In the English study, one can reasonably presuppose that many law students might be surprised or even shocked to learn of the real possibility of a mid-tier firm or any law firm offering them a paralegal role instead of a training contract on graduation, and remaining in this role without progressing to formal qualification. Further research is required on the impact on their well-being as a result of missing out on a training contract. However if this possibility were discussed openly by law schools at the recruitment stage, some students may be deterred from applying to study for a law degree in the first place. Equally however, transparency is vital if potential students and aspiring lawyers are to make informed decisions.

Toxicity, atrocity and acceptance

In the Australian study, the habitus also influences some students who prioritise well-being whilst expressing ambivalence but acceptance of the top-tier culture.

51 Richard Susskind, *The End of Lawyers?* (Oxford University Press, 2008); Richard Susskind, *The Future of the Professions: How Technology Will Transform the Work of Human Experts* (Oxford University Press, 2015).

Abigail, an LLB participant, was drawn to the competitiveness of 'big law firms' placing her 'at the top of her game' working on 'big cases', but conceded she would be 'much happier' in a mid-tier firm with a diverse workload and 'better whole life experience' compared to 'sweating your butt out' in a big law firm. Two LLB participants, Joanna and Phoebe, rationalised aspirations towards top-tier careers. Joanna, despite having no commercial law interest, would 'love to experience the commercial law world' to 'skill-up',[52] coupled with her perception of commercial lawyers being taken 'very seriously'. Even though Phoebe thought top-tier work hours were atrocious with a toxic environment, she still considered it a 'good way to develop skills beyond university' for two or three years before 'burning out'. These competing perspectives illustrate the reproduction of top-tier symbolic dominance lest these students experience marginalisation or symbolic violence by resisting the habitus to maintain their values and identity.

For those law graduates who fail to secure a training contract in England, the habitus frequently influences them to pursue a GLP role instead. This is usually in the hope of being accepted for a training contract in the future. However, the attitude of the recruiters interviewed to GLP recruits was such that these graduates may in fact find themselves joining a separate career track and inadvertently ruling themselves out of selection for future trainee roles. The consequent effect on their well-being is unknown.

Alterity and the next drop

In the Australian study, Dinah and Claudia, both government lawyer participants, shared a poignant exchange highlighting the continuing influence and even symbolic violence of top-tier firms, beyond law school, affecting their well-being. Both recognised with 'only so many roles' at top-tier level, any other job is a 'compromised position' where you've 'taken the next drop' or 'failed'. It is trite to say top-tier firms are not responsible for the well-being of students who won't or cannot secure jobs with them, or for students experiencing low self-esteem or feeling less competent for lacking sufficient grades. Indeed, top-tier firms have the right to utilise capital for their own objectives. However, our data demonstrates this embedded top-tier dominance promotes a notion of limited alterity, potentially affecting well-being. Some undergraduate student participants recognised top-tier firms dominating at careers fairs, with LLB student Abel observing 'I don't see a lot of low to medium firms advertising' and PLT student Tamar rueing 'It was all big firms'. The lawyer participants forthrightly observed the dearth of contrasting career options, with Lois (who practised in top-tier firms) summing up her group's observations by recommending a wider introduction

52 The participants' association of terms such as 'clerkship', 'top', 'big' and 'skill-up' with top-tier firms warrants further research into the top-tiers' use of language as symbolic capital in the field.

of legal practices into the field by increasing awareness of career opportunities at mid-tier, boutique and criminal practices as well as government departments. Miriam's reflection, 'I thought being successful meant working in one of the Big Six firms [but] there's a lot more to commercial law than working in one of those places' highlights the disjunction between shock and awe and reality'. This was a common theme expressed in other focus groups. LLB participant Joanna's observation, 'there are so many other good options there that we don't get exposed to' indicates students desire exposure to broader options. We surmise there are significant challenges for non-top-tier players trying to match the experienced marketing dynamism of top-tier firms, epitomised by lawyer participant Martha's observation, when as an LLB student, she approached government lawyers at career events, 'you don't ever sort of get a feel for it' because of the 'rote responses' when inquiring about government legal practice.

It might be expected that firms would aim to recruit the best candidate, judged by objective criteria, for whatever role they are seeking to fill. However, the data from the English study suggests that their approach is less straightforward. Several participants explained that recruiting candidates who scored highly against their selection criteria for GLP roles posed a risk; such candidates were likely to be 'gone when a better opportunity [came] along'. Instead, firms are recruiting candidates who are unlikely to make the cut for a training contract to GLP roles, on the basis that they are more likely to remain in such roles for long enough to become efficient. Indeed, in some of the participating firms, there were established career routes for paralegals, suggesting that this alterity is becoming embedded in England. The expectation of a graduate lawyer in England accepting a GLP position might therefore be compared with what one of the Australian participants described as a 'compromised position' by taking the 'next drop'. It is possible to speculate that these students are likely to experience similar and possibly more intense feelings of disappointment and cynicism, although further research is required in England to explore this theme.

'Quality' and self-reproduction

The English mid-tier law firms were asked which graduate skills and attributes were most sought after. There were frequent references to 'quality', and identifying candidates of the right 'quality' for trainee roles. This is problematic, as the term 'quality' is often a proxy for other measures of social capital.[53] Bourdieu suggests that as power becomes concentrated in an elite group of decision makers, the field reproduces itself by increasing the value of certain forms of capital,[54] and the tendency of elite lawyers to prefer candidates of a similar profile to

53 Heather Rolfe and Tracy Anderson, 'A Firm Choice: Law Firms' Preferences in the Recruitment of Trainee Solicitors' (2003) 10(3) *International Journal of the Legal Profession* 315.

54 Pierre Bourdieu, 'From the King's House to the Reason of State: A Model of the Genesis of the Bureaucratic Field' (2004) 11(1) *Constellations* 16.

themselves has frequently been noted in the literature.[55] All participants in the English study mentioned 'good academics' or 'strong academics', as the single most important factor in the recruitment decision. Interestingly, all respondents denied that the university attended by a candidate was decisive, although many participants stated that other partners within their respective firms were inclined to favour Russell Group candidates.[56] In other words, there was acknowledgement that this type of reproduction of identity may still be taking place. In the Australian study, some of the LLB participants believed, accurately or not, that top-tier firms tend to favour clerkship applications from students attending law schools with a strong commercial focus, another measure of social capital.

In the English study, strong A-level grades were also cited as desirable, a requirement disadvantaging certain already under-represented groups including ethnic minorities and those from lower social class groups.[57] The resulting suggestion of a self-reproducing bias is borne out by existing empirical data.[58] However in the Australian study the relevance of high school secondary grades was not raised by the participants, and we can surmise this was not considered by the participants to be capital required to secure a clerkship in a top-tier firm.

While legal work experience in the English study was frequently cited as important, several law firms opined that a mixture of short-term placements did not of itself enhance a candidate's employability. The ability to gain relevant work experience is a marker of social capital and the value of contacts in this context is recognised in the literature.[59] However, this kind of social capital is not possessed by all graduates. Citing work experience as a selection prerequisite could equally be seen as rewarding nepotism and even unethical behaviour – offering jobs to friends over objectively better-qualified applicants. Given the known benefits of diversity in the profession, this finding is troubling.[60] The perceived value of work experience for most respondents relates to development of 'commercial awareness' akin to the doxa. Commercial awareness is used indiscriminately to denote a loose collection of knowledge and skills[61] including a general awareness of politics and current affairs and of the current legal landscape and an appreciation of how a firm makes profits. In this context, it is disingenuous to distinguish commercial awareness from work experience since the former refers to a kind of professional socialisation which is usually exclusive to those candidates who can access the latter.[62] Applying this criterion amounts to what Francis and Sommerlad term 'a

55 Cook et al. (n 15).

56 A self-selecting group of 24 top UK universities, including the Universities of Oxford and Cambridge.

57 See e.g. Rolfe and Anderson (n 53).

58 Andrew Francis, 'Legal Education, Social Mobility, and Employability: Possible Selves, Curriculum Intervention, and the Role of Legal Work Experience' (2015) 42(2) *Journal of Law and Society* 173.

59 Ibid.

60 Ashley et al. (n 48).

61 Francis and Sommerlad (n 47).

62 Ibid.

means of reproducing an exclusionary identity',[63] or Bourdieu's elite reproducing itself.[64] However in the Australian study, students seeking clerkships with top-tier firms placed significant weight on being academically successful in undergraduate commercial law subjects, but did not identify the importance of commercial awareness in the same context.

Conclusions

We conclude that the information gap in Australia and England is negatively impacting the well-being of certain sections of the legal community. In Australia it is law students and PLT students who are generally unaware of other career opportunities within the legal profession, the awareness of which may contribute to positively influencing career choices. In England, there is a lack of transparency around the increasingly stratified graduate marketplace which we argue impacts on student well-being. Those lacking the necessary capital to be offered a training contract may be recruited to GLP roles with the data indicating that these positions may amount to career 'dead-ends' because the likelihood of receiving a training contract offer in the future is remote.

The research strongly suggests an augmented field in Australia offering a broader range of career options is required to narrow the information gap. As a result, the field can redefine the doxa and habitus, with new categories of perception and social discussion addressing the identified current deficiencies. We propose that the first steps in attempting to bridge the information gap may involve law schools engaging dedicated staff who possess extensive knowledge of the legal services market to increase students' awareness of the broadness of commercial law careers and legal careers generally beyond top-tiers whose presence already dominate the law school community. Alternatively, having a greater representation of career options, both legal and other, at law careers fairs and career information sessions will also assist students to make more discerning considerations about future career options. In England, law school staff must tread a difficult line, encouraging aspiration and ambition while offering realistic and pragmatic advice to their students whose disappointment of missing out on a training contract is likely to create much anxiety for law graduates. Questions must arise about the well-being of law graduates who opt for GLPs and eventually realise the limited chances of securing a training contract in the same firm. Further, the impact of the realisation that a GLP may be the best position they can ever secure in a legal environment is not yet understood.

It is apparent that unless there is an increased awareness and even challenge of the paradigms of practises of existing and emerging law firm power bases in Australia and England, many individuals seeking careers as legal professionals may encounter incomplete narratives which will significantly impact on notions

63 Ibid 79.
64 Bourdieu (n 54).

of success and future well-being. The adage 'forewarned is forearmed' rings true in determining the extent to which these individuals can confidently define their own success in a highly competitive legal market. Having a more complete factual career matrix will play a significant role in their ability to measure and achieve their legal success paradigm.[65]

Acknowledgements

The researchers thank Alexandra Johnstone, Vivien Holmes, Helen Rodriguez, Courtney Macintosh, Stephen Tang, Pam Foo, the ANU College of Law Small Grant Scheme, Caroline Strevens and the University of Portsmouth Sabbatical Fund.

65 Krieger (n 10) 121.

7 Widening the approach to ethics teaching and positively affecting the ethical professional identity of trainee solicitors in Ireland

Freda Grealy

Irish trainee solicitors, in the context of the apprenticeship model, are moulded by the behaviour, community, and culture of the firm of their traineeship workplace, and also by periods of formal study while undertaking their Professional Practice Course (PPC) at the Law Society of Ireland (LSI) Law School.[1]

The maturation process and assimilation of the profession's own value frameworks are an integral part of professional identity formation for neophyte lawyers,[2] and learning about ethics is an integral part of this professional development process and becoming a lawyer.[3] Learning is part of the collective process of constructing identity in the community.[4] Mead[5] suggests that the way we see ourselves and construct our identity is influenced by our interactions with those around us. The professional vocational journey and period of time studying at the LSI can contribute to this change and can place ethics, morality, and values centrally, thus becoming a potentially powerful and life-changing experience. The notion of a developmental continuum aligns with the traineeship journey that Irish trainees undergo in their two-year apprenticeship. In the context of an intervention course at the Law Society of Ireland, this chapter will discuss the importance of introducing a wide approach to teaching ethics which means going beyond a defensive rule-based approach to learning about professional conduct rules. It outlines the reflections of the trainees who participated in the intervention and the positive impact the teaching and learning approach had on their

1 The Irish apprenticeship model of training means that trainees are obliged to complete a 24-month training contract in a solicitor's office. This is split between time spent in the office and in academic- and skills-based sessions of study, called the Professional Practice Course I (PPCI) and Professional Practice Course II (PPCII), at the Law School in the Law Society of Ireland. All those who attend are graduates but not necessarily law graduates.

2 Adrian Evans, *The Good Lawyer* (Cambridge University Press, 2014).

3 David Luban and Michael Millemann, 'Good Judgment: Ethics Teaching in Dark Times' (1995) 9 *Georgetown Journal of Legal Ethics* 31.

4 Jean Lave and Etienne Wenger, *Situated Learning: Legitimate Peripheral Participation* (Cambridge University Press, 1991); Bente Elkjaer, 'Organizacní Ucení a Napetí Coby Jeho Spoustec v Mnohohlasé Aréne' in Petr Novotny (ed), *Contemporary Issues in Workplace Learning: An Introduction* (Masaryk University, 2009).

5 George Herbert Mead, *Mind, Self, and Society* (University of Chicago Press, 1934).

self-actualisation of personal values, their professional identity and, ultimately, the potential impact on their well-being as future solicitors.

Teaching ethics is difficult, as it requires that trainees engage in a very personal interrogation of their own values and morals and show a willingness to engage with their own development and the values of the profession. Teaching 'identity' is not something you can aim for, since you cannot teach someone else to form identity, which requires internalisation and assimilation. However, you can create an environment that is supportive and facilitates reflection and formation, as outlined below:

> We can design structured experiences in doctrinal courses which engage students in the reflective process from which formation occurs. Developing practical judgment in an ethical context seems tied to identifying and reflecting upon one's own moral as well as ethical reactions and also listening to and understanding the reactions of others.[6]

The impact of legal education, Hall et al. suggest, is not only on how students think and feel, 'but also on *who* they are'.[7] Professional legal education plays a pivotal part in terms of professional socialisation and according to Hall et al., the 'experience of law school has a powerful and, perhaps, under-examined impact on the formation of a lawyer's professional identity'.[8] Whilst these observations are made by Australian authors in relation to legal education generally, they resonate in Ireland at the professional legal education level.[9] Hall criticises law schools and their underlying context, structure, values, and pedagogy for failing to grasp the impact they have on students as they 'become' lawyers. Even worse, law school can, as highlighted by Sheldon and Krieger[10] and by Field, Duffy, and James,[11] have a negative effect and cause changes to their motivation and overall emotional and physical well-being (see also Chapter 3 of this book).

6 David Thomson, *Educating Tomorrow's Lawyers (ETL) Conference* (Institute for the Advancement of the American Legal System, 2012).

7 Kath Hall, Molly Townes O'Brien and Stephen Tang, 'Developing a Professional Identity in Law Schools: A View from Australia' (2010) 4 *Phoenix Law Review* 21.

8 Ibid.

9 Reference is made to literature from the UK, the US and beyond related to the law school throughout this chapter, but there is no intention to conflate law school with professional legal education as the goals of undergraduate legal education are understandably different. It is acknowledged that there are marked differences with the context of US legal education, however, given the dearth of research in the area of professional identity and wellness in Ireland it is useful to refer to the extensive literature, for example, in US postgraduate law schools and internationally; and to discuss the approaches of other universities throughout the world who see professional identity formation as one of their objectives.

10 Kennon M Sheldon and Lawrence S Krieger, 'Understanding the Negative Effects of Legal Education on Law Students: A Longitudinal Test and Extension of Self-Determination Theory' (2007) 33(6) *Personality and Social Psychology Bulletin* 883.

11 Rachael Field, James Duffy and Colin James (eds), *Promoting Law Student and Lawyer Well-Being in Australia and Beyond* (Routledge, 2016).

The challenges of the law school experience for many suggest a need to engage in difficult dialogues that focus not merely on reflecting on ethical dilemmas, but also on students' personal choices, well-being and values, and honest dialogue that recognises the difficulties that many students face. Morin[12] calls for a 'community of truth' approach[13] and she recognises the challenge of opening up classrooms for these types of discussion and the fear of losing control of the room. She suggests that boundaries can be created or that texts and specific questions can be used to maintain focus. Encouraging appreciative inquiry and creative dialogue[14] can address uncomfortable issues, such as the possible disjunction between a lawyer's individual opinion and her duty, and this should begin in law school.[15] Creative dialogue refers to the idea that communication is about hearing another person and finding shared meaning, rather than arguing about who is right or wrong. This is in some ways novel to traditional approaches of studying law, as it's not emphasising persuasion or an adversarial approach. Providing opportunities for open dialogue and creative spaces or a 'community of truth' can encourage talk of personal values and well-being and helps students to not only believe that their own values and morals do matter, but also allows them to recognise the complexities of role morality.[16]

Intervention overview

The intervention course at the Law Society of Ireland was entitled 'Certificate in Legal Ethics and Lawyering Skills' and embraced a wide view of ethics and the notion of professional identity. It was tailored to trainee solicitors at a pivotal stage of their training; namely, when they were at the Law Society of Ireland for their Professional Practice Course II ('PPCII'), after they had spent a period of eleven months in the training firm post-Professional Practice Course I ('PPCI').

12 Laurie A Morin, 'Reflections on Teaching Law as Right Livelihood: Cultivating Ethics, Professionalism and Commitment to Public Service from the Inside Out' (2000) 35 *Tulsa Law Journal* 227.

13 This is a reference to Palmer's 'community of truth', which calls for discourse where 'objective' knowledge is replaced with a notion of truth as 'an eternal conversation about things that matter, conducted with passion and discipline': Parker Palmer, 'Good Teaching: A Matter of Living the Mystery' (1990) 22 *Change: The Magazine of Higher Learning* 11.

14 Alfred C Aman, 'Protecting a Space for Creativity: The Role of a Law School Dean in a Research University' (2000) 31 *University of Toledo Law Review* 557.

15 Susan L Brooks and Inga N Laurent, 'Effective Communication and Professional Relationships' in Leah Wortham et al. (eds), *Learning from Practice* (West Academic Publishing, 2016).

16 The concept of role morality, as distinct from a common morality, suggests that professionals engage in practices that are considered legitimate because of the expressed virtues of the occupational role. Put simply: it is hard to be a lawyer and a human being. As Allegretti puts it: '[T]he standard complaint about lawyers is that they are too disposed to substitute role morality for ordinary morality. They do things that ordinary morality condemns, yet defend their actions on the grounds that their role as a zealous advocate justifies or even demands such actions': Joseph Allegretti, 'Shooting Elephants, Serving Clients: An Essay on George Orwell and the Lawyer-Client Relationship' (1994) 27 *Creighton Law Review* 1.

The ten-week part-time course comprised five evening sessions and two full Saturday sessions. In addition, the various components of the continuous and summative assessments were significant, culminating in a standardised client role play exercise dealing with ethics and an errant solicitor.[17] The Certificate course probed trainees' own motivations, their moral development and their values, encouraging them to reflect on their role as lawyers, their personal values and their future careers in law, in the context of their overall personal and professional well-being. The intense experiential and interactive approach offered ample opportunities for 'peer-to-peer' learning. Small group discussion with exemplars from the profession, role play and simulation, and continuous assessment created the conditions necessary to develop a sense of community and a positive, open learning environment that supported trainees in their ethical identity formation. There are certain similarities with the 'Practical Legal Training' (PLT) course in Australia which focuses on skills, knowledge, and values, with a certain emphasis on well-being at the particular juncture in their career where students transition from student to practitioner.[18]

Teaching ethics 'to the rules' is insufficient and misleads students 'into thinking that ethics are a set of rules for resolving a finite list of the problems that lawyers face'.[19] Traditional approaches to ethics generally do not prepare students adequately for the ethical pressures they will face, as identified by the recent Maharg Report on Professional Legal Education in Ireland.[20] The authors noted the dearth of ethics training at academic stages and the narrow focus at professional training stages with a resultant ethical awareness gap. They noted that the approach to ethics teaching could be complemented and developed further by an educational approach focusing on the 'experiential exploration and development of ethical behaviours and good ethical habits within students'.[21] Being an ethical lawyer involves more than learning and applying a set of rules; it demands the cultivation of a critical reflection upon the professional role and responsibilities of lawyers.[22] This course embraced a wide view of ethics and morality, integrating professionalism, and it advocated a broad approach to thinking about ethics that encouraged an element of social responsibility and public service. Sessions

17 For a full description of the course and the timetable, see Freda Grealy, 'Experiential Training for Real-Life Professional Impact: The Formation of Professional Identity in Trainee Solicitors Through a Discrete Intervention Course on Ethics and Lawyering Skills' (2018) 52(3) *The Law Teacher* 295.

18 Judy Bourke and Maxine Evers, 'Resilience and Wellbeing Programmes: The Practical Legal Training Experience' in Field, Duffy and James (n 11).

19 James E Moliterno, 'An Analysis of Ethics Teaching in Law Schools: Replacing Lost Benefits of the Apprentice System in the Academic Atmosphere' (1992) 60 *University of Cincinnati Law Review* 107.

20 Paul Maharg, Jane Ching and Jenny Crewe, *Solicitor Education in Ireland Review Report* (Law Society of Ireland, 2018).

21 Ibid 138.

22 Allan C Hutchinson, 'Taking It Personally: Legal Ethics and Client Selection' (1998) 1 *Legal Ethics* 168.

on reflection and self-determination theory encouraged trainees to take personal responsibility for their future careers.

The wide view, extending the application of the law beyond 'just' the rules, encompasses moral reasoning, sensitivity, implementation, moral motivation, character, and self-understanding; and connects them with overall professional identity so that ethics is made more tangible and less abstract. Using this broad lens, it was found effective to emphasise the centrality of ethics and show how ethics and personal values pervade the day-to-day role of a solicitor and, in turn, their well-being.

Whilst limitations of the intervention course are acknowledged,[23] the overall demographic proved to be very mixed in terms of geographical spread, size of firm, and type of practice that the participants were involved with.[24] In terms of the geographical spread, some participants hailed from larger commercial firms (which tended to be based in Dublin) and others from smaller city firms and country practices. In terms of the participants undergraduate degree, seven of the group had a pure law degree while the rest had hybrid and other degrees, and this is generally reflective of the wider intake of trainees.

Trainees' reflections

This intervention comprised a mixed method pedagogy with an emphasis on interactive learning approaches, including lecture sessions, workshop sessions, small group discussions, exposure to exemplars, online discussion forums, completion of a career plan, reviewing of journal articles, and a standardised client role play. In terms of feedback, the responses of the trainees to specific pedagogic methods implemented in the blended course framework confirmed unanimous agreement about wanting a 'combination of lectures, workshops, small group discussion, and course forum'. The trainees were specifically asked for feedback on their preferred teaching practices and what they thought was most effective for this type of training, i.e. lecture, workshop, small group discussion, course forum, or a combination of these. They felt that there 'should be more discussions as opposed to assessments' and they valued the opportunity to have the 'time to think' about their values and professional identity. The data from this research

23 It was only possible to work with a group of 21 trainees and they were self-selected. It was not possible to form a control group from amongst the other trainees attending the Professional Practice Course (PPC). However, the pre-test functioned as a baseline test, and post-tests were able to test the impact of the intervention in comparison with this baseline. In terms of pedagogical recommendations, this research does not compare the design of one educational course with another; it simply states that the particular pedagogic approaches were effective and worked in this intervention with this cohort.

24 The gender make-up consisted of four males and seventeen females. The percentage of female to male trainees on the PPC in recent years is 60% female and 40% male. Some of the older participants were women returning to work after child-rearing, as well as others who were changing career, and a good number had worked in law firms for some time and had finally trained as solicitors.

confirms that the intense experiential approach, offering many opportunities for discussion and 'peer-to-peer' learning, active learning, and simulation, when coupled with continuous assessment creates conditions necessary for aiding the learning process. Efforts were made both onsite and via the online discussion forum to draw the trainees out and encourage reflection and deep thought about their values, aspirations, and morals. This is an important element in the coming-of-age process and becoming a practitioner. The following sections look at a number of the pedagogic approaches in turn and the feedback from the trainees on the experience.

Appreciative inquiry

Quaintance, Arnold, and Thompson[25] suggest that in order to assist students to internalise what they are taught in relation to professionalism (and by extension ethics and professional identity), '[c]onstructs such as explicit role modelling, situated learning, and appreciative inquiry can shed light on . . . professionalism'. They outline that to internalise professionalism students need the following:[26]

- To receive explicit teaching about behaviours and values of professionalism within authentic contexts;
- To witness their role models reflect on their own understanding of and experiences with professionalism;
- To reflect on their own experiences; and
- To focus on and be exposed to positive instances of professionalism.

They add that particularly important to the learning process is 'appreciative inquiry' which essentially amounts to the interactions between the students, their peers, and the exemplars; that 'talk' is key to assisting with reflection; and that development follows. The LSI PPC offers a window of opportunity and the challenge for legal educators is to provide opportunities for, and to encourage trainees when they are in, this 'formative space'. Implementing a spirit of appreciative inquiry was forefronted in the intervention by the use of teaching practices such as role play, small group discussion, and encouraging trainees to communicate, discuss, reflect on, and share their experiences around issues that challenge them in their work environment and that they face in their early careers. It is clear from the feedback that the appreciative inquiry approach aided their socialisation into the profession and gave them a greater understanding about their roles as solicitors, and there were many references to their changing views and to their opinions being shaped as a result of the 'talking about'

25 Jennifer L Quaintance, Louise Arnold and George S Thompson, 'What Students Learn About Professionalism from Faculty Stories: An "Appreciative Inquiry" Approach' (2010) 85 *Academic Medicine* 118.

26 Ibid 119.

and 'listening to talk' that Quaintance et al. refer to.[27] Such approaches assist trainees with self-understanding, professional socialisation and acclimatisation to the culture of law and the law firm. This feedback was offered by one of the trainees:

> In particular I found the workshop and group discussions the most engaging, and found they acted as a trigger for thinking about the subject matter long after the class was over.
>
> (Female, 31, small country firm, law degree)

Sharing their experiences gave comfort to other trainees – it reinforced the message that no one traineeship experience is ideal, emphasised the heterogeneous nature of the legal profession, and illustrated the fact that they were interested in one another's experiences.

> I very much enjoyed listening to other people's experiences and how they dealt with situations. I felt I learned a lot from this.
>
> (Female, 27, large Dublin firm, hybrid degree)

Providing opportunities to interact both onsite and online, and a space to reflect on (and sometimes vent about) their concerns, meant that certain themes surfaced, including the work environment, the long hours, motivation (intrinsic and extrinsic) about careers, thinking about what sort of lawyer they will be, how ethical they were, how to make lawyers moral, life in the firm, feeling disillusioned, diversity and gender, wanting to make partner, day-to-day challenges, levels of stress and well-being, wondering whether they were in the right career or type of firm in the first place, and the sometimes random nature of the traineeship regime.

> I find the topics on this course very interesting. I am also interested in the different experiences of students working in the various types of firms. Why they wanted to take this course.
>
> (Female, 31, large Dublin firm, hybrid degree)

One of the emerging themes concerned the level of stress and challenge encountered, with some trainees realising they were in for a shock in relation to the hours and conditions they would have to work in. The expectations that exist in the culture of the firm may not match what they have in mind.

> Stress is an issue in our profession, and I think the more we open up a culture of talking about it rather than putting on a mask and pretending it's not happening, the better for us as individuals and for the profession generally.
>
> (Female, 35, medium Dublin firm, LLM law)

27 Ibid.

Discussion of professional stress and challenge might not, on the face of it, seem to relate to ethics, and may make legal educators uncomfortable, but these conversations are nonetheless important in terms of looking inward, first at personal values and identity, and then building on that to look at professional conduct and professional identity.[28] James (speaking about legal education in Australia) suggests that law schools must recognise the significance of emotions in legal education and training in order 'to inform students of the risks of legal practice and to ensure curricula include exposure to integrated, supervised and reflective clinical practice'.[29] This, he says, 'would help many students begin to develop the self-awareness, interpersonal skills, confidence and integrity they need to endure as legal professionals'.[30]

Provide 'safe space' for discourse and reflection

Moral discourse and reflection are effective in terms of students' ethical professional identity development and in achieving congruence between their inner life and outward behaviour. Engaging in moral discourse is an essential ingredient of moral growth.[31] As Morin states:

> She needs reflection and response (a form of 'moral dialogue') to test her own thoughts about the law and the legal profession, while listening for a collective wisdom that may influence her ideas and beliefs 'from the inside out'.[32]

Schön[33] claims that reflection in action is essentially a mediation between theory and practice, and that legal educators should provide opportunities for students to engage and reflect. Hartwell[34] found both reflection and moral discourse useful in his study, where students were obliged to work in groups to tease out ethical dilemmas and 'take a stand' on a particular issue and defend their moral course of action. Morin advocates the 'community of truth' approach; as she says, it 'takes courage to open up space for discussion of values'.[35] Discussing ethics and morals and providing time and space for both creative dialogue and periods of introspection are vitally important. Not shirking from emotions or challenges and

28 Evans (n 2).
29 Colin James, 'Lawyers' Wellbeing and Professional Legal Education' (2008) 42 *The Law Teacher* 87, 97.
30 Ibid.
31 Evans (n 2); Eleanor W Myers, 'Simple Truths About Moral Education' (1995) 45 *American University Law Review* 823.
32 Morin (n 12) 236.
33 Donald A Schön, *The Reflective Practitioner: How Professionals Think in Action* (Basic Books, 1983).
34 Steven Hartwell, 'Promoting Moral Development Through Experiential Teaching' (1994) 1 *Clinical Law Review* 505.
35 Morin (n 12) 250.

encouraging the negotiation of these difficulties to draw out one's own values and morals are part of the identity construction process and becoming a lawyer.[36]

Literature supports the idea that it is necessary to create an atmosphere of safety and community, particularly in blended or online settings where participants can 'speak and debate their ideas without fear of retribution'.[37] Paloff and Pratt[38] also state that for educators and facilitators, one of the key concepts is to be able to create an atmosphere of safety and community, both in an electronic context and in a face-to-face setting. Fostering an environment of trust is essential for trainee solicitors, bearing in mind that they may be guarded and reticent about displaying any ignorance or lack of knowledge. They need reassurance that any comments and contributions that they make will be confined to the course participants, and that the grounding philosophy of the course is to reinforce an open-minded approach to learning. Garrison and Arbaugh[39] stress the need to foster trust within a community of learning. Thompson and McDonald note that 'for a community to sustain itself, it is essential that the group feels secure to communicate openly and coalesces around a common goal or purpose'.[40]

Fostering an atmosphere that embodies a 'community of truth' cannot fix trainees' problems, but it can help them to become aware that they are not alone in facing these challenges and that there is hope and support for them on their career journey. For some on the course, reflecting and acknowledging their predicament signalled a turning point, as they realised that they could take charge and exercise their own personal autonomy. This, according to James,[41] aligns with Abraham Maslow's notion of 'self-actualisation', which means that they are concerned with 'internal criteria of success, such as having a balanced life, and the integrity to apply one's personal value system in one's professional life'. It appeared that those who internalised the concepts of ethical theory, communication, and role modelling on the course displayed higher levels of self-actualisation than others and saw identity transformation as their own responsibility. The 2007 *Carnegie Report* advocated the introduction of moral discourse, suggesting that 'the primary

36 Timothy L Hall, 'Moral Character, The Practice of Law, and Legal Education' (1990) 60 *Mississippi Law Journal* 511; Myers (n 31) 823; Subha Dhanaraj, 'Making Lawyers Good People: Possibility or Pipedream' (2000) 28 *Fordham Urban Law Journal* 2037; Quaintance, Arnold and Thompson (n 25) 118.

37 Rena M Paloff and Keith Pratt, *Building Learning Communities in Cyberspace: Effective Strategies for the Online Classroom* (Jossey-Bass, 2nd ed, 2007).

38 Ibid.

39 D Randy Garrison and J Ben Arbaugh, 'Researching the Community of Inquiry Framework: Review, Issues, and Future Directions' (2007) 10 *Internet and Higher Education* 157.

40 Terrie Lynn Thompson and Colla J MacDonald, 'Community Building, Emergent Design and Expecting the Unexpected: Creating a Quality eLearning Experience' (2005) 8 *The Internet and Higher Education* 160.

41 James (n 29) 94.

sources of ethical rules include a lawyer's personal sense of morality'.[42] Many of the trainees took the importance of a personal sense of morality on board and, as a result of the intervention, recognised that they had the power to control their own careers and steer them in a particular way – a direction that made sense to them, bearing in mind their own beliefs.

In this intervention, providing journal articles and reading material about the experiences of law students in other jurisdictions resonated with the trainees, and they were a source of comfort to some trainees who felt isolated or those who felt they lacked social, cultural, or intellectual capital. Reflection at this deep personal level requires a high level of willingness and commitment on the part of trainees. It was new ground for them, and there were difficult, perhaps even painful dialogues – one of the trainees, for instance, realised how ill-suited she was to the large firm culture, and felt like an outsider. As Morin[43] notes, if students 'learn how to integrate their personal values with professional norms, they will carry the process of introspection and moral dialogue with them in their careers as lawyers. Thus, what we need to do is to help students develop habits of learning that will lead to a process of ongoing vocational integration' (see also Chapter 3 of this book). Such discussion and engagement are particularly necessary for those trainees who query the values of the firm they are with, particularly if they feel these strike a discord with their own values and ethics.

Making room for uncomfortable conversations

As discussed above, throughout the sessions, both onsite and online, it was important that the participants were encouraged to share their personal experiences of traineeship in order to learn from each other. As Robert Gordon has observed amongst law students, '[t]he minute that a teacher launches a discussion of theory, policy, ethics, or social context that is not immediately and closely tied to resolving a case situation, most of the students tune out and put down their pens'.[44] By asking students to look deeper into their experiences and compare them with others', this intervention aimed to promote deeper learning, or what Mezirow[45] calls transformative learning, which involves assessment and developing a habit of being 'more critically reflective of their assumptions' – in this case by looking at earlier assumptions in relation to ethics and reworking both them and earlier formed meaning perspectives in light of new information. This is also linked to

42 William M Sullivan et al., *Educating Lawyers: Preparation for The Profession of Law* [Carnegie Report] (Jossey-Bass, 2007) 204.

43 Morin (n 12) 241.

44 Robert W Gordon, 'Lawyers, Scholars and the "Middle Ground"' (1993) 91(8) *Michigan Law Review* 2075, 2108 and fn 2181.

45 Jack Mezirow, 'Learning to Think Like an Adult. Core Concepts of Transformation Theory' in Jack Mezirow and Associates (eds), *Learning as Transformation: Critical Perspectives on A Theory in Progress* (Jossey-Bass, 2000) 31.

the Piagetian notion of 'accommodation', which aims for a change or a shift and promotes deeper learning rather than mere assimilation of information. Jean Piaget, in his work focusing on children and their moral development, referred to these notions of 'assimilation' and 'accommodation' to describe how the brain incorporates new information.[46] 'Assimilation' is merely taking in information or experience without it imposing any change or shift in your perception, whereas 'accommodation' means a change or shift has taken place and the learner has thereby adapted to the new situation.

Whilst focusing on moral and professional identity development and cultivating the ability to engage in moral reasoning and doing the 'right thing', awareness was drawn from cognitive processes that take place as people develop and learn. Attempts were made in the design of the course to create the conditions and space to facilitate just such a process of 'accommodation' as described by Piaget – letting certain learnings sit, to allow for periods of confusion and self-questioning, encouraging students to engage in processes of self-reflection in terms of what experiences mean personally and what identity process or transformation is taking place. Given that the overall theme of the educational intervention is ethics and its nexus with professional identity, the course framework was designed around these topics, along with moral development, and well-being, with a view to encouraging growth.

The workshop on ethical dilemmas and the standardised client interview exercise were intended to create 'disorienting moments' for the trainee. Such moments challenge the trainees to reflect on their experience and then perhaps reorient themselves when there is a conflict with their personal view and the reality.[47] Dhanaraj describes the process of moral growth that ensues:[48]

> the lawyer will morally grow if he must reconcile this reality and the motivations with his or her personal views. If such reconciliation does not occur, the lawyer will be motivated to transform the socio-legal order in conjunction with his personal values, whatever they may be. In any event, the tension between personal and legal morality will be recognized and explored by the attorney.

The online course forum provided an opportunity for students to engage at will and in an honest fashion with the absence of overt moderation, and meant that many of the discussion topics were trainee-led and involved an 'airing' or 'outing' of topics, some of which did not reflect well on the traineeship experience or the professional body. It is arguable that such conversations are necessary. They

46 Jean Piaget, *The Origins of Intelligence in Children* (International Universities Press, 1952) 407.

47 Jack Mezirow, 'How Critical Reflection Triggers Transformative Learning' in Jack Mezirow and Associates (eds), *Fostering Critical Reflection in Adulthood: A Guide to Transformative and Emancipatory Learning* (Jossey-Bass, 1990).

48 Dhanaraj (n 36) 2075.

assist with a communal negotiation of meaning and address head-on the trainees' choice of profession. Whilst conversations were moderated, there was no need for any intervention.

Any course aiming to foster a sense of professionalism and identity must take the possible isolation, demoralisation, confusion, and feelings of trainees into account. The potential challenges and hardship of the traineeship need to be aired and acknowledged as more than just a 'rite of passage', although it is not necessarily possible for the professional body to intervene.

Small group discussion with exemplars

The response to the workshop evening entitled '*Putting Ethics into Practice*' and the small group discussions with exposure to exemplars was very positive. The latter took the form of workshop questions which were provided to trainees for them to prepare in advance, and then discussed with tutors over the course of an evening in small groups of five. In line with other studies in this area, Bebeau and Monson note that these case method and questioning strategies can help clarify the role and responsibilities of the professional as well as 'help surface role conflicts and conflicts of interest that professionals often face'.[49]

Eight of the trainees reported that this was their favourite part of the course, and that what they enjoyed most was teasing out issues with experienced colleagues in a safe and non-judgemental atmosphere.

> This was my favourite session. I found the real-life examples very engaging and the discussion with colleagues was very useful in teasing out different perspectives.
>
> (Female, 35, medium Dublin firm, LLM)

> I really learned a lot from this session and really enjoyed it. To be honest I thought the tutor was very informative and helpful.
>
> (Female, 36, small country firm, law degree)

The four tutors who facilitated the sessions had specific expertise and interest in the topics of ethics, professional conduct, and disciplinary matters, and therefore were well placed to speak about the values of the profession. To achieve this effectively, Alexander states that trainees also need guidance from and exposure to exemplars and other experienced practitioners who are respected within the profession with whom they can discuss uncomfortable issues in a safe, supportive environment; and legal education has a role to play in this.[50] The feedback

49 Muriel J Bebeau and Verna E Monson, 'Guided by Theory, Grounded in Evidence: A Way Forward for Business Ethics' in Larry Nucci and Darcia Narvaez (eds), *Handbook of Moral and Character Education* (Mendoza College of Business, Notre Dame University, 2008).

50 Charlotte S Alexander, 'Learning to Be Lawyers: Professional Identity and the Law School Curriculum' (2011) 70 *Maryland Law Review* 465.

affirms the effectiveness of role modelling and how this shapes one's character as a lawyer. This is a further example of the process of 'appreciative inquiry' that aids professional socialisation and it gave trainees a greater understanding about their role as solicitors.

> The most beneficial session for me was 'Putting Ethics into Practice', when we got the opportunity to discuss ethical issues in small groups. It is very easy to sit back and shy away from answering questions when in a bigger group, but everyone in our group contributed during that session. It is thought-provoking to hear the opinions of others and this helped shape my opinions on various matters. We also got the opportunity to ask an experienced lawyer questions about challenges he faced during his career, in what I felt was a comfortable environment. The client interview at the end of the course was, for me, a fantastic way to consolidate what I had learnt.
>
> (Female, 25, large Dublin firm, hybrid degree)

In terms of learning about ethics teaching, the *Carnegie Report* encouraged law schools to enable their students 'to encounter appealing representations of professional ideals, connect in a powerful way with engaging models of ethical commitment within the profession, and reflect on their [own] emerging professional identity in relation to those ideals and models'.[51] Tutors were provided with the material in advance and were guided in terms of the approach required for the evening, which was to discuss and draw out trainees' views and then expose them to the values, ethics, and regulatory role of the profession; thus creating the right environment to assist them in understanding more about their own values and the values of the profession. As one trainee commented:

> I found this session extremely useful in terms of the benefits of having a very experienced practitioner at the table with our group; it was invaluable and unusual to have the opportunity in an informal setting to pick the brains of someone who has seen it all!
>
> (Female, 31, small country firm, law degree)

In addition to discussing ethical dilemmas and working through the material on ethics, a number of groups had time to discuss other issues in the profession. The evening developed organically, and trainees took advantage of the 'safe space' to ask about issues that were of interest to them.

> Useful to get insight into a partner's way of thinking. Very interesting to hear why trainees are expected to work the hours they do and hear it acknowledged that we are worked to the bone.
>
> (Female, 36, small country firm, law degree)

51 Sullivan et al. (n 42) 135.

Conclusion

This chapter has discussed some of the pedagogic approaches that were effective in supporting Irish trainee solicitors to increase their knowledge of ethics, grapple with their own values and professional identity, and highlight issues affecting their well-being. The feedback demonstrates that trainees welcomed the opportunity to have the space and time to reflect and think about their role as solicitors, with many admitting that they were changed by the experience of the intervention. As a result, they had a greater sense of their personal values and who they were as lawyers, and their need to achieve congruence with this. Teaching ethics in tandem with exploring concepts of professional identity appears to be an effective way of demonstrating the importance of ethics and encouraging a process of self-reflection which reinforces personal and professional values for trainee solicitors and, I suggest, ultimately supports their well-being as part of that. One of the goals for the design of the intervention was to create opportunities for dialogue, discussion, and reflection; and the feedback confirms this was achieved in large part. This supports the view that an educational intervention with a wide view of ethics can support the socialisation of an ethical professional identity, so that trainees can become more aware and intentional about their approach to their practice; and as a result develop a level of personal autonomy in being able to influence their professional and personal development and, ultimately, their well-being.

8 Connectivity, socialisation and identity formation

Exploring mental well-being in online distance learning law students

Emma Jones

A distance learning law student who is sitting at home in front of a computer screen is still a law student. They are wrestling with complex concepts and tackling the pressure of assignments, examinations and degree classifications. They are juggling their study with work, family, social and other commitments and have fears, hopes, aspirations and anxieties invested in their studies. However, in addition to these unifying factors, there are also added layers of complexity when considering this particular cohort of students. It may be that their choice to pursue online distance learning has been influenced by their personal circumstances and commitments, from full-time work to family situation to medical issues. Demographically, they may well be older and in a different life stage than the traditional image of a fresh-faced 18 year old beginning their law degree. In addition, their emotions and mental states may be influenced and shaped, at least in part, through the medium of their study.

Given the potential distinctiveness of this cohort and the significance of the online distance mode of delivery, this chapter will consider the application of the literature on law student mental well-being to online distance law students. In particular, it will focus on whether such learners absorb the notion of 'thinking like a lawyer' which is commonly implicated with lower levels of mental well-being, or whether this socialisation process is less significant within their student journey. It will explore the possible implications for both professional identity formation and levels of mental well-being amongst online distance learning law students.

Online distance learning and law students

There is a relatively long lineage of distance learning in law, with the first correspondence law course in the United States of America ('US'), offered by the Blackstone College of Law appearing shortly before the beginning of the 20th century.[1] In Australia, Goldring points to courses offered 'for decades' by institutions

1 Elbridge B Pierce, 'Correspondence Law Schools' (1951) 4(2) *Journal of Legal Education* 160; See also Henry Winthrop Ballantine, 'The Place in Legal Education of Evening and Correspondence Law Schools' (1919) 4(7) *American Law School Review* 369.

such as the University of Queensland;[2] and in England and Wales, during the Second World War, the Society of Public Teachers in Law, the Law Society and the War Office worked together to provide correspondence courses allowing service personnel to continue their legal studies, even obtaining permission for some examinations to be taken in Prisoner of War Camps.[3] However, the growth in popularity of higher education generally, the commensurate expansion of law school provision within universities, and the changing requirements for entry into the legal profession appear to have, in some countries at least, lessened demand for such correspondence courses by the latter half of the 20th century. Aspiring entrants encounter easier access to face-to-face provision and, in the US, accreditation was refused to a number of such provisions, although the reasoning behind this is unclear.[4]

The advent of online learning can be seen as providing a fresh impetus to the provision of distance education in law in jurisdictions including the UK, US and Australia. In terms of online education generally, the overall sector has grown exponentially in recent years with offerings ranging from the inclusion of online content within conventional face-to-face university provision, to wholly online versions of conventional degree courses. Massive Open and Badged Open Online Courses have been designed to provide shorter formal or informal learning opportunities. Although this overall expansion does obscure variations in take-up within different types of course and discipline.[5] In terms of law specifically, there is a vast range of stand-alone online distance learning courses.[6] However, ongoing issues with accreditation for professional purposes seems to continue to impact on law degrees, notably in the context of the US's postgraduate *Juris Doctor* ('JD').[7] In addition, amongst some academic lawyers, there appears to be a continuing lack of acceptance of the notion of studying for a legal qualification at a distance, with some remaining sceptical about the value of such studies.[8]

2 John Goldring, 'Coping with the Virtual Campus – Some Hints and Opportunities for Legal Education' (1995) 6(1) *Legal Education Review* 92.

3 Fiona Cownie and Raymond Cocks, *'A Great and Noble Occupation!' A History of the Society of Legal Scholars* (Hart Publishing, 2009) 60–61.

4 In 1951, Pierce (n 1) 171, in the US context argued that 'the need, the justification, and the value of the correspondence school in the limited field of legal education have definitely ended' citing the reluctance of regional Bar Associations to accredit such courses for entry into the profession. For a discussion on the 20th century development of law schools in England see William Twining, *Blackstone's Tower. The English Law School* (Sweet & Maxwell, 1994).

5 In the US context, Seaman et al., report levels of distance learning rising for the 14th consecutive year: Julia E Seaman, I Elaine Allen and Jeff Seaman, *Grade Increase Tracking Distance Education in the United States* (Babson Survey Research Group, 2018).

6 See, for example, <www.futurelearn.com/courses/categories/law-courses> accessed 7 May 2019.

7 The American Bar Association notes that 'Currently, no law schools that provide a J.D. degree completely via distance education are approved by the ABA' (*American Bar Association Distance Education* (2018) <www.americanbar.org/groups/legal_education/resources/distance_education.html> accessed 7 May 2019). However, in Australia and the UK a number of wholly online law degree programs are accredited.

8 Pasquale, in the US context, suggests such courses are akin to factory assembly lines focused on graduate employability rather than the wider research and social missions of the law school, thus raising questions relating to both quality and purpose: Frank Pasquale, 'Synergy

It is very difficult to identify reliable statistics on the number of law students across the world studying for a law degree via online distance learning, but the number is likely to be significant.[9] The increasing use of technology within face-to-face higher education environments also means many more law students in jurisdictions including the UK, US and Australia will engage in forms of blended learning, utilising online tools and resources within their studies.[10]

There is now a body of general literature on the ways in which studying online engages the student's emotions, feelings and moods, with occasional reference to emotional or mental well-being, although there is a lack of directly comparable data to be drawn upon.[11] Specifically in relation to law, there is now a significant body of work on the mental well-being of law students (much of it from the US and Australia), but the empirical evidence available appears to be largely based on students undertaking face-to-face studies with little focus on online distance learning cohorts.[12] Whilst this chapter draws upon the face-to-face data, it is important to acknowledge that it cannot be simply transposed into the online environment without acknowledging the significant differences in modes of study.

In the US context, the seminal (face-to-face) studies of Sheldon and Kreiger[13] suggest that during their legal studies, law students experienced a decline in mental well-being with elevated levels of stress, anxiety and depression, higher than those found within the general population. Similar findings have also been reported in Australia, with a large-scale study by Kelk et al. across 13 universities and nearly 2,000 members of the legal profession concluding 'that law students and members of the legal profession exhibit higher levels of psychological distress

---

and Tradition: The Unity of Research, Service, and Teaching in Legal Education' (2015) 40(1) *Journal of the Legal Profession* 25, 26.

9 The Open University has the largest LLB program in the UK, delivered largely through online distance learning, with approximately 5,000 students.

10 Anne Hewitt, 'Can You Learn to Lawyer Online? A Blended Learning Environment Case Study' (2015) 49(1) *The Law Teacher* 92.

11 Patricia J Slagter van Tryon and MJ Bishop, 'Theoretical Foundations for Enhancing Social Connectedness in Online Learning Environments' (2009) 30(3) *Distance Education* 291; Marta Arguedos, Thanasis Daradoumis and Fatos Xhafa, 'Analyzing the Effects of Emotion Management on Time and Self-Management in Computer-Based Learning' (2016) 63 *Computers in Human Behavior* 517.

12 For one exception (with no standardised measures) see Lynda Crowley-Cyr, 'Promoting Mental Well-Being of Law Students: Breaking-Down Stigma and Building Bridges with Support Services in the Online Learning Environment' (2014) 40(1) *QUT Law Review* 129.

13 Kenneth S Sheldon and Lawrence S Krieger, 'Does Legal Education Have Undermining Effects on Law Students? Examining Changes in Goals, Values, and Well-Being' (2004) 22 *Behavioral Sciences and the Law* 261; Kenneth S Sheldon and Lawrence S Krieger, 'Understanding the Negative Effects of Legal Education on Law Students: A Longitudinal Study of Self-Determination Theory' (2007) 33(6) *Personality and Social Psychology Bulletin* 883; Kenneth S Sheldon and Lawrence S Krieger, 'Walking the Talk: Value Importance, Value Enactment, and Well-Being' (2014) 38(5) *Motivation and Emotion* 609. It should be noted that these studies focused on post-graduate JD students. This qualification is generally perceived as more vocational in nature than the LLB, which is followed by a period of additional vocational training.

and depression than do community members of a similar age and sex".[14] Since this study, a range of other Australian scholarly studies have also supported this conclusion.[15] The majority of such studies in both the US and Australia also suggest that there is something discipline-specific about the law school experience which contributes to these issues with well-being, although this is not wholly uncontentious.[16]

In the UK-context, the published empirical data focused specifically on law students is very limited. However, the author (with colleagues) recently conducted

14 Norm Kelk et al., *Courting the Blues: Attitudes Towards Depression in Australian Law Students and Lawyers* (Brain & Mind Research Institute, 2009) 42.

15 Catherine Leahy et al., 'Distress Levels and Self-Reported Treatment Rates For Medicine, Law, Psychology and Mechanical Engineering Tertiary Students: Cross-Sectional Study' (2010) 44(7) *Australian and New Zealand Journal of Psychiatry* 608; Molly Townes O'Brien, Stephen Tang and Kath Hall, 'Changing Our Thinking: Empirical Research on Law Student Well-Being, Thinking Styles and the Law Curriculum' (2011) 21(1/2) *Legal Education Review* 149; Molly Townes O'Brien, Stephen Tang and Kath Hall, 'No Time to Lose: Negative Impact on Law Student Well-Being May Begin in Year One' (2011) 2(2) *The International Journal of the First Year in Higher Education* 49; Wendy Larcombe et al., 'Does an Improved Experience of Law School Protect Students against Depression, Anxiety and Stress? An Empirical Study of Well-Being and the Law School Experience of LLB and JD Students' (2013) 35(2) *Sydney Law Review* 407; Natalie Skead and Shane L Rogers, 'Stress, Anxiety and Depression in Law Students: How Student Behaviors Affect Student Wellbeing' (2014) 40 *Monash University Law Review* 565; Wendy Larcombe, Sue Finch and Rachel Sore, 'Who's Distressed? Not Only Law Students: Psychological Distress Levels in University Students across Diverse Fields of Study' (2015) 37(2) *Sydney Law Review* 243; Adele Bergin and Kenneth Pakenham, 'Law Student Stress: Relationships between Academic Demands, Social Isolation, Career Pressure, Study/Life Imbalance and Adjustment Outcomes in Law Students' (2015) 22(3) *Psychiatry, Psychology and Law* 388; Natalie Skead and Shane L Rogers, 'Do Law Students Stand Apart from Other University Students in their Quest for Mental Health: A Comparative Study on Wellbeing and Associated Behaviours in Law and Psychology Students' (2015) 42 *International Journal of Law and Psychiatry* 81; Natalie Skead and Shane L Rogers, 'Running to Well-Being: A Comparative Study on the Impact of Exercise on the Physical and Mental Health of Law and Psychology Students' (2016) 49 *International Journal of Law and Psychiatry* 66; Natalie Skead, Shane L Rogers and Jerome Doraisamy, 'Looking Beyond the Mirror: Psychological Distress, Disordered Eating, Weight and Shape Concerns, and Maladaptive Eating Habits in Lawyers and Law Students' (2018) 61 *International Journal of Law and Psychiatry* 90; Rachael Field, Nickolas James and James Duffy, 'Making Wellness Core Business in Australian Law Schools: Listening to the Student Voice' (Conference Paper Presented to the 2019 Wellness for Law Forum, 14–15 February, Melbourne Australia).

16 In support of this hypothesis, see Mary E Pritchard and Daniel N McIntosh, 'What Predicts Adjustment Among Law Students? A Longitudinal Panel Study' (2003) 143(6) *The Journal of Social Psychology* 727; Natalie Skread and Shane L Rogers, 'Do Law Students Stand Apart from Other University Students in their Quest for Mental Health: A Comparative Study on Well-Being and Associated Behaviours in Law and Psychology Students' (2015) 42 *International Journal of Law and Psychiatry* 81. However, Larcombe et al., 'Who's Distressed? Not Only Law Students' (n 15) have argued that students from other disciplines experience similar levels of psychological distress to those of law students.

an online questionnaire involving 344 student respondents in year 3 (full-time) or years 5 and 6 (part-time) of online distance study for the LLB via The Open University, with the aim of obtaining a snapshot of their well-being.[17] The survey instrument included two standardised self-report measures, the World Health Organisation's WHO-5 Well-Being Index and the Depression, Anxiety and Stress Scales 21 ('DASS-21'), a shortened version of the full 42 item scales, which is frequently used as a clinical assessment to ascertain a range of psychological symptoms and has been used in a range of previous studies on law student well-being.[18] There were also five open-ended items to ascertain: (a) the respondents' main motivation for studying law; (b) whether law school had met their expectations; (c) whether law school had contributed positively or negatively to their well-being; (d) their suggestions for The Open University as to how to improve student well-being; and (e) what sources of support they drew on during their course.

The responses to the open-ended items will be explored later, when considering the traditional norms associated with law degrees and their interplay with mental well-being. However, it is worthy of note that the results of the standardised measures demonstrated striking similarities to those found in previous studies in the US and Australia, despite probable differences in demographics (for example, the mean age of respondents was 40.6 and a portion did not have the educational attainments usually associated with undergraduate level study). Although the majority of respondents were within the normal range on the DASS-21, the mean scores were all higher than those within the general population.[19] Around 12–15% of respondents reported symptoms within the severe and extremely severe ranges whilst between 7–14% fell within the moderate range.[20]

Given that these results indicate that a sizeable minority of respondents were experiencing some form of psychological distress, it could be interpreted as demonstrating that the law school experience has a detrimental effect for a proportion of students regardless of the format and medium of study used. However, a qualitative analysis of the open-ended items suggests a more nuanced reading, indicating that online distance learning law students have a different experience of law school socialisation than those in conventional face-to-face learning environments.

17 See Emma Jones, Rajvinder Samra and Mathijs Lucassen, 'The World at Their Fingertips? The Mental Well-Being of Online Distance-Based Law Students' (2019) 53(1) *The Law Teacher* 49. A total of 742 students were eligible to participate, giving a response rate of 46.4%. 2.8% of respondents had a declared mental health disability or disabilities. The quantitative results were analysed using SPSS (Statistical Package for the Social Sciences, Version 21) software. The qualitative open-ended items were analysed using an inductive thematic analysis. The ethics approval confirmation number is HREC/2017/2502/Jones/1.

18 For example Townes O'Brien et al., "No Time to Lose" (n 15); Larcombe et al., 'Who's Distressed? Not Only Law Students' (n 15).

19 Jones et al. (n 17) 19.

20 Ibid 19.

The role of socialisation and identity formation

There appears to be a range of factors behind the issues law students face with their mental well-being, but many are connected with forms of socialisation into the traditional norms of legal education and practice. The concept of social norms is widely used in the social sciences and, although utilised in a variety of ways, can be explained as 'a term used to refer to a variety of behaviors, and accompanying expectations'[21] or, in other words, 'the rules of the game'.[22] These may be explicitly taught, but can also be perpetuated almost 'by osmosis, or interstitially'.[23] For the purposes of this chapter, it will be argued that traditionally legal education has encouraged, or even required, its students to comply with a number of specific norms, commonly encapsulated in the phrase 'thinking like a lawyer'.[24] Although contemporary law schools are increasingly pluralistic and diverse,[25] significant remnants of these norms still remain and play a significant role in the formation of students' professional identity. In both the US and Australia, the prevalence of emotionally detached, individualistic and combative ways of reasoning amongst law students has been highlighted.[26] Despite less UK data, at postgraduate level, Sommerlad's study of Legal Practice Course students indicated a socialisation process beginning at the LLB stage.[27] This process arguably impacts on law student mental well-being in two key ways: firstly, in the way in which more general pressures on students in higher education translate into the law school environment and, secondly, in terms of the impact of specific norms which are unique to legal education and culture. The impact of both, specifically on distance learning law students, has not been explored.

In relation to the translation of general pressures, a useful example is that of academic stress. The recent Student Minds' Grand Challenges report, identifies

21 Cristina Bicchieri, *The Grammar of Society: The Nature and Dynamics of Social Norms* (Cambridge University Press, 2006) 2.

22 Zanita E Fenton, 'The Paradox of Hierarchy – or Why We Always Choose the Tools of the Master's House (Teaching from the Left: A Conference at Harvard Law School)' (2007) 31(3) *New York University Review of Law & Social Change* 627, 628.

23 Frederick Schauer, *Thinking Like a Lawyer: A New Introduction to Legal Reasoning* (Harvard University Press, 2009) xi.

24 The exact origins of this phrase are unclear, but it has been widely discussed, including Colin James, 'Lawyers' Well-Being and Professional Legal Education' (2008) 42(1) *The Law Teacher* 85; Jess M Krannitch, James R Holbrook and Julie J McAdams, 'Beyond "Thinking Like a Lawyer" and the Traditional Legal Paradigm: Towards a Comprehensive View of Legal Education' (2009) 86(2) *Denver University Law Review* 381; Tony Foley and Stephen Tang, 'On Being, Not Just Thinking Like, A Lawyer. Connections between Uncertainty, Ignorance and Well-Being' in Rachael Field, James Duffy and Colin James (eds), *Promoting Law Student and Lawyer Well-Being in Australia and Beyond* (Routledge, 2016).

25 Emma Jones, 'One Size Fits All? Multiple Intelligences and Legal Education' (2017) 51(1) *The Law Teacher* 56, 56–57.

26 Peggy Cooper Davies and Aderson Belgarde Francois, 'Thinking Like a Lawyer' (2005) 81 *North Dakota Law Review* 795, 797; Townes O'Brien et al., 'Changing Our Thinking' (n 15) 177.

27 Hilary Sommerlad, 'Researching and Theorizing the Processes of Professional Identity Formation' (2007) 34(2) *Journal of Law and Society* 190.

'Academic Pressure and Concerns about Future Employability' as posing a key challenge for students and notes that:

> Many students suffer from more severe stress at uni with all the combined pressures. The changing environment, the harder work, the smaller ability gap causing more academic pressure and multiple other things.[28]

These forms of pressures are replicated within law, with Krieger (in the US context) referring to 'the top-ten-percent tenet', suggesting that there is an 'entirely obvious' belief that to succeed at law school you must fall within the top 10% of your cohort.[29] This can lead to students associating their future happiness and security with their position in the hierarchy of academic success.[30] This is echoed in the Australian setting by Skread and Rogers' findings that one of the 'stand out' subscales for causes of stress was external pressures, including 'competition (on grades and work), deadlines, and work overload'.[31] In the UK-context, anecdotally, there appears to be an implicit understanding amongst students (including distance learners), perhaps based on the recruitment websites of larger firms, that to qualify as a solicitor a 2:1 LLB classification is required (that is, an upper second class honours), generating significant pressure to achieve academically.[32] Entry to the Bar in England and Wales also requires a 2:2 LLB qualification (that is, a lower second class honours).[33]

In relation to those expectations and demands that are unique to legal education and culture, the concept of "thinking like a lawyer" has been identified as vital in shaping professional identity.[34] This concept is heavily promoted throughout face-to-face legal education in the US, Australia and the UK and can be

28 Student Minds Grand Challenges in Student Mental Health (undated) 7 <www.studentminds.org.uk/uploads/3/7/8/4/3784584/grand_challenges_report_for_public.pdf> accessed 7 May 2019.

29 Lawrence S Krieger, 'Institutional Denial About the Dark Side of Law School and Fresh Empirical Guidance for Constructively Breaking the Silence' (2002) 52(1/2) *Journal of Legal Education* 112, 117.

30 Ibid.

31 Skead and Rogers (n 15) 572–573; see also Bergin and Pakenham (n 15) 388.

32 In Bleasdale and Humphrey's recent report on undergraduate resilience at the University of Leeds they noted that out of 11 law students 'four specifically wanted a First; three wanted at least a 2.1; four referenced a 2.1; and three referred to a broader range of indicators of success': Lydia Bleasdale and Sarah Humphreys, *Undergraduate Resilience Research Project. Project Report* (2018) 25 <http://teachingexcellence.leeds.ac.uk/wp-content/uploads/2018/01/LITEbleasdalehumphreys_fullreport_online.pdf> accessed 7 May 2019. See also Chapter 13 of this work. It should be noted that this implicit understanding is, at least to some extent, flawed given the existence of other routes into the profession and the range of Training Contracts available.

33 Bar Standards Board, *Becoming a Barrister* (2019) <www.barstandardsboard.org.uk/qualifying-as-a-barrister/becoming-a-barrister/> accessed 7 May 2019.

34 Terry Hutchinson and Nigel Duncan, 'Defining and Describing What We Do: Doctrinal Legal Research' (2012) 17(1) *Deakin Law Review* 83; James R Elkins, 'Thinking Like a Lawyer: Second Thoughts' 47 *Mercer Law Review* 511; see also Schauer (n 23).

viewed as 'a threshold identity' for law students in such learning environments.[35] It is closely tied to doctrinal forms of legal analysis which developed in the 19th century, at least in part, from a desire to carve out a niche for the academic study of law in universities.[36] The notion of the law as a coherent body of logic and principles discerned through scientific study is largely derived from this and manifests itself today through the promotion of a certain form of thought process identified with legal analysis. This is a way of knowing which elevates a form of rigid, analytical thinking, requiring the suppression or disregard of more experiential, emotionally connected forms of thought.[37]

A number of the factors implicated in low levels of well-being amongst law students appear connected in some way to this seminal concept in legal education. In the Australian context, James argues that rather than being correctly perceived as 'a form of linear analysis in a restrictive paradigm' it has become elevated to a prized way of thinking within law schools which largely disregards holistic problem-solving, along with providing a service and trying to help people.[38] In the same context, Allen and Baron argue that the focus on 'course content that is abstract and unconnected to real experience' and the emphasis on a particular type of reasoning and rationality 'may cause the loss of connection to values, morals, convictions and feelings and suppress the development of creativity and moral reasoning'.[39] One example of this is the way students are discouraged from engaging with the messier, more emotionally involved aspects of the law, focusing instead on abstract problem-solving in the form of analysis of appellate court judgments.[40] Another is the way in which, within Commonwealth jurisdictions, adversarialism pervades the law school, leading to individualistic and competitive tendencies becoming normalised and even encouraged.[41] Although there have been attempts to reinvigorate and redirect the concept, to date these do not appear to have significantly tempered such characteristics.[42]

35 Foley and Tang (n 24) 133. See also Rachael Field and Jan HF Meyer, 'Threshold Concepts in Law: A Key Future Direction for Intentional Curriculum Reform to Support Law Student Learning Success and Well-Being' in Emma Jones and Fiona Cownie (eds), *Key Directions in Legal Education: National and International Perspectives* (forthcoming).

36 David Sugarman, 'Legal Theory, the Common Law Mind and the Making of the Textbook Tradition' in William Twining (ed), *Legal Theory and Common Law* (Blackwell, 1986).

37 Townes O'Brien et al., 'Changing Our Thinking' (n 15).

38 James (n 24) 91.

39 Judy Allen and Paula Baron, 'Buttercup Goes to Law School: Student Well-Being in Stressed Law Schools' (2004) 29(6) *Alternative Law Journal* 285, 286.

40 Lara Dresser, 'Promoting Psychological Health in Law Students' (2005) 24(1/2) *Legal Reference Services Quarterly* 41, 50; Townes O'Brien et al., 'No Time to Lose' (n 15).

41 Jennifer Jolly-Ryan, 'Promoting Mental Health in Law School: What Law Schools Can Do for Law Students to Help them Become Happy, Mentally Healthy Lawyers' (2009) 48(1) *University of Louisville Law Review* 95, 106; Townes O'Brien et al., 'No Time to Lose' (n 15) at 56; Sturm and Guinier (n 30) 528.

42 See, for example Preston et al. who argue that 'thinking like a lawyer' should focus on metacognitive skills: Cheryl B Preston, Penée Wood Stewart and Louise R Moulding, 'Teaching "Thinking Like a Lawyer": Metacognition and Law Students' (2014) *Brigham Young*

Given these examples, it is perhaps not surprising that a study of over 300 law students by Townes O'Brien et al. applying a rational-experiential inventory of their ways of thinking found 'significant differences' between the cohort's scores at the start and end of the first year, with scores on the rational thinking scale becoming 'significantly higher' and scores on the experiential thinking scale becoming 'significantly lower'.[43] A higher score on the rational thinking scale was 'consistently associated' with a more positive anticipated and actual experience of law school.[44] However, students who were higher than the average in rational thinking, but lower than the average in experiential thinking demonstrated 'a significant increase in depressive symptoms' over the course of the first year and a 'clear association' was identified between lower levels of depressive symptoms and higher levels of experiential thinking.[45] A subsequent additional dialogue with 18 law students and 10 faculty members reinforced these findings, as students indicated that law school was making them 'more rational, objectifying, analytical and logical'.[46] At the same time, they reported feeling 'more competitive, adversarial, arrogant and elitist' with increased 'feelings of isolation, disconnection and intolerance'.[47] Such comments reflect two of the other commonly identified causes of well-being issues amongst law students, namely, a lack of social connectedness,[48] and a shift from intrinsic to extrinsic motivations.[49] Although this study focused on students studying face-to-face, echoes of the emphasis on rational thinking and lack of social connectedness can be identified in the comments of distance learning students discussed in the following section.

Socialisation and identity formation at a distance

The research into the notion of 'thinking like a lawyer' and its impact on identity formation and well-being is summed up well by Collier who suggests:

> Studies in this field have highlighted law student perceptions of how the experience of law school can itself tend to make them more rational, objectifying,

University Law Review 1053. Other potential challenges to this adversarial mindset can include a focus on alternative dispute resolution and methodologies such as problem-based learning.

43 Townes O'Brien et al., 'Changing Our Thinking' (n 15) 155.

44 Ibid 163.

45 Ibid 165.

46 Ibid 177.

47 Ibid.

48 Massimiliano Tani and Prue Vines, 'Law Students' Attitudes to Education: Pointers to Depression in the Legal Academy and the Profession?' (2009) 19 *Legal Education Review* 3.

49 Allen and Baron (n 39) 285; Sheldon and Kreiger, 'Undermining Effects on Law Students' (n 13); Sheldon and Kreiger, 'Undermining Effects on Law Students' (n 13); Kath Hall, 'Do We Really Want to Know? Recognising the Importance of Student Psychological Well-Being in Australian Law Schools' (2009) 9(1) *Queensland University of Technology Law and Justice Journal* 18.

> analytical and logical; and yet also, at the same time, more isolated and, often, more insecure, anxious and intolerant.[50]

However, as discussed previously, these studies have focused on the face-to-face law school environment. The question, therefore, is whether this process is mirrored in the journey of online distance learning law students. Although there is a lack of data on this, there have been suggestions that distance learning does not allow students the same access to legal culture. As early as 1919, Ballantine commented that 'the evening law schools unfortunately do not have the cultural atmosphere which surrounds university life', implying that part-time or distance students lacked the form of immersion into the life of the law school which students in a full-time, face-to-face environment experience.[51] Nearly a hundred years later, this sentiment was echoed by Cahak's suggestion that:

> Opponents of online law schools often argue that distance learning can have an isolating effect that is particularly trying for first-year students who need the most guidance. They contend that classroom instruction conveys subtle nonverbal messages that often indicate classroom expectations and information crucial to comprehension.[52]

It is interesting to note that both Ballentine and Cahak refer to the socialisation process of law students as a positive and necessary part of legal education, without seeming to acknowledge the negative impacts on well-being which are now commonly associated with it.

Returning to the author's research with an online distance learning cohort within the UK, there were some indications amongst the open-ended responses to the survey that students had absorbed (and prized) the norms associated with 'thinking like a lawyer'. Indeed, several of the respondents referred explicitly to the notion of a shift in their thought processes:

> I am constantly being asked to make use of rational thought and to look around into the complex web of relationships that we can find in society.
> (Respondent 179)

> It has ushered me into a very different way of looking at issues generally.
> (Respondent 272)

50 Richard Collier, 'Well-Being in the Legal Profession: Reflections on Recent Developments (or, What Do We Talk About, When We Talk About Well-Being?)' (2015) 23(1) *International Journal of the Legal Profession* 1, 5.

51 Ballantine (n 1) 372.

52 Abigail Cahak, 'Beyond Brick-and-Mortar: How (Cautiously) Embracing Internet Law Schools Can Help Bridge the Legal Access Gap' (2012) (2) *University of Illinois Journal of Law, Technology and Policy* 495, 501.

Other responses implicitly suggested a viewpoint or thought process which prized the forms of status or gain commonly associated with shifts in values and motivations in studies of law student well-being.[53] For example, in answer to the question of whether the law school had lived up to their expectations and also the question of how law school had impacted on their well-being, a number of respondents referred to a new sense of status or authority:

> I have a greater awareness of my rights and responsibilities in law. Knowledge is power.
>
> (Respondent 50)

> It has proved advantageous both at work where contracts have been interpreted incorrectly or totally misunderstood and more senior people have come to me for advice which is normally given as 'you need a specialist in this field'.
>
> (Respondent 55)

> I believe yes but I will confirm when get a better paid job.
>
> (Respondent 161)

> I am more organised, rational and I always now look at all sides of the story.
>
> (Respondent 189)

Of course, none of these responses is inherently worrying, or necessarily correlates to lower levels of well-being; indeed, the respondents in question appeared to view these as positive changes. However, it does echo the notion of law students focusing on the (so-called) rational at the expense of the experiential.[54] It also suggests a possible emphasis on extrinsic motivations and rewards which, within self-determination theory, has been potentially linked to lower levels of well-being.[55] Such responses seemed markedly different in nuance than comments by several other respondents which referred to empowerment and tended to focus more on factors commonly associated with intrinsic motivation, such as the attainment of personal goals or growth in self-confidence or self-awareness:

> I view society in a different light with greater perspective, so I find myself helping others and taking the time to listen.
>
> (Respondent 40)

53 Sheldon and Kreiger, 'Undermining Effects on Law Students' (n 13); Sheldon and Kreiger, 'Walking the Talk' (n 13); O'Brien et al., 'Changing Our Thinking' (n 15).

54 Ibid.

55 Richard M Ryan and Edward L Deci, 'Self-Determination Theory and the Facilitation of Intrinsic Motivation, Self-Development and Well-Being' (2000) 55(1) *American Psychologist* 68, 72.

> Law touches every aspect of our lives. Knowing how it is formed and applied, gives you a sense of empowerment and being in control impacts on your well-being.
>
> (Respondent 63)

> I am a more confident character after doing my final module.
>
> (Respondent 84)

Thus, the responses indicated, to a limited extent, an absorption of some of the norms associated with 'thinking like a lawyer' in a way which would perhaps be anticipated from a face-to-face cohort. However, the large majority of responses did not appear to (explicitly or implicitly) focus on these issues. More common themes that emerged were around the stresses and strains of juggling work, family and other commitments with study; along with the levels of support provided by The Open University as a whole, the Law School and individual tutors.[56] Interestingly, there was relatively little reference overall to the online nature of much of the study;[57] instead for those students who referred to the levels of support falling below expectations or impacting negatively on their well-being, they appeared to highlight the distance learning nature of the degree as key: [58]

> Too removed as a student. Left to own devices.
>
> (Respondent 32)

> Lack of support and student interaction is quite depressing.
>
> (Respondent 258)

For a number of respondents, they appeared to view this as being the compromise which enabled them to study for a degree:

> I have enjoyed studying law and the OU pathway has fitted around my life. However, I think it can be quite isolating studying alone at home.
>
> (Respondent 136)

A smaller number indicated they preferred a mode of study offering limited interactions and there were also several respondents who had either had personal experience of a face-to-face university, or had family members who had, and who compared their distance study experience favourably to this. However, overall, the responses indicated that a sense of social isolation or lack of belonging were

56 Jones et al. (n 17) 18.

57 Depending on the year of registration, some students may have also received hard copy materials.

58 It should be noted that there were also a range of positive responses around the levels of support offered, for example, 'fabulous support' (Respondent 208) and 'found it very supportive and flexible' (Respondent 221).

viewed as more significant factors in the respondents' experience and well-being than the socialisation process so often implicated in face-to-face studies.

A unique balance?

The journey of studying for any degree involves students in a process of constructing and developing their identity.[59] Such a process can impact on both their academic and personal development in a range of ways, including on their mental well-being and engagement with their chosen discipline and institution.[60] For law students, many of whom are also seeking (at least at the start of their studies) to become legal professionals,[61] this process commonly involves imbibing the notion of 'thinking like a lawyer' and its associated norms in a manner which can negatively impact their mental well-being.[62] This means that for any law school, there is a balance to be struck between equipping students for a possible career in law and beginning their professional identity formation positively, and preventing the inculcation of negative or rigid traditional legal norms, such as 'thinking like a lawyer' in a manner which could be harmful to individuals' mental well-being. The balance may depend on a variety of factors, such as whether the law degree is undergraduate, postgraduate or vocationally focused in nature, the priorities of the wider institution and whether the law school has been able to develop its own norms (for example, by promoting a more holistic approach to legal education).[63]

For online distance learners it could be argued that the distance nature of their study has potentially beneficial aspects in terms of mental well-being, if the lack of physical proximity means that they are subjected to less pressure to 'think like a lawyer' and comply with problematic characterisations. However, whilst the socialisation process appears potentially less intense because of the lack of physical proximity, one danger appears to be that such students are also missing out on the social connectedness with fellow students which is also seen as essential in promoting well-being.[64]

In addition, they may lack that sense of belonging to the law school as a whole which could enable them to overcome barriers to learning and reduce a possible sense of alienation.[65] Indeed, it was notable that in answer to the question about

59 In relation to adult learners see Phil Askham, 'Context and Identity: Exploring Adult Learners' Experiences of Higher Education' (2008) 32(1) *Journal of Further and Higher Education* 85, 89–90.

60 Sarah J Mann, 'Alternative Perspectives on the Student Experience: Alienation and Engagement' (2001) 26(1) *Studies in Higher Education* 7.

61 Melissa Hardee, *The Cohort Study of the Career Expectations of Students on Qualifying Law Degrees in England and Wales* <http://ials.sas.ac.uk/sites/default/files/files/About%20us/Leadership%20%26%20Collaboration/LERN/LERN_Hardee.pdf> accessed 7 May 2019.

62 Townes O'Brien et al., 'Changing Our Thinking' (n 15); see also James (n 24).

63 James Duffy, Rachael Field and Melinda Shirley, 'Engaging Law Students to Promote Psychological Health' (2011) 36(4) *Alternative Law Journal* 250.

64 Tani and Vines (n 48); Bergin and Pakenham (n 15).

65 Ibid.

law school expectations that several respondents did not identify themselves as having been to a law school, despite having been studying the LLB for at least two years within a law school branded as such both internally and externally:

> I did not have specific expectations and would not describe studying for my degree as 'law school'.
>
> (Respondent 76)

> I wish I could have attended University than trying to teach myself law.
>
> (Respondent 110)

> Haven't been to law school yet.
>
> (Respondent 273)

There is also the question of where, if it is not from their studies, distance learning students are receiving information about the norms (or perceived norms) of law and legal practice. Of survey respondents, 45.1% indicated they wished to go into the legal profession, suggesting professional identity formation would have a particular significance to them.[66] All of the respondents were at a point in their degree where they had invested significant amounts of time, energy and resources into the study of law, and indicated some form of interest or engagement with the discipline and, by implication, its norms. If these are not being provided to a significant number of students during their study, there are dangers that traditional norms may be unquestioningly accepted, for example, via social media and law firm prospectuses.[67]

For any law school providing online distance learning there is a need to begin an explicit conversation about the concept of 'thinking like a lawyer' and the norms they are seeking to develop in their students. This does not mean slavishly following existing tenets, with potentially damaging consequences for mental well-being. Instead, it means exploring how they can best foster healthy and critically aware approaches at a distance which preserve well-being, foster professional identity and provide a sense of belonging. This chapter has begun the discussion by problematising the issue, but much remains to be debated.

66 Jones et al. (n 17).

67 For discussion of the latter, see Richard Collier, 'Be Smart, Be Successful, Be Yourself. . .'?: Representations of the Training Contract and Trainee Solicitor in Advertising by Large Law Firms' (2005) 12(1) *International Journal of the Legal Profession* 51.

9 Which hat shall I wear today? Exploring the professional and ethical implications of law clinic supervision

Margaret Castles and Carol Boothby

Through supervision of students in a law clinic environment, supervisors are able to provide students with an ethical and professional framework which can provide invaluable role modelling, and a foundation for their future legal selves. The formative experiences of students in a clinical environment can provide rich ground for developing reflective skills, and enable them to face challenging situations in a controlled environment. Structuring this self-directed form of learning is a delicate balance, requiring supervisors to adopt a variety of situation-specific roles.

This chapter examines the complex role of clinical supervisors, and relates the value of this form of teaching to ideas of student wellness, for example in greater feelings of relatedness[1] and connectedness.[2] The supervisor role can affect student motivation and capacity, and how far students feel able to assume more responsibility for their own learning as well as service delivery. It may also support students in dealing with uncertainty, as they discover that the practice of lawyering involves exercising reasoned judgment in an unpredictable environment. These learnings are an important element of professional identity formation for new lawyers.

This chapter provides a comparative perspective, drawing common and divergent approaches from opposite sides of the globe using the experience of the writers. We conclude that it is valuable for clinical supervisors to identify and understand the different roles they play with reference to associated professional expectations to ensure that they adopt a mindful and balanced approach to supervision. Reflections on the role of the supervisor together with a mapping of some of the existing work in this area will provide meaningful reference points to those involved in this form of experiential learning.

1 Leah Wortham et al., 'Autonomy-Mastery-Purpose: Structuring Clinical Courses to Enhance these Critical Educational Goals' (2014) 18 *International Journal of Clinical Legal Education* 105.

2 Rachael Field, James Duffy and Colin James (eds), *Promoting Law Student and Lawyer Well-Being in Australia and Beyond* (Routledge, 2016).

Introduction

Clinical Legal Education (CLE) – law students learning through engagement with clients and qualified lawyers in an authentic legal practice context – is a unique pedagogical model that raises diverse challenges for the teachers involved. According to Evans et al.:

> Clinical legal education is a pedagogy that places students in real-life environments. It is a form of experiential learning where students learn by doing and then reflecting[3]

Clinic provides the potential for an experience which leads students to look both inwards, at their own values and skills, as well as outwards, at the community around them. CLE can illuminate not only the application of the law, but also its limitations, and 'demonstrates the role that lawyers can or perhaps ought to play in the lives of others'.[4] Teachers in clinic supervise students' learning in the context of real legal work. They play a multifaceted role that responds to context and student needs and have a much closer and more nuanced relationship with students than is typical in law schools.[5]

Our uniform observation is that students who have already completed most of their undergraduate education experience clinic as a dramatic introduction to the 'real world' – a stark contrast with the academic structure that they have so far experienced. This can occur against the experience of becoming less connected, less autonomous, and less focused on social justice ideals during several years' traditional classroom based learning.[6] In many cases the clinic experience is transformative,[7] immersing students in an active role engaging with clients while developing their lawyering skills and considering broader social and legal challenges.

The focus of this chapter is on the unique influence that clinic supervisors can have both on student learning and on student well-being. We use the example of CLE programs based on live client service models with students supervised by a solicitor clinician throughout their placement.

Our respective clinics operate differently. At Northumbria University's Student Law Office,[8] the clinic experience is compulsory for virtually all students,

3 'Adrian Evans et al., *Australian Clinical Legal Education: Designing and Operating a Best Practice Clinical Program in an Australian Law School* (ANU Press, 2017) 41.

4 Richard Grimes, 'Reflections on Clinical Legal Education' (1995) 29(2) *The Law Teacher* 169, 171.

5 For example, see the detailed discussion using vignettes from clinic in Margaret Martin Barry, 'Clinical Supervision: Walking That Fine Line' (1995) 2 *Clinical Law Review* 137.

6 Wortham et al. (n 1) 129; Evans et al. (n 3) 75.

7 Fran Quigley, 'Seizing the Disorienting Moment: Adult Learning Theory and the Teaching of Social Justice in Law School Clinics' (1995) 2 *Clinical Law Review* 37.

8 Northumbria University is based in Newcastle on Tyne, in the North East of England. The Law School is renowned for the Student Law Office, with as many as 200 students per year participating in the in-house free legal advice provision. For more information, visit <www.northumbria.ac.uk/about-us/academic-departments/northumbria-law-school/study/student-law-office/> accessed 7 May 2019.

who work in 'firms' of 6/8 students under the guidance of a law lecturer who is qualified as a solicitor/barrister, usually on particular types of work (for example, housing, family, commercial, general civil.) All casework including client interviews must be carried out in the Student Law Office, a dedicated workspace located within the Law School. Students generally spend around 10–20 hours per week in the office, are able to come and go between 9 and 5 most days and work on their cases throughout the academic year. At Northumbria, students and supervisor meet at a specified time for a once-weekly 'firm meeting'. This meeting provides a forum for students to reflect with their fellow students on the work with their clients in the past week. Students leave the firm meeting with a plan for the next week, and work in the Law Office drafting letters and research reports.

As mentioned above, the students can come and go as needs dictate. The supervisor receives frequent visits from individual students wishing to discuss various legal and procedural aspects of their cases, or their own learning – from problems in working in pairs, to worrying about their own performance. They might come to discuss errors they fear they have made on their cases, or areas of law they cannot understand. Students generally initiate contact with and make appointments to see supervisors when they need support. This is an assessed module, for which students are graded; indeed, clinic can form around 35% of the final year grade. The assessment encompasses 10 competency areas, as well as reflective skills.[9]

At Adelaide University in South Australia the clinics operate differently. Clinic forms the placement component of the Clinical Legal Education elective, which is not a compulsory part of the degree. Each semester up to 30 students in groups of six are allocated to one of three law school clinics, each dealing with discrete types of practice.[10] The clinics are all off campus, co-located at courts or situated at a community centre. Students and supervisor[11] attend the clinic placement one day per week. 35% of the final grade for the subject is based on placement performance which is assessed by supervisors on specific criteria. Students work in pairs, but only on the allocated clinic day each week. There is no access to files, office or the supervisor on other days. Meetings, discussions about cases, and all other interactions occur in a single open office area throughout the clinic day.

In both the Northumbria University and University of Adelaide clinics, students typically interact with their supervisor to prepare for client interviews, confirm action to be taken when the interview is completed, and check with the supervisor as each step, document, or process progresses. Supervisors support students to find and apply the law, edit and re-edit their written work, explore the challenges for clients engaging with the legal system, and discuss the students' own intellectual, emotional, and social learning.

9 For more information on assessment at Northumbria University Student Law Office, see Carol Boothby, '"Pigs are Not Fattened by Being Weighed" – So Why Assess Clinic – and Can We Defend Our Methods?' (2016) 23 *International Journal of Clinical Legal Education* 137.

10 Minor civil claims; equal opportunity and discrimination; general law. Some of the clinics operate two days per week with different students attending on each day. There are also several externship placements that are not the focus of this chapter.

11 Supervisors are legal practitioners employed by the university on contract.

The student/teacher ratio in clinic creates a professional intimacy not found in other law teaching. Whilst orthodox clinical supervision theory[12] advocates a degree of distance between teacher and student, so that each student can develop autonomously, supervisors can in reality spend hours each day with students. At Adelaide each of the clinics are located in one room – one supervisor with six students. Students work, consult with each other, seek supervision from the supervisor, in the same space, for 8 hours. There is little privacy, and the words, actions, and conduct of students and supervisor are observable by all. Students will consult the supervisor following client interviews, and during client casework, and these discussions will canvas skills, drafting, ethics, case strategy, managing client conduct, different approaches to practice, how students are feeling, and broader issues of justice and legal practice. There are regular 'break out' discussions between supervisor and all students when interesting points arise.

Clinicians have conflicting ethical demands: to ensure service quality, and to manage meaningful experiences for students. As the preceding descriptions demonstrate, in the course of a clinic day, supervisors will be legal practice manager, senior lawyer, risk manager, assessor of written work and performance, counsellor, mentor, advisor, and commentator.

Author Margaret Castles, describes it thus:

> In a typical day in clinic at Adelaide, the supervisor oversees students organising the appointments and follow up work for the day; provides feedback to students on written drafts and legal research; discusses how they managed a client in interview and explores what they have learned from that process. They could be drawn into a discussion about women and the glass ceiling, or the practice of empathy in legal practice or in life generally. They may counsel students after a particularly difficult interview, ask students to deeply consider the ethical implications of proposed case strategies, or to consider how their own emotions or frustration affected their management of a client. They will track students' understanding of the legal concepts in a case through their preparation of verbal or written advice to a client, or the drafting of court documents. They might be asked to speak privately to a student who has confidence, personal, or health dilemmas that they are not coping well with. If they notice difficult dynamics within the group or problematic work practices, they will work out a way to address that without causing shame or distress to any student.

Each response has to be nuanced to the needs of the particular student, but often also re-packaged for the entire cohort. Dealing with students in the midst of raw experience (such as an angry client) requires managing the emotion of the moment to minimise student distress and making sure they can finish the

12 Harriet Katz, 'Reconsidering Collaboration and Modelling: Enriching Clinical Pedagogy' (2005) 41 *Gonzaga Law Review* 315, 316–318, 322–324; Adrian Evans et al., 'Best Practices: Australian Clinical Legal Education' (2013) 47(3) *The Law Teacher* 421.

interview, and then coming back to that experience to check student well-being, whilst supporting the student to analyse and learn from the experience. Clinical teaching is often in the moment, and teaching occurs as a series of scaffolded learning interactions over a period of time. Clinic supervisors will be holding several learning 'threads' in relation to different students at any one time. As a typical clinic day will involve each pair of students interviewing 1–2 clients and doing related casework, it can be demanding, fast paced, and stressful.

Clinicians find out more about students at a personal and academic level than would ever occur in a normal teaching environment. There is a fine line between collegiality, mentoring, and hierarchy. As colleagues we share experiences, opinions, and challenges and seek to create a collegiate team environment where everyone can share leadership, exercise autonomy, and support each other. As a mentor we devise support and engagement of students each according to their level of experience, confidence, and interest. As practice manager, and the ultimate guarantor of quality client service, we must monitor compliance with practice standards and ensure that students are professional, reliable, and accurate in their work. As role model we are closely observed by students in all of these activities.

We focus now on three of the most influential elements of supervisorial impact on clinic students: pedagogy in clinic (including personalising learning and autonomy support), mentoring, and role modelling.

Pedagogy in clinic

Extensive scholarship has developed around clinical pedagogy.[13] Originally grounded in an orthodox view of non-directive supervision,[14] the last decade or so has seen clinical pedagogy enriched with ideas of autonomy, mastery, insight, reflective capacity, and role assumption.[15] Modelling and student/teacher collaboration, ideas which would once have been inconsistent with orthodox understanding of non-directive supervision, are now recognised as critical features.[16] Nuanced guidance and continuous feedback,[17] cognitive development, and social interaction are also recognised as important factors in students forming

13 For the earliest roots of CLE, see Jerome Frank, 'Why Not a Clinical Lawyer School' (1933) 81(8) *University of Pennsylvania Law Review* 907. See also Anthony G Amsterdam, 'Clinical Legal Education – A 21st Century Perspective' (1984) 34(4) *Journal of Legal Education* 612. For an overview see Margaret M Barry, Jon C Dubin and Peter A Joy, 'Clinical Education for this Millennium: The Third Wave' (2000) 7(1) *Clinical Law Review* 1.

14 Katz (n 12) 315, 316; James Stark et al., 'Directiveness in Clinical Supervision' (1993) 3(1) *Boston University Public Interest Law Journal* 35.

15 Kennon M Sheldon and Lawrence S Krieger, 'Understanding the Negative Effects of Legal Education on Law Students: A Longitudinal Test of Self-Determination Theory' (2007) 33(6) *Personality and Social Psychology Bulletin* 883, 885; Wallace J Mlyniec, 'Where to Begin – Training New Teachers in the Art of Clinical Pedagogy' (2012) 18(2) *Clinical Law Review* 505, 518.

16 Katz (n 12) 315, 316, 322; Evans et al. (n 12) 421–423.

17 Roy Stuckey et al., *Best Practices for Legal Education a Vision and a Road Map* (Clinical Legal Education Association, 2007) 176.

a professional identity.[18] Supervisors need to work across these functions to deliver the web of supports that typically hold the clinic experience together for students, and protect their well-being. As described by Mlyniec, clinic supervision 'is an art, requiring multiple teaching tools that will improve with experience'.[19]

Personalising learning

Stuckey recognises as one of his principles of best practice for legal education that each student will have different personal and educational needs and aspirations.[20] Unlike traditional courses with fixed assessment points and standard course coverage, clinical experience allows students to develop in different ways and to different levels, in a malleable and dynamic learning environment. This process echoes Vygotsky's 'zone of proximal development' – creating individual learning 'zones' with each student so that each can reach their optimal development.[21] Part of the role of the clinical supervisor is to enable students to make the links between their theoretical knowledge and the unstructured legal issues presented to them by clients. Over time, they develop methods of tackling legal issues in unfamiliar areas of law. As they develop 'black letter' legal skills, they are also practising a range of broad and often very challenging practice activities. Most of them have never interviewed a client, yet fail to recognise that by their final year of law school they have considerable skills in human interrelationships from all other aspects of their lives. They have not managed a case file, but may have significant skills arising from managing their own work, tax, income, and university lives. They have not had to deal with legal ethical challenges but have made personal ethical judgments throughout their lives. Supervisorial guidance supports students to make connections between existing experience, theory, and legal practice. Supervisors mediate indeterminate situations with multiple possible outcomes, in order to provide a scaffolded learning experience for each student in the clinic.

Autonomy support

Blaustone et al. emphasise structuring supervisorial practice in clinic to meet the psychological need for autonomy and motivation in learning. They contrast

18 These factors are described as part of the 'third apprenticeship' of becoming a lawyer in the influential Carnegie Report. William M Sullivan et al., *Educating Lawyers: Education for the Profession of Law* (Carnegie Foundation for the Advancement of Teaching, 2007) 9.

19 Mlyniec (n 15) 505, 520. For a perspective from the Northumbria clinic, see Angela Macfarlane and Paul McKeown, '10 Lessons for New Clinicians' (2008) 13(13) *International Journal of Clinical Legal Education* 65.

20 Stuckey (n 17) 177.

21 Vygotsky theorised that 'the zone of proximal development is the distance between the actual development level as determined by independent problem solving and the level of potential development as determined through problem solving under adult guidance or in collaboration with more capable peers': Lev S Vygotsky, *Mind in Society: The Development of Higher Psychological Processes* (Harvard University Press, 1980) 86.

typical hierarchical directive practices such as telling, explaining, providing solutions, predicting outcomes, and asking controlling questions, with exploring student views, listening, helping students identify rationales for ideas, asking clarifying questions and supporting and encouraging students, rather than simply using praise and/or criticism.[22] Developing a sense of teamwork around the student–supervisor interrelationship, and exploring values and ethics,[23] are also important. Nurturing intrinsic motivation (such as creativity, competence, relatedness, and autonomy) rather than the more typical goal-focused outcomes, results in better outcomes and in higher reported well-being.[24] Autonomy support is a structured and intentional process, involving providing students with as much choice as possible; providing meaningful rationales when choice is not available; and considering the students' point of view in relation to the particular task in supporting completion.[25]

These pedagogical considerations provide a basic framework for clinic learning, upon which ideas of mentoring, role modelling, and collaboration are built.

Mentoring

Mentoring is typically described as a hierarchical one-on-one developmental relationship between a less experienced individual (the protégé) and more experienced individual (the mentor).[26] Mentoring can take different forms. It can be formal or informal. It can be primarily instrumental, providing challenging assignments, coaching, 'how to' advice, career advice, advancement support, and protection. It can also be a deeper 'psychosocial' process aimed at helping protégés develop a sense of professional identity, self-efficacy, and self-worth.[27] Used together, instrumental and psychosocial support can help protégés to deal with immediate, and be better prepared for future, challenges, whether professional, relational or personal. Clinic supervisors are not in a formal mentoring relationship with students, yet much of their work with students is characteristic of mentoring and reflects some if not all of the above characteristics. Today, where graduate attributes include teamwork and communication skills, career and leadership readiness, and emotional intelligence,[28] as well as academic and discipline knowledge, mentoring is particularly important, but poses challenges of role.

22 Wortham et al. (n 1) 124.

23 Ibid 145 citing the Carnegie Report supporting the proposition that law schools can and should have a role in the development of ethical standards in students.

24 Johnmarshall Reeve, *Understanding Motivation and Emotion* (John Wiley and Sons, 5th ed, 2009) 113; Wortham et al. (n 1) 109.

25 Wortham et al. (n 1) 114.

26 Tammey D Allen et al., 'Taking Stock of Two Relational Aspects of Organizational Life: Tracing the History and Shaping the Future of Socialization and Mentoring Research' (2017) 102(3) *Journal of Applied Psychology* 324.

27 Ibid.

28 Adelaide University, 'Graduate Attributes' <www.adelaide.edu.au/learning/strategy/grad attributes> accessed 7 May 2019.

The role of a mentor is essentially partial, whereas the role of a supervisor must be visibly impartial.[29] Student trust in supervisors will be compromised if they are seen to treat students differently, and ultimately the fairness of marking will be challenged if it seems that markers have different relationships with different students. Temperament, personality, working style, and tacit connectedness will influence the ease and closeness of the working relationship, so supervisors have to self-monitor their own interaction with students to equally share their attention, support, and interest. As practice managers and assessors of student performance, supervisors need to be mindful of 'power asymmetry' in clinic.[30]

Role modelling

Intentional role modelling is a third influential function of clinical supervisors. Students learn from what they see others doing,[31] and it is critical that supervisors send the right messages. Described as being in the 'hot seat' [32] supervisors have to be aware of the overt and tacit messages they send. Attitudes to each other, to students, to clients, and to the way they practice law will be closely observed by students.[33]

Role modelling is consistently in action in the clinical setting. We 'show' students how to deal with interrupters, over-talkers, shy or non-talkative people through our management of clinic meetings. We demonstrate patience and respect in the manner in which we support students to achieve their work. We model respect (or lack thereof) in the way we talk about clients, other lawyers, and each other; we model our capacity to consider other perspectives in case discussions, and in counselling of individual students. We demonstrate interviewing, communication, and conflict management and dispute resolution skills in the way we deal with the students individually and in groups. Our attitudes to legal, political, social, and emotional issues will be visible and influential.[34]

Much role modelling is tacit. But some requires thoughtful explanation. Supervisors will explain their thinking – around ethics, around dealing with repugnant clients, around power dynamics in disputes and around access to justice issues in clinic. Self-disclosure – revealing our own learning journey, our own challenges,

29 For the definition of mentoring as opposed to supervision, see Barry (n 5) 137, 146, drawing on Michael Meltsner et al., 'The Bike Tour Leader's Dilemma: Talking About Supervision' (1989) 13(2) *Vermont Law Review* 399.

30 Jeff Giddings, 'The Assumption of Responsibility: Supervision Practices in Experiential Legal Education' available at SSRN 2740208 (2014) 17.

31 Peter Joy, 'Ethics of Lawyers in Unsupervised Work Experience' (2003) 45 *Southern Texas Law Review* 815.

32 Liz Curran et al., 'Pushing the Boundaries or Preserving the Status Quo: Designing Programs to Teach Law Students a Deep Understanding of Ethical Practice' (2005) 8 *Journal of Legal Education* 104.

33 Susannah Sage-Jacobsen et al., 'Identifying Teaching and Learning Opportunities Within Professional Relationships Between Clinic Supervisors' (2014) 24 *Legal Education Review* 159.

34 Carrie J Menkel-Meadow, 'Can a Law Teacher Avoid Teaching Legal Ethics?' (1991) 41(1) *Journal of Legal Education* 3.

and our own doubts and weaknesses – can also be an important part of an authentic role modelling process. Legal ethics is a fertile area for explanatory role modelling. A supervisor might decide that the relationship between two clinic clients who have had past dealings together is remote enough not to raise conflict concerns. But failure to explicitly address the reasoning and considerations behind this decision will leave students believing that this issue is either not important or that we have acted unethically. The binary approach students can have to the law can be challenged if supervisors can make transparent the process of deciding how to take a case forward, particularly where there may be a number of options.

Clinic and well-being

A combination of pedagogical technique, mentoring, and role modelling demonstrate that learning in clinic is a 'whole of student' endeavour. In the following section we consider how ideas of mental well-being and social wellness are part of this approach.

Statistics indicate that law students and law graduates experience significantly higher levels of mental illness than the rest of the community.[35] Diverse initiatives addressing well-being have been developed in both Australia[36] and the UK.[37] Many of the more recent initiatives are documented and discussed in this work.

Well-being is a diffuse concept. It can mean happiness or contentment;[38] it can relate to basic human needs for community, autonomy, agency, and voice.[39] It can mean absence of psychological distress, uncertainty, lack of confidence, social stress. However, as Strevens and Wilson argue,[40] drawing on the work of Molly Townes O'Brien,[41] it is not the duty of legal educators to shoulder the responsibility for each student's happiness:

> The goal is not to produce relaxed and superficially happy lawyers, but to produce competent lawyers and problem solvers, who have the skills and the creativity to address legal and social problems and make a positive difference.

35 Norm Kelk et al., 'Distress and Depression Among Australian Law Students: Incidence Attitudes and the Role of Universities' (2010) 32(1) *Sydney Law Review* 113; Norm Kelk et al., *Courting the Blues: Attitudes Towards Depression in Australian Law Students and Lawyers* (Brain & Mind Research Institute, 2009) 7.

36 Rachael Field, James Duffy and Anna Huggins, *Lawyering and Positive Professional Identities* (LexisNexis Butterworths, 2014) 21.

37 Caroline Strevens and Clare Wilson, 'Law Student Wellbeing in the UK: A Call for Curriculum Intervention' (2016) 11(1) *Journal of Commonwealth Law and Legal Education* 44.

38 Ibid.

39 See Ronald J Fisher, 'Needs Theory and Social Identity an Eclectic Model of Conflict' in John Burton (ed), *Conflict: Human Needs Theory* (The Macmillan Press Ltd, 1990) 89. Consider also positive psychology's Self-Determination Theory (SDT) which is used in the wellness for law context by many authors – including many in this work. The basic needs theory of SDT focuses on autonomy, competence and relatedness.

40 Strevens and Wilson (n 37) 44.

41 Molly Townes O'Brien and Stephen Tang, 'Stop Struggling for the Struggle's Sake: Make It Meaningful' (Conference paper presented to the 16th International First Year in Higher Education Conference, Wellington, New Zealand, 2013).

Well-being has direct professional impact. It affects both the ethical and relational elements of legal practice – ranging from the clinically depressed lawyer who misses deadlines, ignores clients, and compromises critical transactions, to the uncertain young lawyer who has not developed a professional support network and does not know where to turn to get advice. Day-to-day experiences – compassion fatigue, angry or tearful clients, aggressive opponents, personal circumstances, work stress, difficult work colleagues – that typically arise in clinic provide fertile ground for considering these issues that we know impact on students and practitioners alike.

Well-being awareness in the UK and Australia

In 2009 the Australian Brain and Mind Institute published the ground-breaking report *Courting the Blues*,[42] prompted by the tragic suicide of young solicitor Tristran Jepson. Law students disclosed consistently higher stress scores, in relation to academic performance, time pressure, fear of failure, classroom and economic stress, higher depression and anger, and lower levels of contentment and feelings of friendliness.[43] This and subsequent reports[44] have been influential in the development of initiatives to embed well-being in both curricular and extra-curricular models in various universities in Australia.[45]

In the UK there has been less focus on student well-being in general, and little empirical data particularly in relation to law students. However, this is changing. The recently published Institute of Public Policy Research think-tank study found increasing levels of mental illness, mental distress, and low well-being among students in higher education in the UK, with levels higher than the general population.[46] The report concludes with a number of recommendations for reform, including 'Designing course content and delivery in a way which promotes positive mental health and well-being, while maintaining an emphasis on academic rigour'.[47]

42 Kelk et al. *Courting the Blues* (n 35).

43 The study compared law and medical students in Australia. Kelk et al. *Courting the Blues* (n 35) 2–3. See also Wendy Larcombe et al., 'Does an Improved Experience of Law School Protect Students Against Depression, Anxiety and Stress: An Empirical Study of Wellbeing and the Law School Experience of LLB and JD Students' (2013) 35 *Sydney Law Review* 407.

44 See for example, Larcombe et al., (n 43).

45 Michael Appleby and Judy Bourke, 'Promoting Law Student Mental Health Literacy and Wellbeing: A Case Study from the College of Law' (2014) 21 *International Journal of Clinical Legal Education* 461; Katherine Lindsay et al., 'Oh the Places You'll Go! Newcastle Law School's Partnership Interventions for Well Being in First Year Law' (2015) 8(2) *Journal of Learning Design* 11.

46 Craig Thorley, 'Not by Degrees: Improving Student Mental Health in the UK's Universities' (2017) *Institute for Public Policy Research* <www.ippr.org/publications/not-by-degrees> accessed 7 May 2019.

47 Ibid 68.

Cause and effect: Well-being and the role of traditional legal education models

Whilst there are many possible reasons for low well-being amongst law students,[48] the causes are not yet fully understood.[49] There is however increasing support for the idea that typical legal education is partly to blame.[50] With high academic entry requirements, there is fierce competition to get a place in law school. Complex materials, tight deadlines, large workloads, and the competitive nature of legal argument all contribute to this stress.[51] Large classes, pressure to cover complex course material in short timeframes, and a focus on assessment performance can deplete autonomy, creativity, and reflexivity in student learning,[52] with consequential impact on student well-being.[53] Similar pressures are repeated in legal practice. A growing body of research recognises the significance of close student–teacher interactions in primary and secondary education, and the importance of the affective dimensions of the bond between student and teacher in creating an effective learning relationship.[54] Less well researched in the higher education context, there is no reason to believe that the demonstrable impact on motivation, social competence, and well-being of forming and maintaining enduring personal relationships[55] is any less influential at tertiary level.[56] Law schools in Australia and the UK take in large numbers of first year students. Core teaching normally occurs in large non-compulsory lectures, and smaller one or two-hour weekly learning groups (tutorials or seminars) which still contain between 30 and 50 students. There is little opportunity for anything other than brief academic engagement between teacher and student. The sustained one-on-one interaction that supports connectedness is often absent.

48 These typically include high achieving personality types, focus on grades, self-criticism, social isolation, unrealistic expectations, and perfectionism. See, for example, Massimiliano Tani and Prue Vines, 'Law Students' Attitudes to Education: Pointers to Depression in the Legal Academy and the Profession?' (2009) 19(1–2) *Legal Education Review* 3. See also Susan Daicoff, 'The Future of the Legal Profession' (2011) 37(1) *Monash University Law Review* 7.

49 Appleby and Bourke (n 45) 461.

50 One Australian study concluded that student well-being reduces markedly in the first year of law study: Molly Townes O'Brien et al., 'Changing Our Thinking: Empirical Research on Law Student Wellbeing, Thinking Styles and the Law Curriculum' (2011) 21(2) *International Journal of the First Year in Higher Education* 1, 49.

51 Field, Duffy and Huggins (n 36) 242.

52 James Duffy et al., 'Engaging Law Students to Promote Psychological Health' (2011) 36(4) *Alternative Law Journal* 250.

53 Larcombe et al. (n 43) 407.

54 Wallace J Mlyniec, 'Developing a Teacher Training Program for New Clinical Teachers' (2012) 19(1) *Clinical Law Review* 327.

55 Gerda Hagenauer and Simone E Volet, 'Teacher-Student Relationship at University: An Important Yet Under-Researched Field' (2014) *Oxford Review of Education* 370.

56 Hagenauer and Violet (ibid, 373) point out that empirical evaluations of the impact of the student-teacher relationship tend to be superficial, focusing on access to teachers or timeliness of feedback. They argue for deeper research on the identifiable benefits to students of more complex personal relationships with teachers.

The need for holistic teaching models, which connect theory to skills and practice,[57] and the importance of dispute resolution and communication skills,[58] are identified as, but are not yet typical features of, law teaching. Ideas of connectedness and a sense of belonging have also moved into the spotlight in legal education. Students today are increasingly remote from law schools, with lectures available online, voluntary seminars/tutorials, and increased demands from outside work and other activities. Many students do not develop friendships or academic collaborations with their peers, nor have any personal contact with teachers. Huggins sees lack of autonomy – the subjective experience that one's behaviour is self-governed, volitional, and congruent with one's true beliefs, values, and interests – as a significant factor in law student distress.[59] Clinic may be the first time some students find themselves in an environment where all of these needs are addressed, working in a peer group and forming friendships. It may be the first-time students have encountered a teacher with whom they will form a professional relationship. 'Caring for students' is commonly identified as an important influence in well-being.[60] The smaller student–teacher ratio and the more intimate relationships in clinic create natural opportunities for supervisors to demonstrate 'care' at a personal, educational, and intellectual level.

Dissecting the idea of 'well-being' in legal education discloses several desirable elements.

- Curriculum content that acknowledges well-being and goes beyond the traditional paradigm of legal problem-solving;
- Curriculum delivery that encourages creative, autonomous and positive relationships with other participants; and
- Collegiality and a sense of relatedness in the work team.[61]

The first of these elements can be met by explicitly addressing well-being in teaching and course materials. The Adelaide CLE program weaves this topic through the 'Clinical Legal Education' elective course from the first day, emphasising the imperative of self-monitoring and supporting others, with reference to psychological resources, reflective exercises, and student discussion. Discussions

57 Sally Kift, 'Lawyering Skills: Finding their Place in Legal Education' (1997) 8(1) *Legal Education Review* 43; Sally Kift, '21st Century Climate for Change: Curriculum Design for Quality Learning Engagement in Law'(2008) 18 *Legal Education Review* 1.

58 See also, David Weisbrot, 'Taking Skills Seriously: Reforming Australian Legal Education' (2004) 29(6) *Alternative Law Journal* 266; Andrea Flynn et al., 'Law School Stress: Moving from Narratives to Measurement' (2017) 56 *Washburn Law Journal* 259; Kelk, et al. (n 35) 7.

59 Anna Huggins, 'Autonomy Supportive Curriculum Design: A Salient Factor in Promoting Student Wellbeing' (2012) 35(3) *University of New South Wales Law Journal* 683.

60 Townes and O'Brien et al. (n 50) 3, report that in a study of first year students at the Australian National University, students identified more time to engage with staff personally and socially as an important factor.

61 Wortham et al. (n 1) 129; Harry T Reis et al., 'Daily Well-Being: The Role of Autonomy, Competence, and Relatedness' (2000) 26(4) *Personality and Social Psychology Bulletin* 419.

of well-being then become a normal part of interaction in the student cohort and with supervisors. In addition to incorporating well-being into the curriculum, clinic provides an excellent vehicle for the second element, development of a sense of autonomy, with students having a high level of responsibility in relation to clients, as well as receiving ongoing support and feedback from each other and from supervisors. Finally, clinic can provide the close interpersonal bonds that define relatedness. At the Northumbria clinic, there is a strong emphasis on reflection, working cooperatively, and creating a sense of 'belonging' so that students start to feel part of a community of practice. The approach to well-being is framed as a need to develop professional and personal resilience, in managing workload and competing demands on students' time, as well as the emotional impact live client work can have on well-being.[62] Supervisors have an important role to play here. Take the example of a client who is about to be evicted, failing to attend an appointment with students. Students may be frustrated, distressed, and feel personally responsible for the client. The supervisor can help students to broaden their perspective and more clearly appreciate the limits of their influence – the client may lack funds to get there, experience a chaotic life as they struggle with debt, and dread discussing the problem with the students. The supervisor can also explore how students feel, and how to put those emotions into a professional perspective.

Conclusion

According to Townes O'Brien and Tang, 'Legal education should be experientially and emotionally grounded so that lawyers can embrace the idea of struggle and change'.[63] Clinical teaching can, at its best, encompass these requirements. However, the available evidence points to CLE providing the key elements of autonomy competence and relatedness, identified by Ryan and Deci as essential for 'growth and integration as well as for constructive social development and personal well-being'.[64]

Supervisors occupy a difficult space. Whilst modelling collaboration, there remains an enduring and explicit power differential, arising from the imperatives of quality client service, targeted learning outcomes, and clinical management. Supervisors are not friends or counsellors. They are not peers, and not quite colleagues. They must be aware that the power differential, and the relative inequality between inexperienced and often naive students, means their words, actions, and attitudes will often be deeply influential. This wearing of many hats comes with many challenges.

62 For a vivid account of one student's very individual struggle to maintain emotional equilibrium, and the fine line supervisors in clinic tread, see Jennifer Howard, 'Learning to Think Like a Lawyer Through Experience' (1995) 2(1) *Clinical Law Review* 167.

63 O'Brien and Tang (n 41) 8.

64 Richard Ryan and Edward Deci, 'Self-Determination Theory and the Facilitation of Intrinsic Motivation, Social Development, and Well-Being' (2000) 55(1) *American Psychologist* 68.

As universities respond to the increasing demands to deal with the issue of student well-being, those involved in the area of CLE need to ensure that this message is driven home – that part of the battle to improve student well-being must lie with improvements to the curriculum, and that by embedding forms of teaching and learning that encourage self-development and well-being, we can ensure that students emerge more ready to face the world of work. The complex and diverse demands of clinical pedagogy demonstrate that the quality of supervision within clinic is critical. In clinic, three aspects of well-being converge: course content that acknowledges well-being beyond the traditional paradigm of legal problem-solving; curriculum delivery that encourages creativity, autonomy, and confidence; and an environment of connectedness that engenders positive interrelationships with others The dynamic and multifaceted setting of CLE not only provides a unique experience for students in support of their professional identity formation, but valuable insights that can be translated back into the more traditional law teaching model.

10 Clinical legal education and the hidden curriculum in the neoliberal university in England and Wales

Caroline Gibby

Introduction

This is an uncertain time for students and lecturers in legal education in England and Wales. Political influence in the development of higher education (HE), and the emergence of the 'neoliberal university', demands greater awareness of value for money from University programs. These pressures are transferred to lecturers to meet organisational demands, sector evolution and student expectations, which represent academic success.[1] Students face their own profound pressures to ensure that their investment is wise, which are driven by social and parental expectation, increasing choice, cost, debt and aspiration that higher education brings.[2] These factors provide both challenge and opportunity for law lecturers in equal measure to ensure that programs offer support for the well-being of law students.[3] This chapter considers student well-being and health through the lens of clinical legal education's hidden curriculum, drawing on cross-jurisdictional practices to inform support for embedding wellness and well-being practices, that in turn support and promote the professional identity formation of law students.

Background

In England and Wales, the existing methods of training lawyers through higher education (HE) focus on a triple stage approach which for graduates includes the qualifying law degree (QLD), vocational course and a period of training. The

1 David Palfreyman and Ted Tapper, 'The Marketization of English Higher Education and the Financing of Tuition Fees' (2016) 14 *London Review of Education* 47.
2 Rebecca Huxley-Binns, 'Tripping Over Thresholds: A Reflection on Legal Andragogy' (2016) 50 *The Law Teacher* 1.
3 Enid Rowlands, *Training for Tomorrow: Assessing Competence* (SRA, 2015) <https://www.sra.org.uk/sra/consultations/t4t-assessing-competence.page access> accessed 7 May 2019. See also various other commentaries and reports from the SRA as set out at <www.sra.org.uk/sra/policy/sqe.page> accessed 7 May 2019.

academic program focuses on seven core/mandatory subjects,[4] mostly taught in the first two years of the three-year degree.[5] On completion, students' progress to vocational study – and finally to a period of work-based training.[6] The QLD and vocational course revisions have become increasingly aligned to a centralised professional mandate which focuses on the business of practice rather than the exercise of law in practice. The development of Clinical Legal Education (CLE) has created opportunities for authentic learning experiences for students, not only in terms of the law, but also for their well-being.[7]

Universities are therefore keen to capture capable and independent law students with significant drive and motivation with an eye to a professional career. Student expectations, fuelled by carefully crafted marketing, anticipate immersion in professional etiquette, codes and practices whilst studying their degree. Some align their degrees closely with law and practice – with the ever-present reference to images of practitioners reinforcing that connection. The current degree curriculum sees students completing half of the credit-bearing element of their program set by the professions.[8] Therefore opportunities to promote well-being within the curriculum are often hard to see or indeed for some to value.[9] Yet it has become widely apparent within universities and the legal services sector that engaging in discussion of mental health and well-being is a necessity rather than a flight of fancy.[10]

Despite this there is little direct collaboration between universities and the profession, with the result that there has been minimal real engagement in identifying and embedding values, well-being and ethics of practice within programs.[11] It is understood that students who progress into the profession are likely to face

4 The SRA Training Regulations 2014 set out the practical aspects of training: <www.sra.org.uk/students/academic-stage.page> accessed 7 May 2019.

5 Legal Education Training Review (LETR), *Setting Standards: The Future of Legal Services Education and Training Regulation in England and Wales* (LETR, 2013).

6 Since drafting this chapter, the SRA reforms in relation to solicitor training progression have gathered momentum and will take effect in 2020/21. The implications for law degrees are unclear.

7 Neil Gold, 'Clinic is the Basis for a Complete Legal Education: Quality Assurance, Learning Outcomes and the Clinical Method' (2015) 22 *International Journal of Clinical Legal Education* 1.

8 Patricia Leighton, 'The Legal Education Training Review (LETR): Where Are We Now?' (2012) 46 *The Law Teacher* 281. The law degree requires 180 credits of the 360 overall credits to be devoted to the foundation subjects.

9 Keystone Law, *Lawyers and the Pursuit of Happiness* (Keystone Law, 2016). See Gerry Kearns, 'Ensuring Staff Wellbeing is a Commercial Necessity' (2013) *Law Society Gazette* (9 September); Richard Collier, 'Wellbeing in the Legal Profession: Reflections on Recent Developments (or, What Do We Talk About, When We Talk About Wellbeing)?' (2016) 23 *International Journal of the Legal Profession* 41.

10 See for example, *Junior Lawyers Division, Resilience and Wellbeing Survey Report*, <http://communities.lawsociety.org.uk/junior-lawyers/news/jld-resilience-and-wellbeing-survey-report-2018/5064876.article> accessed 7 May 2019.

11 Ibid.

significant and profound challenges to their mental health and well-being.[12] The implication of this is that the lack of access to practitioners' experiences restricts sharing professional discourse and secondly, it reduces the opportunity to use these experiences to address issues of well-being and mental health.[13]

The issue is, however, where and how to locate this within legal education, to ensure recognition of well-being in terms of both academic but also professional development at this early stage of their legal careers.

The gaps

In England and Wales, as in other parts of the world, government policies and practices influence the direction of higher education, encouraging competition as much as quality improvement. This is evidenced through league tables, and progression data, as well as through the Research Excellence Framework (REF) and the Teaching Excellence Framework (TEF) grading.[14] The application of technology and pressures on lecturers to carry out organisational demands have begun to affect face-to-face student contact, which leads to a distance between student and teacher as well as content and context.[15] The outcome of this is that social learning and collegiality is eroded, and access to academic as well as professional language development and discourses, and professional identity formation, becomes tightly focused in bursts of teaching. Further, cost cutting and the centralisation of support services has increased the disconnection between staff, student and professional supports services in universities.[16]

Law schools feel the additional pressure of meeting sector expectations leading to fundamental changes to curriculum – seeking to balance institutional demands with improvements to teaching practice, more positive student learning experiences and exposure to practice-based education.[17] The quiet evolution of the degree has been led by the law subject benchmark,[18] but what is often left to the

12 Ibid. See also, Paula Baron, 'The Elephant in the Room? Lawyer Wellbeing and the Impact of Unethical Behaviours' (2015) 41 *Australian Feminist Law Journal* 87.

13 Paul Temple, 'What Has the Coalition Government Done for Higher Education?' (2015) 13 *London Review of Education* 174; Brendan Bartram, 'Student Support in Higher Education: Understandings, Implications and Challenges' (2009) 63 *Higher Education Quarterly* 308.

14 Justin Cruickshank, 'Putting Business at the Heart of Higher Education: On Neoliberal Interventionism and Audit Culture in UK Universities' (2016) 2(1) *Open Library of Humanities* 1.

15 Alina Ciobanu, 'The Role of Student Services in the Improving of Student Experience in Higher Education' (2013) 92 *Procedia – Social and Behavioral Sciences* 169; Gervas Huxley and Mike Peacey, 'Measuring Teaching Intensity: The Authors Respond to the Critics' (HEPI, 7 August 2017) <www.hepi.ac.uk/2017/08/07/4519/> accessed 7 May 2019.

16 Temple (n 13) 174; Bartram (n 13) 308.

17 The Law Society, *The Future of Legal Services* (The Law Society of England and Wales, 2016).

18 See Law subject benchmark at <www.qaa.ac.uk/quality-code/subject-benchmark-statements> accessed 7 May 2019.

hidden curriculum is the introduction of values, emotion and understanding.[19] The current cramped curriculum crowds out the potential of the hidden curriculum to introduce such values and attitudes.[20] There is clearly opportunity to support challenge and change in the content of legal education as well as the teaching approaches adopted.[21]

For legal education, which has a tradition of non-collaborative and content heavy learning, there is little scope for integrating mental health literacy. Collier rightly implies that how we teach needs to be refocused away from the adversarial and individualistic, moving towards a more collective, collaborative approach to resolving legal issues, reducing the need to add tension to already volatile situations.[22]

Reinforcing this, Hall suggests that 'It is the responsibility of legal educators to support student learning, to create constructive learning experiences, and to promote the development of positive personal and professional identities for students of law'.[23] In calling out legal educators in this way she indicates that there is a fundamental need to change the culture of suppression of feelings of stress which law students report.

Hall is echoing the time-honoured views of Wendell Holmes[24] and his challenge to legal educators to frame their teaching to ensure that students engage with more than case law. The comment that 'The life of law has not been logic: it has been experience,'[25] affirms that whilst there is a need for foundational knowledge, experience confirms that law is not a paper exercise, but real people with real problems who need real solutions. It is this authenticity of the law that provides an opening to engage students in understanding their world in its wider context and to explore their values, emotions and understanding.[26] In doing so

19 CLE programs introduce students to authentic client-based law, with some providers using this to support teaching of the LPC (see n 5). See also, for example, Chapters 8, 9 and 11 of this book.

20 Kate Bloch, 'Cognition and Star Trek(r): Learning and Legal Education' (2009) 42 *John Marshall Law Review* 959.

21 See for example, Robin Wellford Slocum, 'An Inconvenient Truth: The Need to Educate Emotionally Competent Lawyers' (2012) 45 *Creighton Law Review* 827; Colin James and Felicity Wardhaugh, 'Enhancing Emotional Competencies with Law Students' (2016) 23 *International Journal of Clinical Legal Education* 53; Maniam Kaliannan and Suseela Devi Chandran, 'Empowering Students Through Outcome-Based Education (OBE)' (2012) 87 *Research in Education* 50.

22 Collier (n 9) 41; Kate Galloway and Peter Jones, 'Guarding Our Identities: The Dilemma of Transformation in the Legal Academy' (2014) 14(1) *QUT Law Review* 15.

23 James Duffy, Rachael Field and Melinda Shirley, 'Engaging Law Students to Promote Psychological Health' (2011) 36(4) *Alternative Law Journal* 250; Kath Hall, 'Do We Really Want to Know – Recognising the Importance of Student Psychological Wellbeing in Australian Law Schools' (2009) 9(1) *Queensland University of Technology Law and Justice Journal* 1.

24 Oliver Wendell Holmes, 'Book Notices' (1880) 14 *American Law Review* 233.

25 Ibid 234.

26 See for example, the Junior Lawyers Division (n 10); Baron (n 12) 87.

one can hypothesise a concomitant support for student well-being and mental health which might better ready them for whatever career their future may hold.

Despite this, university recruitment and selection practices for lecturers often mean that practitioners with the capacity to share professional reflections are rarely recruited, unless for a role in a legal clinic.[27] This means that any exposure to an authentic voice of the profession is limited within law faculties, and access to valuable experience is lost.[28] The implication of this is that the lack of access to practitioners' experiences reduces student understanding of legal professional discourse, along with the opportunity to use these experiences to address issues of law student well-being and mental health.[29]

Clinical legal education (CLE)

This section explores CLE, its context within tertiary legal education and its relevance as a well-being supportive pedagogy.

In England and Wales, the development of CLE has been encouraged as a method to engage students in experiential legal learning. Interestingly, there is little evidence of legal practices providing direct support for CLE programs – such as a hospital trust might for trainee doctors or schools might for trainee teachers. Yet it is the legal profession that ostensibly has the most to gain from CLE; not just in terms of the way it contributes to the skill development of emergent lawyers, but also in relation to the potential benefits it offers in terms of making students aware of the importance of having strategies to manage the pressures of practice.

Where CLE in the UK differs from some jurisdictions is that its focus has initially been on the educational experience of the student. Clinic teaching is commonly based on small group or firm work, where a practitioner supports students' professionalisation whilst working with authentic legal matters. Clinics usually provide free services across a narrow range of practice areas. There are different models of CLE, but what is also increasingly evident is that cuts in legal aid funding will challenge CLE clinics to expand their services – in order to address the access to justice and service gap.

The implication here is that where students are faced with a more politicised approach to their work, this may influence not only what they do but the way in which they do it. This is an issue which has plagued CLE – is it a social service, should it replace legal aid, should it provide campaigning vehicles for reform, or is it simply somewhere that students can begin their professional identity formation and transformation to becoming a legal practitioner? CLE potentially has a part to play in fulfilling any or all of these purposes. A key issue is that whatever

27 Caroline Gibby, 'Constructing the Role of the Law Teacher in the Changing Context of Higher Education Policy and Practice' (Doctoral Thesis, Newcastle, 2018).

28 See (n 5).

29 Temple (n 13) 174; Bartram (n 13) 308.

the role of CLE, students will need access to support which recognises the high-risk nature to student well-being of this type of experiential learning.[30]

In CLE the lecturer/student relationship appears to enhance experiential legal education.[31] Unlike traditional law teaching, CLE addresses the application of the law to authentic situations. In doing so, the student is engaged in very different types of learning and teaching activities from the traditional subject-centred doctrinal teaching approaches found in most law schools. The law comes alive, and the practice of law is made real. Students are exposed to the complex layers of the real world application of the law, and become aware of the potential personal impact that this may have on their own emotional and cognitive development.[32] CLE is therefore high-risk, not only in pedagogic terms, but personally for all stakeholders – the client, the student and the educator/practitioner.

My way of teaching has always favoured the relational and contextual – solution focused but mindful of the client. Like many practitioner/lecturers, I consider that the law is there as a tool not an absolute, and that clients are not consistent and need to be listened to carefully. In practice we develop professional skills such as listening to, assessing and evaluating clients,[33] as well as evaluating the information they provide and how this relates to the law and possible solutions to their legal problems. The learning of such skills in practice takes time, learning from colleagues, clients and competitors. So, exposing students to such lessons through CLE opens up opportunities for educator/practitioners to share experiences, and highlight the importance of engagement with values, emotions and knowledge.

CLE programs are often designed, managed and delivered by practitioners – solicitors or barristers. The teaching approaches focus on a combination of centrally delivered professional conduct sessions, coupled with facilitative teaching by practitioners using small groups. This incorporates a narrative, and experiential approach to pedagogy – which in many cases practitioners develop without direct access to specific training. In this way, CLE provides a link to narrative and social learning, which focusses on discourse, collaboration and collective approaches to learning.

CLE is expensive to manage as the staff–student ratio is likely to be lower than traditional group-based teaching. However, it provides students with a potentially richer learning experience not only in relation to emotional intelligence but in terms of connecting with professional values in an immersive way. This

30 On this point, compare, for example, with medical health workers: Cameron Johnston, 'Medical Students Talk Openly About Their Mental Health Challenges' (2015) 18 *Canadian Medical Association Journal* 187. See also Janice Carello and Lisa D Butler, 'Potentially Perilous Pedagogies: Teaching Trauma Is Not the Same as Trauma-Informed Teaching' (2014) 15 *Journal of Trauma & Dissociation* 153.

31 Emma Jones, 'Connectivity, Confidentiality and Confidence: Key Issues in the Provision of Online Pro Bono Activities' (2018) 25 *International Journal of Clinical Legal Education* 48. See also Chapter 9 of this book.

32 Bloch (n 20) 959.

33 These are remarkably like the therapeutic competences within counselling; see ibid 962.

small group mechanism with a loosely defined curriculum provides opportunity to engage in what is understood as the hidden curriculum and so to develop sustainable practices which address key issues such as well-being, mental health and of course practice knowledge. Using the frame of the hidden curriculum, this chapter now turns to examine how values, emotions and understanding have become immersed within the pedagogy of CLE.

The hidden curriculum and well-being

Using the frame of the hidden curriculum, this section examines how values, emotions and understanding have become immersed within the pedagogy of CLE, thus creating opportunities to engage students in their own transformation,[34] and consequently addressing elements of student well-being.

Emotions: Emotional intelligence

Heath affirms that legal education is focused on academic and professional demands;[35] each place at its centre the law as a process. The implication is that these demands encourage a remoteness or disconnection between law, society and individuals. So, an emotionally distant, objective lawyer is perceived as more effective than a passionate socially aware lawyer.[36] However, feelings and connected emotions are now being recognised as relevant for the development of professional identity and resilience which are understood as necessary characteristics for survival within the profession.[37] Sommerlad indicates that the reality of practice has been substantially impacted by the pressures of the neoliberal 'turn'. Coping with these pressures demands a range of skills which doctrinal or even socio-legal teaching may not support.[38] Montgomery suggests that students should develop

> a set of emotional competencies involving self-awareness of emotions, empathetic awareness of the emotions of others, and the ability to use this awareness to influence the behaviour of others.[39]

34 Donald Nicholson, 'Making Lawyers Moral: Ethical Codes and Moral Character' (2005) 25 *Legal Studies* 601; Gold (n 7).

35 Mary Heath et al., 'Learning to Feel Like a Lawyer: Law Teachers, Sessional Teaching and Emotional Labour in Legal Education' (2017) 26 *Griffith Law Review* 430.

36 Ibid 430.

37 Chalen Westaby, 'A Qualitative Study of the Impact of Law Clinics on Students' Perceptions of Emotional Labour Expectations' (2014) 48 *The Law Teacher* 248.

38 Hilary Sommerlad, 'Researching and Theorizing the Processes of Professional Identity Formation' (2007) 34 *Journal of Law and Society* 190; Collier (n 9) 41.

39 John Montgomery, 'Incorporating Emotional Intelligence Concepts into Legal Education: Strengthening the Professionalism of Law Students' (2008) 39 *University of Toledo Law Review* 323, 326.

Students in clinics encounter experiential practices, problem-based learning and simulation, where they are encouraged to develop these emotional competencies.[40] Teaching in a supportive social learning environment encourages students to reach a deeper level of understanding of themselves, of the law and also potentially of their client. In doing so the power relationship between content and context is likely to change for the student, with greater ownership of how they learn being afforded to the student. This facilitative approach provides a learning culture which encourages personal and professional student transformation. However, what is evident is that these competencies alone do not provide a mechanism for individuals to balance the range of feelings that a lawyer may face with the diverse challenging situations that arise in practice.

Empathy

Gerarda Brown makes a persuasive argument that empathy in all its guises can be integrated with cognition, thereby providing a persuasive perspective as to why lawyers should approach clients and their issues with a caring attitude.[41] Empathy in this sense in the CLE context has two levels: firstly, where the student mirrors the client language providing acknowledgement, affirmation and resonance for the client and secondly, more challenging, where the student stands in the shoes of the client seeking to understand what the client feels. In many cases practitioners may aspire to the latter, but in practice what may occur is the former.

For students, with a notional age of 20 in many cases, asking them to reach this latter level of depth of empathy may be too much to expect, but talking about and exploring the case, along with the student's experience of it, is key to the CLE teacher's role. Where students understand the importance of navigating the clients' emotions they reflect on their interviewing and advice-giving techniques.

The combination of emotion and knowledge helps to build the students' capacity to understand and manage the feelings of others as well as their own feelings.[42] These important professional as well as personal skills inevitably place pressures on students' emotional intelligence – a pressure which is not easily measured or managed within the curriculum or indeed in the legal environment. Such experiences in CLE can awaken concerns or issues within students which may require support. As elements of the neoliberal university – such as a rise in student numbers and a reduction in support staff numbers – increase their impact, law lecturers may find that time is squeezed between research, wider university obligations and developing curricula and teaching practices, thus potentially reducing their

40 Ibid 326; Chalen Westaby and Emma Jones, 'Empathy: An Essential Element of Legal Practice or "Never the Twain Shall Meet"?' (2018) 25 *International Journal of the Legal Profession* 107.

41 Jennifer Gerarda Brown, 'Empowering Students to Create and Claim Value Through the Thomas Kilmann Conflict Mode Instrument' (2012) 28 *Negotiation Journal* 79.

42 Heath et al. (n 35) 433.

capacity to support students appropriately. As the demands of tertiary institutions grow, it becomes less possible to get to know students. As a result, in CLE where non-didactic discourse is powerful, the social aspect of learning is curtailed.

Cognition/understanding

Learning, knowledge and understanding are vital cogs in any tertiary level degree. Law school learning environments place significant demands on students and lecturers to embrace strategies that encourage active and deep learning. Legal pedagogy is multidimensional, and it is beyond the scope of this chapter to examine all its elements here. However, it is evident that how we teach students is often affected by our own learning approach, institutional expectations and disciplinary traditions. Law, unlike English, history or geography or indeed pure sciences, has been significantly influenced by government policy and professional expectations.[43]

Cognition expects that students' learning becomes part of them – as Bonwell and Eison have indicated, learning is not a spectator sport.[44] Increasingly what is evident is that lecturers are encouraged to seek different methods of assessing just what learning has gone on. In so doing they are aware that learning can no longer be teacher led, but opportunities to develop these approaches are often limited by time or capacity.

The segregation of legal subject disciplines and their infrequent inter-connection results in students often siloing their knowledge without being encouraged to consider that legal problems commonly have multiple, complex layers.[45] Therefore, to provide opportunities for students to understand the complexity of law, narrative pedagogies have developed to support a more contextual approach to learning.[46] Such approaches use constructivist methods of teaching – which recognise that students do not come to law school as a blank slate, not only in terms of how they learn, but also in terms of their understanding and expectations of their legal education.[47] So, students may believe that all that they need to be able to do is to argue, have a prodigious memory and be determined, when in fact far more may be expected of them in terms of being active participants in their own learning experience, particularly in the CLE context.

43 William Twining, 'Professionalism in Legal Education' (2011) 18 *International Journal of the Legal Profession* 165.

44 Charles C Bonwell and James A Eison, *Active Learning: Creating Excitement in the Classroom* (ASHE-ERIC HigherEducation Report No 1, 1991).

45 Paul Maharg, 'Convergence and Fragmentation: Legal Research, Legal Informatics and Legal Education' (2014) 5(3) *European Journal of Law and Technology* 2.

46 Such as problem-based learning, simulation, active learning and clinical legal education.

47 Lee Shulman, 'Knowledge and Teaching: Foundations of the New Reform' (1987) 57 *Harvard Educational Review* 1.

Values

Turning now to consider the relevance of values within the hidden law curriculum: this has been variously defined as phronesis[48] or practical wisdom, ethical conduct,[49] professionalism,[50] and professional values.[51] As indicated earlier, teaching in CLE is often based on a small group, mentoring method which encourages an immersive approach to absorbing such values. In some cases, this may create tensions and expectations of performance that students used to traditional teaching practices – and who seek a 'right' answer – may find hard to navigate.

As lecturers of doctrinal subjects, there is little obvious opportunity to find space in an already crowded knowledge-based curriculum to share and explore values in the wider sense. Indeed, it is interesting that in terms of curriculum order the knowledge-based, core subjects are taught to students mostly in the first two years of the degree. As a result, students are inculcated by the teaching subtext of knowledge rather than criticality, acceptance rather than questioning the reasoning behind the law, or the values that constitute its foundations.

The Aristotelian adage 'law is reason, free from passion'[52] is often relied on to support an expectation of objectivity within legal education. Creativity, dealing with different layers of the law and questioning the law which go beyond knowledge, may not be delivered easily within a curriculum without context. The implication for students is that they may find that knowledge is prized more than the exploration of the nature of values which lie within the law.

Therefore, the use of CLE to unpack the values which lie within the law, not only for the students as law students, but also for them as emergent lawyers forming their professional identity, creates different learning environments for developing the threshold concept of thinking like a lawyer.[53] James and Wardhaugh suggest that 'well-developed self-awareness and the kind of good communication skills that require emotional capacities'[54] are expected by practitioners. Silver also argues that 'legal education should prepare students for the emotional dimension of law'.[55] Learning and teaching practice in the context of CLE has a role to play in ensuring that this occurs by exposing students to issues of how understanding

48 Nicholson (n 34).

49 Graham Ferris, 'Values Ethics and Legal Ethics: The QLD and LETR Recommendations 6, 7, 10, and 11' (2014) 48 *The Law Teacher* 20.

50 David M Moss, 'The Hidden Curriculum of Legal Education: Toward a Holistic Model for Reform (Symposium)' (2013) *Journal of Dispute Resolution* 19.

51 Linda A McGuire and Julie Phye, 'The Hidden Curriculum in Medical and Law Schools: A Role for Student Affairs Professionals' (2006) *New Directions for Student Services* 59.

52 Aristotle, Politika III.

53 James and Wardhaugh (n 21) 36. See also Rachael Field and Jan HF Meyer, 'Threshold Concepts in Law: A Key Future Direction for Intentional Curriculum Reform to Support Law Student Learning Success and Well-Being' in Emma Jones and Fiona Cownie (eds), *Future Directions in Legal Education* (Routledge, forthcoming).

54 James and Wardhaugh (n 21) 38.

55 Marjorie A Silver, 'Emotional Intelligence and Legal Education' (1999) 5 *Psychology, Public Policy and Law* 1173.

the values inherent in the law can support the development of a positive professional identity.

Teaching developments

As indicated at the outset of this chapter, the neoliberal university creates significant challenges for law lecturers and their role which affect their capacity to research, as well as develop new and contextual curricula.[56] Further, the centralising approach to student services within tertiary legal education often means that the connection between lecturer and student is diluted and the relationship is reframed to meet the exigencies of organisational practice. Therefore, opportunities to reach out to students, and to support their well-being is perhaps determined more by exception than as a rule.

The disjunction between what teachers feel they need to do, and what they have the capacity to do in reality, in terms of student support and innovative curriculum design, is challenging.[57] Whilst student support is taken seriously, it may not always be enacted adequately or integrated within the curriculum. As a result, there needs to be more effective communication between student support and teaching teams. Law lecturers also need to feel confident that they can develop a curriculum where student well-being and mental health is as intrinsic as introducing students to knowledge and critical thinking. To support this, teacher learning and understanding of new methods of teaching, such as those used in CLE which encourage collaboration and collective approaches to learning, is vital.

Conclusion

Law and legal practice are about people and this means that lawyers inevitably have to deal with emotions, as Chandler rightly identifies 'these may be their own and others'.[58] As indicated earlier, there is increasing recognition that the legal services sector at large, and the profession in particular, struggle in dealing with issues of mental health and well-being for practitioners. The CLE environment reflects similar challenges that other disciplines such as medicine, health care and social work also face, but perhaps with fewer of the support mechanisms or overt curricula engagement that help to develop the necessary well-being characteristics in those other disciplines.[59] Reliance on individual practitioners to nurture these skill-sets within themselves is problematic.

56 See Heath et al. (n 35).

57 Ibid.

58 Sara Chandler, 'Can Litigators Let Go? The Role of Practitioner Supervisors in Clinical Legal Education Programmes' in Paul Maharg and Caroline Maughan (eds), *Affect and Legal Education: Emotion in Learning and Teaching the Law* (Ashgate, 2011) 88.

59 Andrew Grant et al., *Identifying Good Practice Among Medical Schools in the Support of Students with Mental Health Concern* (General Medical Council, 2013).

However, there are more fundamental problems which need to be addressed within law schools, and higher education more broadly. Firstly, inadequate overt teaching of the hidden curriculum places too much reliance on law students as independent learners to acquire the relevant skills and attitudes and this places all the well-being and mental health eggs in a single basket. To avoid this, we can learn from other professions which develop a more cohesive attitude to supporting student well-being by improving wider discourse around the relevant issues through intentional curriculum design and experiential learning methods. Secondly, by building proactive reflective sessions into teaching and learning activities in the core curriculum students may become more confident with understanding, rather than judging, themselves when faced with critical incidents. Everything that can be done at law school, including positive CLE approaches in the curriculum, to support and develop resilience for law students is now more pressing than ever.

11 Resilience, positive motivation and professional identity

The experience of law clinic students working with real clients

Nigel Duncan

On the Bar Professional Training Course (BPTC) taught at City, University of London, students may choose options which require them to work with real clients. This exposes them at an early stage in their progress towards full professional status to challenging experiences as they interact with clients, opponents and judges. This chapter presents findings from a research program that explores their experiences and perceptions of their development and the factors that influence their achieving creative and constructive responses. It explores students' views as to how they might best develop the skills of effective practitioners and the personal insights that will help them to enhance their resilience without losing their capacity for empathy as they develop their professional identity.

The three clinical options on the BPTC

The BPTC is the one-year vocational course authorised by the Bar Standards Board for the training of barristers between their undergraduate degree and their work experience (pupillage).[1] City Law School (CLS) introduced a live clinic option in 1992, the first such module on a professional course in the UK.[2] This, the FRU (Free Representation Unit) (Employment) Option, has since been joined by the Domestic Violence and the FRU (Social Security) Option. The three options operate in slightly different ways.

FRU (employment) option

This option operates in conjunction with the Free Representation Unit (FRU), a charity that provides free representation to clients in employment and social security tribunals.[3] Students attend a training day organised by FRU and complete a test. If they pass the test they may then apply for the option. CLS provides them

1 Details are at <https://www.barstandardsboard.org.uk/qualifying-as-a-barrister/bar-training-requirements/> accessed 7 May 2019.

2 For an early report on this initiative see Nigel Duncan, 'On Your Feet in the Industrial Tribunal' (1996) 2 *Contemporary Issues in Law* 53.

3 Details of FRU and its work are at <www.thefru.org.uk/> accessed 7 May 2019.

with workshops in conference skills, in the emotional issues arising from working with clients and how they might develop their own empathic responses, and in technicalities such as calculating compensation. They may then take out a case.

Many cases settle, although most students have experience of advocacy at case management or procedural hearings. Some proceed to a full hearing and students on the option have won compensation of over £20,000 or a tribunal order of re-engagement for their clients. All will experience one or more client conferences, interactions with the tribunal and opponents, drafting of documents, and they may experience negotiation or various degrees of trial advocacy.

Students are required to undertake at least one case and are assessed on a file which contains two reports. One is the analytical report of their work on the case, evidenced by documentation including the case papers, attendance notes and their own plans and notes. The second report is a reflective report in which students critically consider their own learning from the option.

FRU (social security) option

This operates in much the same way as the FRU (Employment) option except that students are required to undertake at least two cases for submission, because social security cases tend to be factually less complex, and rarely involve cross-examination. Since cases do not settle students are guaranteed an advocacy experience although it differs in nature from that in employment cases.

Domestic violence option

This option is a similar mutually beneficial collaboration with an external organisation, in this case the National Centre for Domestic Violence (NCDV).[4] Students go through a similar process of training and application. Their work on this option involves acting as McKenzie Friends[5] in telephone conferences with clients who are the victims of domestic violence and who are usually seeking urgent injunctive relief. This is not an advisory task. Instead students take instructions from their client in order to draft witness statements and other documents. These will be checked by NCDV legal officers and the client before being submitted. As a result, training in conference skills is more developed. Students' attention is drawn to the problems faced by many victims of domestic violence, the chaotic lifestyles many have and the trauma of living with a coercive or violent partner. They are trained in addressing inconsistencies in stories, how to explore the client's account without suggesting the client is lying, and yet to recognise when what they are told indicates (for example) that children may be at risk. They may telephone or email supervisors for advice immediately after such a conference, or

4 Details of NCDV and its work are at <www.ncdv.org.uk/> accessed 7 May 2019.

5 McKenzie Friends advise clients in the preparation for, and during, a hearing. Judges sometimes permit them to advocate for their client.

indicate in the email that covers their draft witness statement that there are particular issues that concern them. It is then a matter for the experienced lawyers at NCDV to finalise the documents with the client.

Students are required to submit three cases for assessment. They submit a file with analytical and reflective components as with the two FRU options.

The research program

For the last three years I have conducted research into the experience of the students undertaking these options, approved by City, University of London's research ethics committee,[6] subject to the voluntary participation of students, and normal conditions as to explanations of the research, the anonymisation of participants and secure transcription and storage of data. The research in each year has taken the form of online surveys and one or more focus group meetings. However, the participants are far from being a random group. They are all postgraduate Bar students who have opted for an approach to learning that requires work with real clients. Each has chosen a significantly different option which may reflect prior interests and life experiences. Response rates have been reasonable, averaging some 50% of a small cohort of around 50 students, but this provides a self-selecting group. Therefore, I make no claim to statistical significance, especially as the goals of the research in each year shifted slightly. In the first year my main goal was to explore students' experience in order to identify areas where support could be improved, leading to changes in the information and the teaching and learning sessions provided. Student responses identified a variety of concerns, including some relating to the emotional impact of working with clients who were often in distressing circumstances, or working with aggressive opponents or challenging judges. Subsequent iterations of the survey therefore explored these areas in more depth and were informed by my reading of the research into self-determination theory (SDT). I used a thematic approach to the analysis, seeking insights into my research questions from student responses to the survey and to the focus group discussions. This chapter reports on the findings that relate in particular to students' experience of interactions with these others.

In presenting these findings I initially identify the nature of the challenging experiences students faced, in their own words where possible. Students are identified by gender, the chosen option (DV, Emp or SS) and the year of their experience. I then consider, informed by SDT, what this suggests in terms of the use of different learning approaches for the development of well-being and resilience as individuals develop their professional identity in transition from law students into legal practitioners.

6 Approval was obtained from City's Research Ethics Committee – Ref: LREC17002 – and the project was funded by a small grant from City's Centre for the Study of Legal Professional Practice.

Working with clients

Our students' clients sought their help at times of enormous stress and usually experienced feelings of helplessness in the face of their circumstances and the formality of the procedures that they had to use to seek a remedy. DV clients generally experienced violence from a partner in their homes and sought urgent relief in the form of a non-molestation order or an ouster order. Many Emp clients had lost their livelihoods, often putting the security of their homes in jeopardy. They generally felt that they had been treated unfairly by their employers and in some cases had faced discrimination. Most SS clients were challenging refusals of disability-related benefits. Their physical or mental suffering was exacerbated in many cases by facing extreme poverty where their disability made employment difficult or impossible to find. What was common across all three categories was living in a precarious world characterised by a lack of personal control and a feeling of injustice perpetuated by an unfeeling bureaucracy.

One student was concerned that the limited conference skills training had left him unprepared for his client conference:

> [I]t was particularly pronounced I think because of the particular client I had in my first case. She suffered from schizophrenia and heard voices. That was their primary medical condition. I got into the conference with her and about 20 minutes in, with me having written three pages worth of questions I was going to go through with her really pressing the details on various points. She basically stood up and said 'I don't want to do this anymore. I'm going to go'.
>
> At first, I was worried that I'd sort of said something to offend her or done something wrong. It transpired that she was actually hearing voices during the conference and she just didn't feel comfortable staying in the room. So we rescheduled it. . . . Same thing ultimately happened but I was so intent on being able to represent her and trying to take the most basic instructions I possibly could from her in order to be able to represent her that in effect I came very close to leading and coaching her in that second conference just to get to the point of being able to continue the case. And at the time that felt like the most pragmatic and sensible thing to do but actually now having studied conference skills I realise it was a borderline unethical thing to do.
>
> (M1, SS, 18)

All lawyers recognise that they sometimes encounter clients who are not entirely truthful. The ethical rules are clear: they are required to present their client's case regardless of their personal beliefs as to its accuracy. However, if they notice discrepancies, they owe a duty to their client to draw their attention to them in conference. This could be a significant source of stress. One DV student was told a variety of things by her client that did not seem to fit together. She paused the conference and drew up a chronology.

> I was basically going to have to say to her, 'I understand it's very difficult talking about your children being abused but your account doesn't make

> sense. The judge is going to look at this and instantly go, "This doesn't add up. What happened where?" ' And also, in the back of my head, I'm thinking the local authority is going to get an interim care order review. If this is the witness statement, they're going to see that's going to be disclosed to them, they're going to go, 'Her account is inconsistent,' and all the other evidence, they're probably going to go, 'She hasn't protected her children. She's potentially a risk for having not protected them.' In which case, they'd probably be saying, 'Okay, we want an interim care order. We'll have all three of your children.' You're going, 'You need to get your account quite straight, otherwise, this could have quite serious implications if it doesn't already.'
>
> (F1, DV, 16)[7]

This student is working through her understanding of ethical practice, but here appears to be struggling to combine providing sound professional advice with effectively and empathically communicating with a victim of domestic violence. Another student represented a SS client who appeared to be feigning a degree of disability he did not really suffer.

> [The client] showed up at tribunal looking like they were half dead. And I like ran a purely procedural argument on it because I didn't think the judges would believe that. And like I've confirmed with my client that it's the way his instructions were. Ran the procedural argument, won the procedural argument and walked out. And my client basically ran home well after that and it was actually kind of sickening to me because I mean you do the best for your client and like you have a duty to act in their best interest and to advocate for them. But I guess sometimes yeah. Sometimes philosophy and the academics of it sort of crash into the real world.
>
> (M2, SS, 18)

This student had clearly learnt from the study of professional ethics how to address the conflicting duties that can arise when advocating for a client whose account they mistrust. His reflection on his moral discomfort gave him greater confidence to direct the professional career he intended to pursue.

Working with opponents

The Employment Option involves the most clearly adversarial work. Early interactions with opposing solicitors were usually constructive and useful, helping students to develop an understanding of how the preliminary stages of litigation

7 This student is reporting in the focus group meeting what went through her mind at the time. In fact, in supervision, she had reported her concerns and had recognised that it was not her role to advise the client, but simply to explore the accuracy of the account while maintaining a trust relationship.

were meant to work. By contrast, others experienced opponents whose work was minimal, often late and of poor quality. This was a different learning experience altogether in that the problems caused by poor practice became evident when the matter came to the hearing. Students came to realise how thorough preparation, prompt response to tribunal directions and a willingness to consider settlement could save time and costs in the long run.

Students sometimes found themselves challenged by their professional opponents. This could be a positive experience:

> I think because the better your opponent I think it brings out sort of a better side of you – wakes you up a bit. I mean it scares you right in the beginning when you realize 'Oh man I have senior counsel like opposing me. . . .' That's something that you know you have to get over it because it's this guy's life right. And this actually means a lot to him because . . . from what my client was saying getting a good outcome was the difference between keeping a roof over his head and his family first.
>
> (M2, Emp, 18)

This student rose to the occasion and felt that he had grown from the experience. So did this student:

> And the source of stress being on my case an opponent who is perhaps the most aggressive person I've ever met in my life who threatened costs in every phone call and email. I understand it's probably a strategy, but you know from the perspective of never having done something like this before or thinking crap will my client get costs? Am I going to screw up here?
>
> (M1, Emp, 18)

Training had alerted students to opponents' tactics of threatening costs whether or not justified, while also needing to be cautious to alert clients to costs risks in appropriate cases.

Working with judges

Students' experience of judges was generally positive, but there were some exceptions. Here is the experience of one student in a Social Security tribunal.[8]

> After the judge has done the introductions and the immediate preliminaries he handed it to the doctor to ask questions who launched into a 30 to 40 minute barrage of interrogation almost of questions which went far beyond anything I've seen before both in terms of sort of tone and attitude and

8 These tribunals are generally constituted of three members, one a doctor, with another who is legally qualified and usually chairs the hearing.

> style of questioning. It's incredibly hostile and aggressive but also far beyond what she should have been asking about because she was asking effectively the claimant to try and justify the doctor's decisions and why she had been prescribed certain things. So it was a really awful situation for the claimant to bear. And somewhat surprisingly the claimant ultimately broke down completely. . . . She burst into tears. . . . And I tried to intervene a couple of times during the questioning to try and tame things a bit and bring it back. And the doctor had shut me down.
>
> (M1, SS, 18)

The client ran from the tribunal room and the judges told M1, SS, 18 to follow her to the waiting room. However,

> I basically stood firm and said 'No my client is a really vulnerable individual – this style of questioning has not been appropriate. We need to resolve this.' And I basically just made submissions on her behalf in the room. God knows whether I did the right thing procedurally but ultimately it worked out. The judge said okay fine we'll have a quick discussion and then they agreed without having to reconvene – they agreed to grant the application.
>
> (M1, SS, 18)

This student was conscious of a lack of preparation by not knowing the extent to which he could challenge the panel. However, he showed great moral courage after his client had left and achieved the desired outcome. On further reflection of how the experience had changed how he would approach such situations in the future he said: 'I probably would be more forceful in the tribunal' (M1, SS, 18). Had he done so he may have avoided the dilemma of leaving his client upset and unsupported in order to challenge the direction the tribunal was taking.

Resilience

If we are to prepare practitioners who will be able to sustain themselves, they will need to develop resilience[9] in the face of the challenges they will encounter. This concept is currently popular but should not be accepted uncritically. Many of the sources of damaging stress on clinic students and lawyers might themselves be addressed. Focusing on resilience risks individualising problems and placing the onus on the person who is facing the excessively stressful situation.[10] Employers are inclined to exploit individualistic solutions in order to avoid making structural

9 Psychologists have developed working definitions of resilience. For a useful overview see Sandra Prince-Embury, 'Review of Resilience Conceptual and Assessment Issues' in Sandra Prince-Embury and Donald H Safloske (eds), *Resilience Interventions for Youth in Diverse Populations* (Springer, 2014), 13. See also, for example, Chapters 10 and 13 of this book.

10 Christine Parker, 'The "Moral Panic" Over Psychological Wellbeing in the Legal Profession: A Personal or Political Ethical Response?' (2014) 37(3) *UNSW Law Journal* 1103, and in

or cultural change within the workplace as they may be concerned that it will affect their competitivity. We need to be alert to this and recognise that the need for resilience should in no way inhibit our challenging things that might be improved.[11] That said, it is in the nature of much professional work that people will have to engage with stressful situations and difficult encounters. It is therefore important to address resilience in a way that enhances the capacity of individuals to respond professionally to inevitable challenges while retaining a critical perspective on stressors which might be changed. This has been done with some success in the context of nursing continuing professional development. An intervention of six workshops with a group of nurses introduced to a participatory mentoring environment was shown to be effective both in developing personal resilience and making positive changes to the workplace.[12] There is limited evidence of this being addressed in the legal practice context.[13] Thus the experience of colleagues working in the medical context provides a valuable guide for legal continuing professional development. The context of a short optional module in a one-year professional program, however, does not allow for such a developed intervention. This, I suggest, is therefore a matter for regulators to require as an element of continuing professional development, as many stressors could, as suggested previously, be reduced or eliminated.

We did introduce changes as a result of the insights that our research gave us.

Interventions

In the light of the responses received in 2016 we introduced an early session on conference skills, initially focusing on practical matters and the ethics of client conferences with some discussion of the emotional issues that clients might bring to their conference and approaches to responding to those. This seems to have been effective (recognising the limited reliability of the small numbers surveyed). In 2016 only 45% of students felt that they had responded well to clients' emotional difficulties, but the following year this had risen to 79%. The percentage who felt they had responded badly dropped from 30% to 7%. Interestingly, in this context, the number who responded 'very well' actually fell (from 23% to 17%). This may have been because they had a greater awareness of the issue and were more critical of themselves, though this, inevitably, is speculation and with these small numbers has no broader significance.

---

the medical field, Caroline Barratt, 'Developing Resilience: The Role of Nurses, Healthcare Teams and Organisations' (2018) 33(8) *Nursing Standard* 43.

11 See, for example Dave Webster's blog, *Critiquing Discourses of Resilience* <https://davewebster.org/2017/05/14/a-contrary-view-critiquing-discourses-of-resilience-in-education/> accessed 7 May 2019.

12 Glenda MacDonald et al., 'A Work-Based Educational Intervention to Support the Development of Personal Resilience in Nurses and Midwives' (2012) 32(4) *Nurse Education Today* 378, 383.

13 A list of Australian responses as at 2014 can be found in Parker (n 10) at Appendix 2. These tend to focus on the individual rather than the structural, thus risking the criticism identified earlier.

Subsequently we have developed the conference skills session by adding a self-study module that helps students to understand the nature of empathy, techniques that they might practise and use to demonstrate empathy and how this relates to professional practice.[14]

Developing resilience

While it is clear that we should do what we can in terms of module and assessment design to minimise unnecessary stress on students, it remains the case that legal practice inherently carries stressors. How do we best help students to develop the necessary resilience? In one focus group the facilitator related an experience where, facing bullying from a student, her line manager had, in effect told her to 'toughen up'. Student responses included:

> You need to be resilient because I think that it's something that you might have to find within you and having someone tell you toughen up and be stronger, it's not really going to – it's such a horrid thing to tell someone. I would hate it.
>
> (F1, DV, 17)

> I think experience was what really helps you with this.
>
> (F1, SS, 17)

> I think what helped was that [supervisor] told us practical steps to take rather than tell us to be tough and to be resilient because those things would not have helped us. But taking these practical steps would be telling us how to do it.
>
> (F2, DV, 17)

Students recognised that resilience came, in part, from 'something within' them and saw the most effective way of helping them to develop resilience being to provide practical guidance and opportunities to develop competence through experience. This is what all professional development programs should be seeking to achieve and live clinical work is an important component of that process.

Research into student perceptions of resilience was undertaken with undergraduates studying several different disciplines.[15] Amongst the conclusions drawn is the proposition that:

- Resilience is about the individual, and the context in which they are operating:
    - **Internal factors**: optimism, control, dealing with change and uncertainty, dealing with failure, competence, self-care, goalsetting, expectations of self;

14 The essential elements of that module are presented in the Empathy section.

15 Lydia Bleasdale and Sarah Humphreys, *Undergraduate Resilience Research Project Report* (Leeds Institute for Teaching Excellence, 2018) <http://teachingexcellence.leeds.ac.uk/wp-content/uploads/2018/01/LITEbleasdalehumphreys_fullreport_online.pdf> accessed 7 May 2019.

- **External factors:** relationships (personal and professional), transitions, expectations, formal support, organisational processes, expectations of others.[16]

These factors suggest that in order to assist students to develop the necessary degree of resilience we may be assisted by self-determination theory.

Self-determination theory

SDT[17] has been used to develop understanding of the social environments that best support our individual well-being and development.[18] According to SDT there are three basic psychological needs which, if satisfied, will enhance intrinsic motivation: autonomy, competence and relatedness. Cognitive evaluation theory (CET) has been developed as a sub-theory by Ryan and Deci[19] and explains how the fulfilment of these three basic needs supports the maintenance of intrinsic motivation. Students would be described as intrinsically motivated where they have chosen activities 'that have the appeal of novelty, challenge or aesthetic value'.[20] Having intrinsic goals has been found to be positively associated with well-being and negatively associated with depression and anxiety.[21]

As Sheldon and Krieger explain, writing in the context of the well-being of law students,

> people need to feel that they are good at what they do or at least can become good at it (competence); that they are doing what they choose and want to be doing, that is, what they enjoy or at least believe in (autonomy); and that they are relating meaningfully to others in the process, that is, connecting with the selves of other people (relatedness).[22]

Students who are intrinsically motivated and have intrinsic goals will demonstrate greater resilience.

With this in mind, clinic students at City were asked about their motivation for choosing a clinic option. The strongest motivator was the desire to improve

16 Lydia Bleasdale, 'Undergraduate Resilience Research Project: University of Leeds' (17 November 2017, London & South East PFHEA Meeting).

17 For a fuller explanation, see earlier chapters of this volume.

18 Richard M Ryan and Edward L Deci, 'Self-Determination Theory and the Facilitation of Intrinsic Motivation, Social Development, and Well-Being' (2000) 55(1) *American Psychologist* 68.

19 Richard M Ryan and Edward L Deci, *Intrinsic Motivation and Self-Determination in Human Behaviour* (Plenum, 1985).

20 Deci and Ryan, (n 18) 71.

21 Tim Kasser and Richard M Ryan, 'Further Examining the American Dream: Differential Correlates of Intrinsic and Extrinsic Goals' (1996) 22 *Personality and Social Psychology Bulletin* 280.

22 Kennon M Sheldon and Lawrence S Krieger, 'Understanding the Negative Effects of Legal Education on Law Students: A Longitudinal Test of Self-Determination Theory' (2007) 33(6) *Personality and Social Psychology Bulletin* 883, 885.

competence. No student thought this unimportant or slightly important. The next most highly rated was 'to achieve justice for my clients', a powerful intrinsic motivator for the challenging work these students will be doing. Third comes communication skills – related to competence but introducing a recognition of the importance of relatedness: the ability to communicate with others. By contrast, the concept of working with others towards a goal received a relatively low rating. This may be because of the culture of the Bar, in which there is a real pride in independence. Before encountering the team-working realities of practice, students may not recognise the importance of effective collaboration. Indeed, the relatively high rating given to 'take decisions within a limited field of activity' is consistent with this perspective and shows some self-awareness of the importance of autonomy.

Two low-rated motivators may tell different stories. Participants may have assumed that down-rating 'Enhance my CV' was the 'correct answer' and given the answer they thought I wanted to hear. By contrast, the low rating given to 'understand myself better' was personally disappointing, given that these students had just submitted a reflective report as part of their assessment task.

Students were also asked about what motivated them in their actual work with clients. The three top-rated options (to 'please my client'; 'achieve justice' and 'win the case') may have been hard to distinguish. However, they were all clearly more highly rated than self-interested motivators. As one student observed:

> although my motivation for selecting the option was connected to my studies and my CV; when conducting actual work with clients, these (and the connected statements above) were completely unimportant to the conduct of my work. Once involved in a client's case, the motivation became about them – not born out of any self interest.
>
> (M, SS, 18)

However, one motivator, 'the freedom to make decisions', included to explore students' evaluation of autonomy, was relatively lowly rated. It divided opinion, with six students rating it 'extremely important' but nine rating it as 'unimportant' or 'slightly important'. One student explained:

> I tend to be motivated by a desire to do my best rather than please the client. Often by doing my best for a client, this will result in my pleasing them, but sometimes I have to provide them with bad news and the case may not go well for them. I am very competitive, hence why my main motivators are winning, achieving justice and making my own decisions – each of which this module enabled me to achieve.
>
> (F, Emp, 18)

This led me to think that the three psychological needs (competence, autonomy and relatedness) identified in Self-Determination Theory, do not work in a hierarchy but are better thought of as interacting factors, all of which are significant, but which different individuals may prioritise differently. Discussions in one focus group tended to confirm this. Students were introduced to SDT and asked their thoughts about the three needs. One quickly suggested that for her, relatedness was the most important.

> I think [relatedness] is more important for me than the others. . . . Because I think what really drives me is helping others and I think . . . being competent feeds into [relatedness] for me. So, being competent is very necessary, being good at something is necessary in order to help people better.
>
> (F1, DV, 17)

This raised an immediate response:

> I think competence is the most important thing because especially with the Bar, you need to know your stuff otherwise you're going to get terrible barristers, so I think competency is the main thing and autonomy as well because it's a self-employed profession. And I'm someone that's always enjoyed working independently. . . . And meaningful relationships I think that is a less important thing.
>
> (F, SS, 17)

This student also explained how she had hated group work at university, where others took the credit for her hard work. She added:

> This is why I want to be a barrister because . . . if I do something badly, I should suffer the consequences; if I do something well, I should have all the consequences.
>
> (F, SS, 17)

Students then discussed their experiences of barristers they had known who had succeeded or failed to relate openly to them even when undertaking demanding work.

> I bumped into a barrister yesterday who I did my very first mini-pupillage with. . . . it was really bizarre, because he was busy, you know he was about to go into court. But he couldn't just say, 'Oh okay, good to see you.' He can't really sort of stop for five seconds and I see other barristers who are brilliant and just switching just like, they'll say something, really communicate with you, and then get on with what they do. . . . Those are the ones I aspire to be.
>
> (F2, DV, 17)

Further discussion addressed the interaction between autonomy and relatedness.

> I'd complicate that autonomy element. I think it's kind of a balance of autonomy and then working with other people.[23] I think that's the agenda, sort of unfettered autonomy is – (interrupted)
>
> (M, SS, 17)

23 This suggests that this student had misunderstood the concept of autonomy to mean working alone. However, his observation and the ensuing discussion do raise insights into students' perceptions as to how the elements of SDT interact.

> So, autonomy needs to be balanced with a meaningful relatedness. You can't just be autonomous on your own. Yeah, there should be a sort of balance on those and then the other things that you were saying and things like empathy also would feed into those things and also would be influenced by those things.
>
> (F, SS, 17)

This, however, was getting too comfortable for M, SS, 17 who said:

> These are a bit motherhood and apple pie though. Of course, these are important – but sorry, to me 1) might be intellectual fulfilment, so 2) might be remuneration whether that's monetary or psychological or status in society. I think people are different in terms of what they look for. These three might be particularly common but there are other factors that people are looking for too.
>
> (M, SS, 17)

He may have been thinking of the three elements as motivators rather than needs.

The final student comment before the group had to finish was:

> I think for me relatedness or relationships that's particularly key. I think in general specifically at the Bar I always think one of the things that resonates with me is the sort of point how you can build your whole career, your reputation that you can lose in five seconds at the Bar. And once it's gone, you're not going to get it back but based on it, you can't be trusted perhaps.[24]
>
> (M, Emp, 17)

This student discussion tends to support the view that the three needs identified by SDT act together to encourage intrinsically motivated behaviours as opposed to operating in any hierarchy (even a hierarchy that differs between individuals). Of the three, relatedness was the one that produced more equivocal responses from students. As a result, we have introduced training designed to give students insight into the significance of empathy when working with clients and how it develops both their professionalism and their resilience.

Empathy

Students are first reminded that empathy is a professional responsibility: '[barristers] will know how and where to demonstrate empathy and act accordingly.'[25]

24 This is something of a trope at the Bar of England and Wales. It is a small profession and reputation is enormously significant if barristers are to be able to conduct negotiations or litigation effectively on behalf of their clients.

25 Bar Standards Board, *Professional Statement for Barristers*, Rule 3.4, <www.barstandardsboard.org.uk/media/1787559/bsb_professional_statement_and_competences_2016.pdf> accessed 7 May 2019.

They often confuse empathy with sympathy, so are given an explanation such as: 'Sympathy refers to the heightened awareness of another's plight as something to be alleviated. . . . Empathy . . . refers to the attempt of one's self-aware self to understand the subjective experiences of another self. . . . Empathy is a way of "knowing". Sympathy is a way of "relating" '.[26]

Two main types of empathy are generally recognised. Affective empathy is a spontaneous process which works more strongly with family, friends and people who share our background, culture or experiences. The firing of 'mirror neurons' partially activates the same emotion as observed in the other.[27] Cognitive empathy is the appraisal of another's emotional state or situation with focus, reflection and thought as key elements. It can lead us to act and respond in constructive ways. This is necessary for professional empathy which involves:

- Understanding the client's situation, perspective and feelings;
- Communicating that understanding and checking its accuracy;
- Acting on that understanding with the client in a helpful (professional) way.[28]

Research into the lawyer-client relationship suggests that this is key to client satisfaction. Cunningham found that client satisfaction is concerned more with the process than with the outcome of representation.[29] Research by the Law Society showed the importance of the client feeling listened to and respected: 'She talked to me, as a person, with respect'.[30] In order to ensure that clients know we are empathising we can use non-verbal behaviour such as nodding, eye contact, raised eyebrows, appropriate expressions and non-judgmental reactions. We can explore what the client has said with further questions and make verbal statements showing or describing what we have understood. In this way a client-centred interview should seek to do the following:

- Explore and clarify the client's perspective, circumstances and feelings;
- Listen to understand, using eye contact and mirroring body language;
- Recognise an empathic opportunity;
- Communicate genuine empathic understanding – ideally verbally as well as non-verbally (unconsciously);
- Act on that understanding in a professionally helpful way.[31]

26 Lauren Wispé, 'The Distinction Between Sympathy and Empathy: To Call Forth a Concept, a Word Is Needed' (1986) 50(2) *Journal of Personality and Social Psychology* 314, 318.

27 Vilayanur S Ramachandran, 'The Neurology of Self-Awareness' (2007) *The Edge* <www.edge.org/3rd_culture/ramachandran07/ramachandran07_index.html> accessed 7 May 2019.

28 Stewart W Mercer and William J Reynolds, 'Empathy and Quality of Care' (2002) 52 *British Journal of General Practice* S9–13.

29 Clark D Cunningham, 'What do Clients want from their Lawyers?' (2013) *Journal of Dispute Resolution* 143.

30 Hilary Sommerlad and David Wall, 'Legally Aided Clients and their Solicitors: Qualitative Perspectives on Quality and Legal Aid' The Law Society, *Research Study No 34*, 1999.

31 Mercer and Reynolds (n 28) 1; Eliska Prochazkova and Mariska E Kret, 'Connecting Minds and Sharing Emotions Through Mimicry: A Neurocognitive Model of Emotional

Developing this particular communication skill provides a better experience for the client and also helps the lawyer to understand the client's position better and enable more appropriate, better-focussed advice. There is also evidence that it can provide personal benefits as well. Researching the use of empathy by general medical practitioners, Roter discovered that increased expressions of empathy are associated with improvements in relationships and increased job satisfaction.[32] Working with a similar group of medical professionals, Krasner found that participating in a mindfulness program that addressed expressing empathy can protect against burnout.[33] Thus students and lawyers can, by providing a better, more empathetic service to clients, take more care of themselves while developing the resilience that they will need to practise effectively and with reduced risk of burnout. This is more the responsibility of employers and regulators than of individuals as it is hard for new entrants to challenge the culture of an existing organisation.[34]

Conclusion

Given the methodological limitations of this study, any conclusions must be tentative. Further research could seek a larger participant group by developing collaboration between law schools offering similar live client programs and explore the potential impact of variables such as age, gender, race, orientation or social background. Students' perceptions of their interactions could be verified (to a degree) by exploring how they came across to clients: whether they effectively demonstrated empathy and whether they appeared to be under stress.

For the present, findings suggest that we might take useful steps towards helping our students to maintain their intrinsic goals and motivation in the face of challenging interactions by combining a number of interventions. We clearly need to develop their competence, a matter that all our programs are designed to achieve. We can provide them with simulated learning experiences that progressively develop their competence, giving them safe spaces within which they may exercise a degree of agency without risk to themselves or clients. Once they have achieved a necessary level of competence (and under proper supervision) they may undertake work with real clients. They can be assisted in doing this if we introduce them to the value of, and the techniques that support the development of, professional empathy. This should become a key element of their professional identity if we encourage a reflective approach to their learning informed by an understanding of the value of intrinsic motivation and what might support it.

Contagion' (2017) 80 *Neuroscience & Biobehavioral Reviews* 99. In the context of legal education and practice see Chalen Westaby and Emma Jones, 'Empathy an Essential Element of Legal Practice or "Never the Twain Shall Meet"?' (2018) 25(1) *International Journal of the Legal Profession* 107.

32 Debra L Roter et al., 'Communication Patterns of Primary Care Physicians' (1997) 277(4) *Journal of the American Medical Association* 350.

33 Michael S Krasner et al., 'Association of an Educational Program in Mindful Communication with Burnout, Empathy, and Attitudes Among Primary Care Physicians' (2009) 302(12) *Journal of the American Medical Association* 1284.

34 See Richard Moorhead, Steven Vaughan and Cristina Godinho, *In-House Lawyers' Ethics: Institutional Logics, Legal Risk and the Tournament of Influence* (Hart, 2018).

12 Meditation in legal education

The value added toward the well-being of law students

Anthony Cullen and Lughaidh Kerin

Introduction

This chapter will consider the potential value that meditation adds to legal education. It will begin by defining what meditation consists of as a contemplative practice. It will then explore the introduction of meditation in law schools and review the rationale for its use in this context. Next, the chapter will focus on the potential for meditation to develop student resilience. In light of the beneficial effects for resilience and the enhancement of well-being more generally, broader institutional responsibility for issues of well-being are examined followed by the possibilities for further research on the efficacy of meditation. Overall, the chapter seeks to provide insight into the practice of meditation and to reflect on the potential value added to student well-being in the context of law student professional identity formation.

Defining meditation

A dictionary definition of the verb 'meditate' states that it is 'to focus your mind and free it of uncontrolled thoughts'.[1] To understand what meditation consists of as a contemplative practice, it is important to appreciate that it takes many different forms. Practices with a global following include transcendental meditation, loving-kindness meditation, vipassana meditation, mindfulness meditation and heartfulness meditation. Given the differences that exist between systems of meditation, there is no single comprehensive definition that would cover all. According to Daniel Goleman and Richard Davidson, '*Meditation* is a catch-all word for myriad varieties of contemplative practice, just as *sports* refers to a wide range of athletic activities. For both sports and meditation, the end results vary depending on what you actually do'.[2] The end results relevant to the enhancement of student well-being will be explored further in the sections that follow. For the purposes of understanding the function that meditation serves generally

1 Maurice Waite and Sara Hawker, *Oxford Paperback Dictionary & Thesaurus* (Oxford University Press, 3rd ed, 2009) 577.

2 Daniel Goleman and Richard Davidson, *The Science of Meditation: How to Change Your Brain, Mind and Body* (Penguin, 2017) 9. Emphasis in original.

for a practitioner, it is important to bear in mind that most systems of meditation involve the continued training of a person's attention – regulation of the mind on a particular point of focus or a concentrated state of general awareness.

The use of meditation in law schools

In recent years, the attention given to meditation in the context of legal education has grown exponentially. This has been most notably observed in US law schools and publications authored by law professors based in the United States. Although similar issues of law student well-being have been reported in the United Kingdom,[3] Australia,[4] and elsewhere,[5] the use of meditation does not appear to have received the same attention. In the United States, law schools making provision for students to engage in meditation include Harvard Law School,[6] Berkeley Law,[7] Columbia Law School,[8] University of Virginia School of Law,[9] the University of Miami School of Law,[10] the University of San Francisco School of Law,[11] and Stanford Law School.[12] As noted by Shailini George, 'Mindfulness meditation has begun appearing on law school curricula as well, sometimes as a

3 For the first mixed methods study on law student well-being from the UK see: Emma Jones, Samra Rajvinder and Lucassen Mathijs, 'The World at Their Fingertips? The Mental Wellbeing of Online Distance-Based Law Students' (2019) 53(1) *The Law Teacher* 49. Jones et al. note that '[i]n the UK, the issue of law student wellbeing has only recently been acknowledged and hence there is relatively little published work on this topic': ibid 55. See also, Caroline Strevens and Clare Wilson, 'Law Student Wellbeing in the UK: A Call for Curriculum Intervention' (2016) 11 *Journal of Commonwealth Law and Legal Education* 44.

4 See generally: Rachael Field, James Duffy and Colin James (eds), *Promoting Law Student and Lawyer Well-Being in Australia and Beyond* (Routledge, 2016).

5 Shivan Chimnan, 'In Law Schools, a Case of Mental Health: On Campus, Suicide Has Become the Leading Cause of Death Among India's Youth' (12 March 2018) <www.newslaundry.com/2018/03/12/law-schools-india-students-mental-health-counselling> accessed 7 May 2019.

6 See <http://hls.harvard.edu/meditation-and-mindfulness/> accessed 7 May 2019.

7 See <www.law.berkeley.edu/students/mindfulness-at-berkeley-law/> accessed 7 May 2019.

8 See <www.law.columbia.edu/events/cls-weekly-mindful-meditation> accessed 7 May 2019.

9 See <http://libguides.law.virginia.edu/mindfulness> accessed 7 May 2019. See also the incorporation of contemplative practices including meditation into Seminars in Ethical Values delivered in the fall of 2015 by Michael Livermore: <https://content.law.virginia.edu/past-courses/view/115819862> accessed 7 May 2019. See also Kristin Glover, 'Mindfulness in Law Schools and Legal Practice' (2015) 64 *Virginia Lawyer* 47.

10 See <www.law.miami.edu/academics/mindfulness-in-law-program> accessed 7 May 2019. See also, Scott Rogers, 'The Mindful Law School: An Integrative Approach to Transforming Legal Education' (2012) 28 *Touro Law Review* 1189.

11 Karmah Elmusa, 'Law Schools Teach the Practice of Meditation' (2013) *California Lawyer* (June) <http://ww2.callawyer.com/clstory.cfm?eid=929087&wteid=929087_Law_Schools_Teach_the_Practice_of_Meditation> accessed 7 May 2019. See also the profile page of Rhonda Magee, 'a teacher of mindfulness-based stress reduction interventions for lawyers, law students, and for minimizing social-identity-based bias' <www.usfca.edu/law/faculty/rhonda-magee> accessed 7 May 2019.

12 See <https://law.stanford.edu/event/mindfulness-meditation-law-students/> accessed 7 May 2019.

course on its own or often as part of another course'.[13] Interest in the area has been fuelled by concerns about mental health of law students and the detrimental effect that the study of law has on student well-being. Teresa Brostoff states that:

> Research, statistical, and anecdotal data have established that the study and practice of law are stressful. Until recently, stress has been considered part of the law learning and practice experience without regard to the damage that such stress can inflict. Now, many commentators and researchers have documented the detrimental effects of the stress endured by students in law schools. Further, some say that stress can be almost universal among law students in varying degrees, and that stress increases as lawyers enter the practice of law. Law students seem to grow less happy as they proceed through law school.[14]

Likewise, Peter Huang comments that:

> Empirical evidence finds that law schools do not select unhappy students. Yet within the first semester of law school, many students report feeling adrift, anxious, apathetic, cynical, dejected, disaffected, disheartened, disillusioned, dispirited, frustrated, irritable, isolated, jaded, lost, overwhelmed, overworked, stressed, unhappy, and withdrawn.[15]

In the context of such concerns for student well-being, the rationale commonly employed for the use of meditation in law schools concerns the management of stress. Katerina Lewinbuk states that:

> High levels of stress can distract students from their studies and disrupt the processing of information. It can also leave them unable to connect and empathize with others and, in turn, hinder personal and professional relationships. In the end, the tremendous demands of legal studies and the profession can take away from the lawyer's mission and personal satisfaction.
>
> In an effort to improve the experience, law schools should arm students with the ability to care for their minds and well-being and reduce stress so they can obtain practice-ready legal skills while maintaining a healthy – or at least a semi-healthy – emotional balance.[16]

13 Shailini George, 'The Cure for the Distracted Mind: Why Law Schools Should Teach Mindfulness' (2015) 53 *Duquesne Law Review* 215, 242.

14 Teresa Brostoff, 'Meditation for Law Students: Mindfulness Practice as Experiential Learning' (2017) 41 *Law and Psychology Review* 157, 157.

15 Peter Huang, 'Adventures in Higher Education, Happiness, and Mindfulness' (2018) 7(2) *British Journal of American Legal Studies* 425.

16 Katerina Lewinbuk, 'Mindfulness Meditation: Is the Practice a Saving Grace for Law Students' (2015) 78(6) *Texas Bar Journal* 454, 454.

As unhealthy levels of stress impact on all aspects of student experience,[17] it is clear that measures that effectively address the issue have the potential to strengthen institutional metrics of student satisfaction, retention, progression, and achievement. Although student well-being is recognisable as an intrinsically worthwhile end in itself, there are other reasons why law schools make programs of meditation available to students. It is arguable that emotionally balanced, resilient students make better lawyers. Such students are better placed to succeed in the study of law and are psychologically more prepared to cope with the demands of legal practice.[18] In light of his experience of Miami Law's Mindfulness in Law Program, Scott Rogers highlights the function that initiatives incorporating meditation can potentially serve in addressing issues of well-being and equipping students for the practice of law:

> As the prevalence of anxiety, depression, and suicide ideation among law students continues to exceed not only levels found in the general population, but also among students in other demanding graduate programs, law schools are recognizing their crucial role in providing students with services that help them relate more effectively to the high stress conditions in which they study, and that they will encounter as practitioners. Importantly, while mindfulness is often regarded as a method of stress reduction; it is, in fact, a practice rooted in the concentration of attention, the skillful treatment of agitated emotions, and the cultivation of compassion, all of which are fundamental skills for the study and practice of law.[19]

In addition to constituting a method of stress reduction, there is evidence to suggest that the practice of meditation enhances resilience.[20] Recognised as one

17 *Mosby's Pocket Dictionary of Medicine, Nursing and Health Professions* defines 'stress' as follows: 'any emotional, physical, social, economic, or other factor that requires a response or change. Stress can be positive or negative. Ongoing chronic stress can result in physical illness.' See Marie O'Toole (ed), *Mosby's Pocket Dictionary of Medicine, Nursing and Health Professions* (Elsevier, 7th ed, 2014) 1277. See also Chris Brooker (ed), *Mosby's Dictionary of Medicine, Nursing & Health Professions* (Elsevier, UK ed, 2010) 741; Harvey Marcovitch, *Black's Medical Dictionary* (A & C Black Publishers, 42nd ed, 2010) 632.

18 Rachel Van Cleave, 'Future of the Legal Profession' in *Daily Journal* (7 May 2013) <http://digitalcommons.law.ggu.edu/pubs/569> accessed 7 May 2019).

19 Rogers (n 10) 1189–1190.

20 Brian Rees, 'Overview of Outcome Data of Potential Meditation Training for Soldier Resilience' (2011) 176 *Military Medicine* 1232; Emma Seppala, et al., 'Loving-Kindness Meditation: A Tool to Improve Healthcare Provider Compassion, Resilience, and Patient Care' (2014) 1 *Journal of Compassionate Health Care* 5; Jayaram Thimmapuram et al, 'Effect of Heartfulness Meditation on Burnout, Emotional Wellness, and Telomere Length in Health Care Professionals' (2017) 7 *Journal of Community Hospital Internal Medicine Perspectives* 21; Holly Rogers, 'Mindfulness Meditation for Increasing Resilience in College Students' (2013) 43 *Psychiatric Annals* 545, 546.

of the attributes necessary for a career at the bar,[21] resilience is an essential prerequisite for the sustainability of a career in legal practice. The section that follows examines research on meditation being utilised as a means of developing resilience, reducing instances of psychological ill-health and burnout.

Development of student resilience

Reflecting the capacity to cope and recover quickly from setbacks,[22] resilience is closely connected with the mental health and overall well-being of students. However, Holly Rogers, a Staff Psychiatrist and Clinical Associate at Duke University, notes:

> The focus on resilience as a key aspect of mental health is relatively new. As the pendulum has swung away from an emphasis on what constitutes mental illness towards focusing instead on what constitutes mental health, it has become increasingly clear that resilience is a key component of mental health.[23]

The use of meditation as a means of enhancing resilience has been the subject of a number of studies. In the context of soldier training, Colonel Brian Rees, a former US Army Medical Corps Officer, produced a study for the journal *Military Medicine* in 2011 exploring different ways of making soldiers more resilient. Following a survey of research focusing on different domains of resilience – including physical, emotional, social, and family life – he concluded transcendental meditation, mindfulness, and progressive muscle relaxation to be the most suitable potential options for improving soldier resilience.[24]

In the context of heath care, another study assessed the benefits of loving-kindness meditation to those involved in the provision of care for patients. Noting that 'the

21 For example, see UK Bar Council, *Professional Statement for Barristers: Incorporating the Threshold Standard and Competencies* (Bar Standards Board, September 2016) 12, para 1.18.

22 There is no one authoritative definition of what resilience consists of as matter of general human psychology. Alex Zautra, John Hall and Kate Murray note that '[a]cross research and practice, there has been considerable debate over the definition and operationalization of resilience': Alex Zautra, John Hall and Kate Murray, 'Resilience: A New Definition of Health for People and Communities' in John Reich, Alex Zautra and John Stuart (eds), *Handbook of Adult Resilience* (Guilford Press, 2010) 3–29, 4. Zautra, Hall and Murray define resilience as 'an outcome of successful adaptation to adversary': ibid. For Ann Masten, Karin Best and Norman Garmezy, resilience refers to 'the process of, capacity for, or outcome of successful adaptation despite challenging or threatening circumstances': Ann Masten, Karin Best and Norman Garmezy, 'Resilience and Development: Contributions from the Study of Children Who Overcome Adversity' (1990) 2 *Development and Psychopathology* 425, 426. In the context of the legal profession, resilience may be characterised as the ability to cope with the demands of legal practice in a sustainable way, with mistakes and setbacks serving to strengthen rather than to undermine an individual's professional and personal development. See also Chapter 13 of this book.

23 Rogers (n 20) 546.

24 Rees (n 20) 1232.

consequence of stress increased provider burnout and decreased quality of care for patients', the study sought to address the question of 'what practical steps can be taken to increase compassion, thereby benefitting both provider well-being and patient care'.[25] The research examined the effectiveness of short, ten-minute sessions of loving-kindness meditation. At Stanford University, 134 undergraduate students participated in the study. The findings, published in the *Journal of Compassionate Health Care* in 2014, suggested that loving-kindness meditation could provide 'a viable, practical, and time-effective solution for preventing burnout and promoting resilience in healthcare providers and for improving quality of care in patients'.[26]

A further study assessed 'the effects of a 12-week "Heartfulness Meditation" program on burnout, emotional wellness, and telomere length in residents, faculty members, and nurses at a large community teaching hospital' in York, Pennsylvania.[27] After 12 weeks of regular meditation, the study found a statistically significant improvement with regard to indicators of burnout and emotional wellness. It concluded: 'results indicate that meditation offers an accessible and efficient method by which physician and nurse burnout can be ameliorated and wellness can be enhanced'.[28]

Other studies have focused on the use of mindfulness meditation.[29] In an article titled 'Mindfulness Meditation for Increasing Resilience in College Students' for *Psychiatric Annals*, Holly Rogers reasoned:

> Mindfulness, the ability to focus one's attention on his or her present-moment experience, releasing worries about the future and regrets about

25 Seppala et al. (n 20).

26 Ibid.

27 'Telomeres are protective protein complexes at the end of chromosomes that promote chromosomal stability and protect chromosomes from cellular senescence. Telomere length influences overall longevity and telomere shortening is a hallmark of molecular aging. Psychological stress has been associated with accelerated telomere shortening in leukocytes, while meditation practices have shown to be associated with increased telomere length.' Thimmapuram et al. (n 20) 21, 22.

28 Thimmapuram et al. (n 20).

29 One of the most widely cited publications on the use of mindfulness meditation in this context is Leonard Riskin's, 'The Contemplative Lawyer: On the Potential Contributions of Mindfulness Meditation to Law Students, Lawyers, and Their Clients' (2002) 7 *Harvard Negotiation Law Review* 1. Since the publication of Riskin's article the literature on the topic has expanded exponentially. See, for example, William Blatt, 'What's Special About Meditation? Contemplative Practice for American Lawyers' (2002) 7 *Harvard Negotiation Law Review* 125; Douglas Codiga, 'Reflections on the Potential Growth of Mindfulness Meditation in the Law' (2002) 7 *Harvard Negotiation Law Review* 109; Clark Freshman, Adele Hayes and Greg Feldman, 'Adapting Meditation to Promote Negotiation Success: A Guide to Varieties and Scientific Support' (2002) 7 *Harvard Negotiation Law Review* 67; Dennis Warren, 'Using Meditation to Enhance the Practice of Law' (2002) 16 *Ohio Law* 12; Van Pounds, 'Promoting Truthfulness in Negotiation: A Mindful Approach' (2004) 40 *Willamette Law Review* 181; Leonard Riskin, 'Mindfulness: Foundational Training for Dispute Resolution' (2004) 54 *Journal of Legal Education* 79; Leonard Riskin, 'Awareness and

the past has been shown to produce a host of benefits for both physical and mental health . . . One specific benefit of mindfulness meditation is the augmenting effect it has on the experience of positive affect. Experienced meditators have been shown to have more positive emotions . . . Since increasing

---

Ethics in Dispute Resolution and Law: Why Mindfulness Tends to Foster Ethical Behavior' (2009) 50 *South Texas Law Review* 493; Scott Rogers, *Mindfulness for Law Students: Using the Power of Mindful Awareness to Achieve Balance and Success in Law School* (Mindful Living Press, 2009); Rhonda Magee, 'Educating Lawyers to Meditate?' (2010) 79 *University of Missouri – Kansas City Law Review* 1; Joel Orenstein, 'The Mindful Lawyer: Meditation and the Practice of Law' (2011) 87 *Law Institute Journal* 40; Charles Halpern, 'The Mindful Lawyer: Why Contemporary Lawyers Are Practicing Meditation' (2012) 61 *Journal of Legal Education* 641; Richard Reuben, 'Bringing Mindfulness into the Classroom: A Personal Journey' (2012) 61 *Journal of Legal Education* 674; Leonard Riskin, 'Awareness and the Legal Profession: An Introduction to the Mindful Lawyer Symposium' (2012) 61 *Journal of Legal Education* 634; Rogers (n 10) 1189; David Zlotnick, 'Integrating Mindfulness Theory and Practice into Trial Advocacy' (2012) 61 *Journal of Legal Education* 654; Scott Rogers and Jan Jacobowitz, *Mindfulness & Professional Responsibility: A Guidebook for Integrating Mindfulness into the Law School Curriculum* (Mindful Living Press, 2012); Pamela Casey, Kevin Burke and Steve Leben, 'Minding the Court: Enhancing the Decision-Making Process' (2013) 5 *International Journal For Court Administration* 45; Jan Jacobowitz, 'The Benefits of Mindfulness for Litigators' (2013) 39 *Litigation* 1; Rhonda Magee, 'Contemplative Practices and the Renewal of Legal Education' (2013) *New Directions for Teaching and Learning* 31; Scott Rogers, 'The Role of Mindfulness in the Ongoing Evolution of Legal Education' (2013) 36 *University of Arkansas at Little Rock Law Review* 387; Shailini George, 'The Cure for the Distracted Mind: Why Law Schools Should Teach Mindfulness' (2014) 53 *Duquesne Law Review* 215; Jan Jacobowitz and Scott Rogers, 'Mindful Ethics – A Pedagogical and Practical Approach to Teaching Legal Ethics, Developing Professional Identity, and Encouraging Civility' (2014) 4 *St Mary's Journal on Legal Malpractice & Ethics* 198; Tamara Kuennen, 'The M Word' (2014) 43 *Hofstra Law Review* 325; Filippa Marullo Anzalone, 'Zen and the Art of Multitasking: Mindfulness for Law Librarians' (2015) 107 *Law Librarian Journal* 561; Lauren Newell, 'Redefining Attention (and Revamping the Legal Profession) for the Digital Generation' (2014) 15 *Nevada Law Journal* 754; Glover (n 9) 47; Peter Huang, 'How Improving Decision-Making and Mindfulness Can Improve Legal Ethics and Professionalism' (2015) 21 *Journal of Law, Business & Ethics* 35; Lewinbuk (n 16) 454; Leonard Riskin and Rachel Wohl, 'Mindfulness in the Heat of Conflict: Taking Stock' (2015) 20 *Harvard Negotiation Law Review* 121; Scott Rogers and Jan Jacobowitz, 'Mindful Ethics and the Cultivation of Concentration' (2015) 15 *Nevada Law Journal* 730; Peter Nicholson, 'You and Whose Mind?' (2015) 60 *Journal of the Law Society of Scotland* 12; Katerina Lewinbuk, 'Lawyer Heal Thyself: Incorporating Mindfulness into Legal Education and Profession' (2015) 40(1) *Journal of the Legal Profession* 1; Katerina Lewinbuk and Christy Gilbert, 'Law Student Heal Thyself: Teaching Mindfulness as a Legal Skill' (2016) 41(1) *Journal of the Legal Profession* 37; Katrina Lee, 'A Call for Law Schools to Link the Curricular Trends of Legal Tech and Mindfulness' (2016) 48 *University of Toledo Law Review* 55; Jeena Cho and Karen Gifford, *The Anxious Lawyer: An 8-Week Guide to a Joyful and Satisfying Law Practice Through Mindfulness and Meditation* (American Bar Association, 2016); Thalia Gonzalez, 'Root to Rise: Mindful Lawyering for Social Justice' (2017) 41 *NYU Review of Law & Social Change* 91; Peter Huang, 'Can Practicing Mindfulness Improve Lawyer Decision-Making, Ethics, and Leadership?' (2017) 55 *Houston Law Review* 63; Brostoff (n 14) 157; Huang (n 15); Debra Austin, 'Positive Legal Education: Flourishing Law Students and Thriving Law Schools' (2018) 77 *Maryland Law Review* 649, 708–9; Nathalie Martin, *Lawyering from the Inside Out: Learning Professional Development Through Mindfulness and Emotional Intelligence* (Cambridge University Press, 2018).

one's experience of positive emotions confers increased resilience, it makes sense that engaging in a practice that increases positive affect will lead to improved resilience.[30]

Rogers examined the use of mindfulness meditation with 'emerging adults'; students ranging in age from 18–29.[31] She concluded, on the basis of the research relating to the neurobiology of stress and resilience, that mindfulness meditation could be considered a 'viable option for enhancing resilience' in the age group.[32]

The studies mentioned here are included by way of example to illustrate the potential that exists for the use of meditation as a means of enhancing the resilience of law students. Although a relatively new area of scientific enquiry, it is difficult to overstate the significance of resilience for the study and practice of law. As unhealthy levels of stress continue to affect the well-being of both law students and legal practitioners, it is important that appropriate consideration is given to practices that address the issue.

Although there is evidence to suggest that the practice of meditation enhances resilience, it must not to be approached as a panacea for issues of student well-being. The conditions that give rise to unhealthy levels of stress need to be considered. The section that follows discusses the broader context of institutional responsibility for student well-being.

The broader context of responsibility for student well-being

In assessing the potential of any well-being initiative, it is important to bear in mind the conditions that give rise to issues of poor mental health. The high levels of stress experienced in the study of law are often compounded by other issues, including concerns relating to personal finances, debt and insecurity of employment upon graduation. While the practice of meditation is helpful in placing such concerns in context, it is not a substitute for other forms of support or for institutional reform. Teresa Brostoff emphasises the importance of rethinking law school culture: 'To assist students in achieving a sense of satisfaction or well-being in law school requires rethinking law school as we know it. This rethinking requires an understanding of what is creating the toxic culture in law schools

30 Rogers (n 20) 547. See also the report published by the US National Task Force on Lawyer Well-Being: Bree Buchanan et al., *The Path to Lawyer Well-Being: Practical Recommendations for Positive Change* (American Bar Association, 2017). The report recommended mindfulness meditation as 'a practice that can enhance cognitive reframing (and thus resilience) by aiding our ability to monitor our thoughts and avoid becoming emotionally overwhelmed': ibid 52.

31 Rogers (n 20) 545.

32 Ibid 548. See also a study of the impact of mindfulness training for psychology students at the University of Naples: Maria Rosaria Strollo, Mariarosaria De Simone and Alessandra Romano, 'Mindfulness in University Education: A Pilot Study' ICERI2014 Proceedings: 7th International Conference of Education, Research and Innovation, Seville, Spain, 17–19 November 2014 (Siviglia: IATED Academy) 6036–6044.

that results in the plethora of psychologically distressed students'.[33] Although the practice of meditation enhances wellness, strengthens resilience and provides a measure of protection against unhealthy levels of stress leading to burnout, it does not address the source of the problem. Peter Huang comments that:

> Legal education often implicitly and even sometimes explicitly trains and socializes law students to be amoral, if not immoral. It is by now quite well-known that many law students come into law schools bright-eyed and bushy-tailed with intrinsic values to do good, help the vulnerable and underprivileged in our society, and make our world a better place. Yet, too many law students end up obsessing in law schools about extrinsic values of comparative worth, such as their class rank, grades, honors, and salary offers. Law school often alters law students in many truly fundamental ways, some that are very undesirable personally and societally. The displacement of intrinsic values by extrinsic values that happens to many law students reduces their subjective well-being, deep sense of meaning or purpose, and self-concordance. It should be unsurprising that emotionally impaired and mentally unhealthy law students graduate to become emotionally impaired and mentally unhealthy lawyers.[34]

If the issues that give rise to unhealthy levels of stress are not addressed, initiatives introduced to deal with the ill effects of such stress will rest on weak foundations. A responsibility exists on the part of the institution to consider student well-being in broad, holistic terms. While the practice of meditation has the potential to enhance well-being in meaningful ways, it is important to appreciate that the introduction of such practices should not be approached in such a way as to shift the duty of care which rests with the institution to individual students. Here it is instructive to consider some of the criticisms that have arisen from the introduction of meditation in a corporate setting. According to Ron Purser and David Loy, '[m]any corporate advocates argue that transformational change starts with oneself: if one's mind can become more focused and peaceful, then social and organizational transformation will naturally follow'.[35] Insofar as meditation makes an individual a more focused and harmonious co-worker, it also has the potential to strengthen productivity, serving better the interests of the organisation. However, the actual source of the stress necessitating intervention is not addressed:

> Up to now, the mindfulness movement has avoided any serious consideration of why stress is so pervasive in modern business institutions. Instead, corporations have jumped on the mindfulness bandwagon because it

33 Brostoff (n 14) 159.
34 Huang (n 15) 32.
35 Ron Purser and David Loy, 'Beyond McMindfulness' (7 January 2013) <www.huffingtonpost.com/ron-purser/beyond-mcmindfulness_b_3519289.html> accessed 7 May 2019.

> conveniently shifts the burden onto the individual employee: stress is framed as a personal problem, and mindfulness is offered as just the right medicine to help employees work more efficiently and calmly within toxic environments. Cloaked in an aura of care and humanity, mindfulness is refashioned into a safety valve, as a way to let off steam – a technique for coping with and adapting to the stresses and strains of corporate life.
>
> The result is an atomized and highly privatized version of mindfulness practice, which is easily co-opted and confined to what Jeremy Carrette and Richard King, in their book *Selling Spirituality: The Silent Takeover of Religion*, describe as an 'accommodationist' orientation. Mindfulness training has wide appeal because it has become a trendy method for subduing employee unrest, promoting a tacit acceptance of the status quo, and as an instrumental tool for keeping attention focused on institutional goals.[36]

Writing in a similar vein, Margaret Thornton refers to the 'neoliberalist assumption that individuals are expected to take responsibility for their own wellbeing'.[37] One of the issues with this approach to student well-being is that attention is deflected away from the duty of care that exists with the institution. Paula Baron states that '[u]ntil the structural issues within law and legal education that impact negatively on lawyer well-being are acknowledged, these issues will continue'.[38] Accordingly, '[w]hile individual techniques of self-management may help the individual to endure the issues that lead to their distress, no amount of antidepressants, time management workshops, or resilience training will ultimately solve the problem for the profession as a whole'.[39]

Interventions enhancing resilience – including meditation – are not designed to address the conditions that give rise to unhealthy levels of stress. While such interventions may ameliorate their ill effects, issues that adversely affect well-being – such as excessive workload – will continue to take a toll if not addressed directly. Accordingly, the broader context of student well-being must be conceived in terms that include those responsible for making decisions at various levels within an institution.[40] For Wendy Larcombe, the promotion of student

36 Ibid.

37 Margaret Thornton, 'Law Student Wellbeing: A Neoliberal Conundrum' (2016) 58(2) *Australian Universities Review* 42, 45. Thornton comments critically that 'the wellbeing discourse deflects attention away from the prevailing political economy as the underlying cause of stress. This leads students to believe that they need to resort to counselling or some other form of therapy to effect a resolution': ibid 48.

38 Paula Baron, 'Althusser's Mirror: Lawyer Distress and the Process of Interpellation' (2015) 24 *Griffith Law Review* 157, 176. Michael Coper states 'there are endemic structural issues that must be addressed'. 'Foreword' in Margaret Thornton, *Privatising the Public University* (Routledge, 2011) x–xi, xi.

39 Baron (n 38) 176.

40 Richard Collier is also critical of the focus on individual responsibility for 'diverting attention from broader models of talent management that might position accountability for poor wellbeing more effectively': Richard Collier, 'Wellbeing in the Legal Profession: Reflections

well-being requires 'an integrated, whole-school approach'.[41] Noting that 'isolated or one-off measures designed to promote mental well-being may be undermined by other practices within a law school',[42] she argues that 'student wellbeing must be addressed as a learning and teaching issue, not only as a matter for student service professionals'.[43]

In the context of higher education, it is important to appreciate the enhancement of student well-being as an end in itself. Although initiatives that effectively support student well-being are likely to improve metrics of student satisfaction, retention, progression, and achievement, care should be taken to avoid the instrumentalist approach highlighted by Purser and Loy. As rates of suicide among students increase,[44] so too does the institutional responsibility to address conditions affecting student well-being. In providing an opportunity to learn a system of meditation, students can be equipped with an important transferable skill of life-long value; one that has the potential to add value not only to the study of law but also to its practice. As noted above, in choosing a method of meditation, it is instructive to consider that different systems of meditation serve the realisation of different ends; some are available on a proprietary basis and others free of charge. The section that follows considers the utility of further research on the efficacy of meditation and its potential for the enhancement of student well-being and professional identity.

Future research on the efficacy of meditation

The utility of high-quality research on the efficacy of meditation is underscored by the prevalence of false or misleading claims made about benefits of particular practices. As noted by Daniel Goleman and Richard Davidson,

> The mix of meditation and monetizing has a sorry track record as a recipe for hucksterism, disappointment, and even scandal. All too often, gross

---

on Recent Developments (or, What Do We Talk About, When We Talk About Wellbeing?)' 23 *International Journal of the Legal Profession* 41, 54.

41 Wendy Larcombe, 'Towards an Integrated, Whole-School Approach to Promoting Law Student Wellbeing' in Field, Duffy and James (n 4) 24–36, 24.

42 Ibid 26.

43 Ibid 24.

44 For rates of student suicide in the context of UK higher education, see Craig Thorley, *Not By Degrees: Improving Student Mental Health in the UK's Universities* (Institute for Public Policy Research, 2017) 4; Sarah Marsh, 'Suicide is at Record Level Among Students at UK Universities, Study Finds' *The Guardian* (2 September 2017) <www.theguardian.com/education/2017/sep/02/suicide-record-level-students-uk-universities-study> accessed 7 May 2019. A rise in mental health problems has also been reported in an Irish context: Sylvia Thompson, 'There Is a Tsunami of Third-Level Students with Mental Health Problems' *The Irish Times* (10 January 2017) <www.irishtimes.com/news/education/there-is-a-tsunami-of-third-level-students-with-mental-health-problems-1.2924516> accessed 7 May 2019.

> misrepresentations, questionable claims, distortions of scientific studies are used to sell meditation.[45]

It is also worth bearing in mind that '[w]ellness initiatives, whether voluntary or mandatory, are now seen by many individual academics as part of a suite of unwelcome educationalist regulations'.[46] On account of this, and considering the nature of meditation as a contemplative practice, gaining first-hand experience of a particular method is invaluable. This is essential for purposes of clarity on the nature of the practice employed, the commitment required and, insofar as possible, how its efficacy is to be evidenced. While a substantial body of research exists on transcendental meditation and mindfulness meditation, the literature comparing different systems of meditation is relatively sparse. In the absence of more concrete points of reference, it is necessary to acquire experience in the practice of a particular system to make a truly useful assessment of its potential.

Although a significant body of research evidences various benefits arising from the practice of meditation,[47] the reasons why such benefits exist is not clear. This has been highlighted by Peter Sedlmeier, Juliane Eberth and Maika Puta:

> Why does meditation have . . . beneficial consequences? The sobering answer to this question is that we do not know, despite the fact that there have been many studies on the effects of meditation. These studies differ widely in focus and methods but almost all contain little or no theoretical background. This lack of theory and, consequently, of precise hypotheses has led researchers to look at how meditation changes a wide range of both physiological and psychological measures. Although the psychological (beneficial) effects can be regarded as established, results in brain research are not clear-cut. There is some indication that meditation affects brain processes and even brain structure . . . but as yet there is no satisfactory theoretical account for these changes.[48]

Sedlmeier et al. state that for 'a comprehensive understanding of why and how meditation works, emphasis should be placed on the development of more precise

45 Goleman and Davidson (n 2) 11.

46 Nick James, 'Dealing with Resistance to Change by Legal Academics' in Field, Duffy and James (n 4) 204–217, 225.

47 From a meta-analysis of 163 studies on the psychological effects of meditation, Peter Sedlmeier, Juliane Eberth and Maika Puta state: 'Meditating improves relationships, reduces anxiety and negative emotions, and strengthens positive aspects of personality; it helps people stay more concentrated and boosts learning and memory': Peter Sedlmeier, Juliane Eberth and Maika Puta, 'Meditation: Future Theory and Research' in Michael West (ed), *The Psychology of Meditation: Research and Practice* (Oxford University Press, 2016) 285–310, 285. See also, Peter Sedlmeier et al, 'The Psychological Effects of Meditation: A Meta-Analysis' (2012) 138 *Psychological Bulletin* 1139.

48 Sedlmeier, Eberth and Puta (n 47) 285–310, 285.

theories and measurement devices'.[49] Given the nature of the benefits reported, there is significant potential for such research to yield insights of value to the study and practice of law. According to the cognitive neuroscientist Dusana Dorjee, 'despite the exponential increase in research and applications of meditation-based approaches over the last three decades, we are still only scratching the surface of the potential that these techniques have for transforming our sense of meaning and purpose in life with broad societal implications'.[50]

As different types of meditation change different areas of the brain,[51] longitudinal research on law students and legal practitioners would be useful. Dorjee notes that 'despite the recent boom in studies on meditation, most of them apply a short-term perspective of meditation'.[52] While additional studies would be useful, it is important to recognise that sufficient research already exists to evidence the beneficial effects of meditation for the well-being of law students. Although further research would be helpful to clarify *why* meditation has beneficial effects (such as the reduction of anxiety and negative emotions), it is not necessary to confirm such benefits exist. In terms of general health and well-being, the value added has been substantially evidenced in a number of studies.[53]

Conclusion

Given the rise of mental health problems among the student population, initiatives to help address the crisis should be considered as a matter of priority. The use of meditation in legal education is one such initiative which has considerable potential. Teresa Brostoff states:

> Now, in the twenty-first century, the 2,600-year-old practice of meditation and mindfulness is recognized as a valuable tool for law students and lawyers. As law schools evolve to include experiential learning, all law schools should consider making secular mindfulness and meditation training part of their curricula. While substantive experiential learning experiences such as clinics and externships are crucial to developing student skills, students need more than substantive legal practice experience to be fully prepared for the professional practice of law.[54]

49 Sedlmeier et al. (n 47) 1139, 1139.

50 Dusana Dorjee, *Neuroscience and Psychology of Meditation in Everyday Life: Searching for the Essence of Mind* (Routledge, 2018) 179.

51 Sofie Valk et al., 'Structural Plasticity of the Social Brain: Differential Change After Socio-Affective and Cognitive Mental Training' (2017) 3 *Science Advances* e1700489 <http://advances.sciencemag.org/content/3/10/e1700489/tab-pdf> accessed 7 May 2019.

52 Dorjee (n 50) iix.

53 For examples of studies on the health benefits of meditation, see the webpages of the US Department of Health and Human Services: <https://nccih.nih.gov/health/meditation/overview.htm> accessed 7 May 2019.

54 Brostoff (n 14) 157.

To fully equip students for the practice of law, a holistic approach is required. The practice of meditation adds value to the experience of studying law, including through the reduction of stress, negative emotions and the development of resilience. While meditation is not a panacea for the unhealthy levels of stress experienced in the study of law, it can serve a purpose in preparing students to meet the demands of legal education and practice in a more sustainable way.[55]

55 In his *Principles of Psychology*, William James states that 'the faculty of voluntarily bringing back a wandering attention, over and over again, is the very root of judgment, character, and will. No one is *compos sui* if he have it not. An education which should improve this faculty would be the education *par excellence*': William James, *The Principles of Psychology* (Henry Holt and Company, 1890) 424.

13 Identity, well-being and law students

Lydia Bleasdale and Sarah Humphreys

Introduction

There is international evidence that levels of psychological distress seen amongst law students are higher than those seen amongst other students.[1] Numerous reasons have been suggested for this, including particular qualities of law students;[2] adversarial law school curricula;[3] and law school pedagogies.[4] For example, writing in the Australian context, Skead and Rogers found that, even when controlling for a range of factors, 'simply being a law student continued to be an independent predictor of anxiety'.[5] Such research is rarer within the UK,[6] which partly informed the authors' decision to undertake research into student resilience in 2016. Another influence was the rise in references to 'resilience', a concept which

1 See, for example, Kennon M Sheldon and Lawrence S Krieger, 'Does Legal Education Have Undermining Effects on Law Students? Evaluating Changes in Motivation, Values and Well-being' (2004) 22 *Behavioural Sciences and the Law* 261. For extensive discussion of a range of Australian research see, Rachael Field, James Duffy and Colin James (eds), *Promoting Law Student and Lawyer Well-Being in Australia and Beyond* (Routledge, 2016).

2 Marilyn Heins, Shirley Nickols Fahey and Roger C Henderson, 'Law Students and Medical Students: A Comparison of Perceived Stress' (1983) 33 *Journal of Legal Education* 511; Norm Kelk, Sharon Medlow and Ian Hickie, 'Distress and Depression Among Australian Law Students: Incidence, Attitudes and the Roles of Universities' (2010) 31 *Sydney Law Review* 113.

3 Molly Townes O'Brien, 'Facing Down the Gladiators: Addressing Law School's Hidden Adversarial Curriculum' (2011) 37 *Monash University Law Review* 43. For a US-based critique of legal education, see William M Sullivan et al. (eds), *Educating Lawyers: Preparation for the Profession of Law* (Jossey-Bass, 2007).

4 Anthony Lester, Lloyd England and Natalia Antolak-Saper, 'Health and Wellbeing in the First Year: The Law School Experience' (2011) 36 *Alternative Law Journal* 47; Wendy Larcombe and Katherine Fethers, 'Schooling the Blues: An Investigation of Factors Associated with Psychological Distress Among Law Students' (2013) 36 *University of New South Wales Law Journal* 390.

5 Natalie K Skead and Shane L Rogers, 'Do Law Students Stand Apart from Other University Students in their Quest for Mental Health: A Comparative Study on Wellbeing and Associated Behaviours in Law and Psychology Students' (2015) 42 *International Journal of Law and Psychiatry* 81, 88.

6 See Caroline Strevens and Clare Wilson, 'Law Student Wellbeing in the UK: A Call for Curriculum Intervention' (2016) 11 *The Journal of Commonwealth Law and Legal Education* 44.

has entered the lexicon of higher education. The term has no universally agreed definition, but in popular discourse is used as shorthand for withstanding pressure, and emerging unharmed or 'stronger' after a challenging or difficult period. Historically, resilience literature was more concerned with how individuals could 'gain' resilience than with the structural factors which could shape their response to challenges.[7] More recently, contextual, 'protective factors' such as self-care, formal support systems and social connections have been viewed as important.[8] This 'ecological' model of resilience sees it as dependent upon factors internal and external to the individual; subject to change; and simultaneously variable within different contexts.[9]

This approach to resilience was the starting point for the Undergraduate Resilience Research Project, conducted at the University of Leeds. The project sought to understand how the university could better support its students, including by examining how factors significant to resilience were supported or undermined within the educational context. Although initially focused upon resilience (which, although related, is distinct from well-being),[10] the project drew upon broader well-being literature, such as the roles communities and relationships play in supporting physical and mental health,[11] the importance of structured leisure

7 For a review of 'resilience' definitions see Ryan S Santos, '"Why Resilience?" A Review of Literature of Resilience and Implications for Further Educational Research' (2012) [Online] <https://go.sdsu.edu/education/doc/files/01370-ResiliencyLiteratureReview(SDSU).pdf> accessed 7 May 2019.

8 Margaret McAllister and Jessica McKinnon, 'The Importance of Teaching and Learning Resilience in the Health Disciplines: A Critical Review of the Literature' (2009) 29 *Nurse Education Today* 371; Jacqueline Stevenson, 'Reconceptualising Student Resilience in Higher Education: Problematising Deficit Discourses' (Presentation at the University of Sheffield, 2016) [Online] slides <www.sheffield.ac.uk/polopoly_fs/1.659638!/file/Reconceptualising_Resiliance_-_Prof_Jacqueline_Stevenson.pptx> accessed 7 May 2019.

9 Gemma Aburn, Merryn Gott and Karen Hoare, 'What is Resilience? An Integrative Review of the Empirical Literature' (2016) 72 *Journal of Advanced Nursing* 980; Stevenson (n 8); Emily McIntosh and Jenny Shaw, *Student Resilience: Exploring the Positive Case for Resilience* (Unite Students, 2017).

10 See Nina Mguni, Nicola Bacon and John F Brown, 'The Wellbeing and Resilience Paradox' (Young Foundation, 2012); Diana F Wood, 'Mens Sana in Corpore Sano: Student Well-Being and the Development of Resilience' (2016) 50 *Medical Education* 20.

11 Harry T Reis et al., 'Daily Well-Being: The Role of Autonomy, Competence, and Relatedness' (2000) 26 *Personality and Social Psychology Bulletin* 419; Scott E Wilks and Christina A Spivey, 'Resilience in Undergraduate Social Work Students: Social Support and Adjustment to Academic Stress' (2010) 29 *Social Work Education* 276; William P Burdick, 'Social Networks (and More) Are Necessary for Student and Faculty Resilience' (2014) 49 *Medical Education* 7; Kenneth I Mavor et al., 'Beyond Prevalence to Process: The Role of Self and Identity in Medical Student Well-Being' (2014) 48 *Medical Education* 351; Susan Armstrong and Michelle Sanson, 'From Confusion to Confidence: Transitioning to Law School' (2015) 12 *QUT Law and Justice Journal* 21; Ben Lovell, '"We are a Tight Community": Social Groups and Social Identity in Medical Students' (2015) 49 *Medical Education* 1016; Mark Robinson et al., 'Peer Support as a Resilience Building Practice with Men' (2015) 14 *Journal of Public Mental Health* 196.

activities,[12] and self-care.[13] 'Well-being' – a term as nebulous and open to criticism as 'resilience'[14] – encompasses a range of physical, spiritual, emotional and mental processes, including how individuals perceive themselves and their role within the world.

This chapter contrasts interview findings from law students with those from other sites, in order to understand why the law school experience may prove particularly deleterious to well-being. It focuses upon two features of law student identities which arose during interviews: concerns about future professional identity, and the influence of past identity as a high academic achiever. The authors argue that the influence of distinctive past and future identities experienced by law students creates particular pressures inimical to well-being.

The chapter begins with an overview of the importance of – and links between – well-being and identity. Key interview findings relating to identities are reviewed, then implications for student well-being are summarised, alongside recommendations for law schools.

Methodology

The project involved three stages of data collection. Firstly, 35 staff across six disciplines (Biological Sciences, Geography, Law, Mechanical Engineering, Medicine and Music) were interviewed about the educational context in which their students were operating (including questions about feedback, student support and assessment, as well as their own views on academic and personal challenges facing their students). Secondly, second year undergraduate students from across those disciplines were invited to complete the Connor-Davidson Resilience Scale online.[15] This scale measures a respondent's self-reported experience of, and response to, stress over the previous month, and was chosen on the basis that it had been widely used internationally with a large range of individuals.[16] A total of 185 students completed the online survey. Of those, 55 were interviewed in the third and final stage of the project. Interviewees were selected on the basis of their resilience 'score' on the Resilience Scale (a mixture of those at the upper, lower and middle parts of the scale were invited to take part in interviews);

12 Eshkol Rafaeli and Atara Hiller, 'Self-Complexity: A Source of Resilience?' in John W Reich, Alex J Zautra and John Stuart Hall (eds), *Handbook of Adult Resilience* (Guilford Press, 2010); Lovell (n 11); Ben Lovell, 'How to Build a Resilient Surgeon: Communities, Cultures and Complexity' (2016) 50 *Medical Education* 798.

13 Andrew J Martin and Herbert W Marsh, 'Academic Resilience and its Psychological and Educational Correlates: A Construct Validity Approach' (2006) 43 *Psychology in the Schools* 267.

14 For an excellent account of deficiencies within the individualised view of resilience, see Paul Michael Garrett, 'Questioning Tales of "Ordinary Magic": "Resilience" and Neo-Liberal Reasoning' (2016) 46 *The British Journal of Social Work* 1909.

15 Jonathan RT Davidson and Kathryn M Connor, *Connor-Davidson Resilience Scale* (CD-RISC Manual, Unpublished, 2018) <www.cd-risc.com> accessed 7 May 2019. This scale was selected primarily on the basis that it had been used with the widest group of participants on an international basis.

16 Ibid.

contextual factors including their age, gender and entry route into university; and the extent to which those personal background features were representative of the student body within their discipline at the university.

At interview, students were asked questions designed to establish the areas of their lives at university which were likely to be supportive, or undermining, of resilience.[17] The questions were devised following a review of the resilience literature and were an 'audit' of resilience within university life. However, additional questions were also asked where appropriate – to that extent, the interviews were semi-structured and adopted a phenomenographical approach. A thematic analysis of the interview transcripts was then undertaken with identity, the subject of discussion within this chapter, emerging as a theme from the data.

The majority of this chapter focuses upon the findings from within the School of Law, University of Leeds. Fifteen law students were interviewed: the majority were female (12); were students from the UK (11), as opposed to International or from the European Union; had completed the standard pre-university qualification (A-levels) immediately prior to entering the program of study (10 – the others had undertaken a mixture of various types of study or were in employment); declared no disability (14 – 1 stated they preferred not to say); had entered the university through the standard access route, as opposed to through a foundation degree, for example (8); and did not have caring responsibilities (13).

The methodological limitations of the study are explored in greater depth within the full report[18] (which also provides a fuller set of findings into how universities can and should support and enhance student resilience), but it must be noted that the authors recognise that this is a small sample from within a particular type of law school. The school has high entry requirements and had a national ranking of 8th in *The Times* and *Sunday Times* Good University Guide 2018. The authors do not claim that the students interviewed for this project are representative of students at all Russell Group universities,[19] the broader university sector, nor indeed of all of the students within the school of law itself. Nevertheless, the work provides an insight into why law students in particular might experience challenges to their identity and therefore with their well-being, in an area where there is not a great deal of literature. Furthermore, although the sample size was small, this was a clearly defined research topic and the students interviewed were selected on a particular basis to discuss experiences which they were in a good position to reflect upon (having been a university student for at least 18 months by the time of interview). For those reasons, a small sample size is not necessarily problematic, and within the law sample saturation was arguably reached.[20]

17 Lydia Bleasdale and Sarah Humphreys, 'Undergraduate Resilience Research Report' (LITE, University of Leeds, 2018) <http://teachingexcellence.leeds.ac.uk/wp-content/uploads/2018/01/LITEbleasdalehumphreys_fullreport_online.pdf> accessed 7 May 2019.
18 Ibid 10–12.
19 A group of 24 self-selected typically research-intensive UK universities.
20 Michelle Cleary, Jan Horsfall and Mark Hayter, 'Data Collection and Sampling in Qualitative Research: Does Size Matter?' (2014) 70 *Journal of Advanced Nursing* 473, 473.

Well-being and identity

Notions of identity are complex and distinct usages of the term exist.[21] Within this chapter identity is concerned with our understanding of who we are, where we belong in the world and our purpose – including our potential future identity. Individuals will have several identities relating to membership of different groups. Understanding of our (multiple) identities is a dynamic process formed through interactions with the social environment: 'it is the interactions in social settings that construct who we are'.[22] A person's identity changes over time and they will have (potentially competing) past, present and future identities.[23]

Consideration should be given to the influence of socio-cultural contexts on identity formation and salience ('defined as the probability that an identity will be invoked across a variety of situations, or alternatively across persons in a given situation'[24]); relationships are key to an individual's understanding of self. This is of particular relevance within this chapter as many undergraduates experience change in significant relationships at university. Weidman's Undergraduate Model of Socialisation[25] offers a framework for understanding the experiences and processes that shape students' identities, including relationships. The model describes students entering university with certain values, aspirations and goals; being exposed to significant influencers; and subsequently changing or maintaining the values, aspirations and goals held on entrance.[26] These influences exist in formal and informal settings within university, for example academic settings, or socialisation with peer groups, but also in interactions with external groups, e.g. with parents or employers. Students are also affected by their experiences prior to university and ideas about their future. Weidman et al. describe the structures students are exposed to as 'value-laden'.[27] Those involved in shaping higher education must understand that academic and social environments will affect students' values and aspirations, as well as their understanding of themselves. It is desirable to reflect on significant relationships during students' university years and seek to understand how situational interactions can reinforce or challenge existing identities.[28]

Students' multiple, and potentially conflicting, identities include personal and social identities. Personal identities (parts of self that make them unique) are

21 Sheldon Stryker and Peter J Burke, 'The Past, Present, and Future of an Identity Theory' (2000) 63 *Social Psychology Quarterly* 284.

22 Peter Kaufman, 'The Sociology of College Students' Identity Formation' (2014) 166 *New Directions for Higher Education* 35, 36.

23 Daphna Oyserman and Mesmin Destin, 'Identity-Based Motivation: Implications for Intervention' (2010) 38 *The Counseling Psychologist* 1001.

24 Stryker and Burke (n 21) 286.

25 John C Weidman, Linda DeAngelo and Kathryn A Bethea, 'Understanding Student Identity From a Socialization Perspective' (2014) 166 *New Directions for Higher Education* 43.

26 Ibid 44–45.

27 Ibid 45.

28 Stryker and Burke (n 21).

often understood as self-declarations ('I am'),[29] and it is crucial that these aspects of self are reflected back in social contexts if they are to persist. Social identities are related to group and categorial memberships.[30] For example, an individual might regard themselves as academically able and personable (personal identities) as well as a law student and proficient footballer (group identities), but must receive acknowledgement of these self-aspects from social environments for the identities to remain. In this project, it was evident that messages from the social environment meant some interviewees experienced threats to dominant academic identities which affected confidence in their ability to succeed as a law student and future lawyer.

Undergraduate years are therefore pivotal to identity formation as many students experience large-scale change in their lives. Variations in the social context (such as moving away from home) will impact on their understanding of self, the salience of their identities, and their behaviour. For example, an undergraduate may have been a school student (past identity), currently be a law student (present identity), and wish to be a lawyer (future identity). The university environment may enable them to enact these roles, thereby confirming these academic and career identities, which in turn reinforces their salience.[31] Conversely, an identity may persist over time but social experiences might reduce its prominence: for example, leaving home may diminish a student's 'older sibling' identity salience.

Identity formation processes can result in negative emotion. This can arise from discrepancies between self-perception and feedback from the social environment, or can be related to coping strategies employed at times of challenge linked to particular identities. Social interactions may reinforce or undermine the sense of self, with failure in self-verification resulting in stress and anxiety.[32] Doubts about present and future law-related identities may impact on an individual's sense of belonging in law school and consequently harm well-being.[33] Feeling connected within university is associated with increased motivation, increased success and better mental health.[34] Membership of the 'law student' group could offer further benefits as 'a strong sense of shared identity promotes positive self-esteem and is associated with higher levels of well-being', but if an individual is to benefit from the protective factors of group memberships, they must be 'central to how they define themselves'.[35] Threats to identity which result in estrangement from the group may have an adverse effect on well-being and can affect a student's ability to manage academic challenge: Oyserman and Destin argue that people are motivated to behave in ways which feel congruent with their identity

29 Kaufman (n 22).
30 Ibid.
31 Stryker and Burke (n 21).
32 Ibid.
33 John Goldie, 'The Formation of Professional Identity in Medical Students: Considerations for Educators' (2012) 34 *Medical Teacher* 641, 645.
34 Aileen M Pidgeon et al., 'Examining Characteristics of Resilience among University Students: An International Study' (2014) 2(11) *Journal of the Social Sciences* 14.
35 Mavor et al. (n 11) 355.

and, consequently, will not pursue actions at odds with their self-concept or will lack motivation to overcome difficulties.[36]

Strong group identification is not, however, unproblematic as it is 'associated with stronger adherence to the social norms of the group'[37] and those norms may undermine well-being. Some 'law student norms' described by interviewees included preoccupation with academic success and an arguably injurious tendency to compare oneself with others.

Attention should also be paid to whether law students have identities outside of their discipline, or predominantly focus on the law student identity. Linville's theory of 'self-complexity' – concerned with the number and diversity of a person's 'self-aspects' (including roles, relationships and activities) – argues that 'greater self-complexity is a protective factor for people under stress'.[38] Conversely, 'when self-aspects are few and undifferentiated, a stressful event in one aspect tends to spill over and color thoughts and feelings about other aspects'.[39] For example, a law student may have friendships within the school, volunteer at a law clinic, and have goals related to a career in law. A negative event in one area may leave them vulnerable to negative thoughts about them all due to their close associations. In contrast, a law student who is a musician, has non-law friends and works in a restaurant is likely to be better protected against such vulnerability: their greater self-complexity provides a buffer at times of challenge.[40]

Student interview findings

Two interview themes concerning law student identity will be examined here: academic identity, and future lawyer identity. Of particular interest is how past, present and future identities affect a student's current sense of self and implications for well-being.

Future lawyer identity

The process through which students gain future professional identities is complex. Weidman et al. highlight the influence of 'non-college reference groups', emphasising that universities are not 'encapsulated environments'.[41] Here, interviewees' ideas about 'lawyer identity' had been influenced by peers, the academic environment and legal work experience. Most interviewees were considering a future in law, and had internalised significant messages about the profession. Students clearly viewed the sector as one requiring the very best of applicants:

36 Oyserman and Destin (n 23).
37 Mavor et al. (n 11) 356.
38 Patricia W Linville, 'Self-Complexity as a Cognitive Buffer Against Stress-Related Illness and Depression' (1987) 52 *Journal of Personality and Social Psychology* 663, 663.
39 Ibid 664.
40 Lovell (n 11 and n 12).
41 Weidman, DeAngelo and Bethea (n 25) 44.

> It is not really about doing well but being the best.
>
> (W23)[42]

> You've got to be amazing . . . everything around you just makes you think, are we good enough.
>
> (W35)

Furthermore, the establishment of a legal career alone was not regarded as sufficient by some: students regarded working in law as requiring achievement at the upper echelons of the sector:

> I'd like to be a Court of Appeal judge which I think is the ultimate goal.
>
> (W27)

> When I get to 'lawyer' my goal is I want to be the best lawyer.
>
> (W31)

Ibarra, observing consultants and investment bankers intent upon career progression, notes three 'rough categories of behaviours' which are particularly influential in helping individuals to form future identities: 'observing role models to identify possible identities . . . experimenting with one's own image, and . . . evaluating image and identity based on internal and external feedback'.[43] Furthermore, 'people conduct internal assessments by comparing their public persona with their representations of the kind of person they "really" are or would like to be: conclusions about what selves to keep or reject depend on feelings of congruence or authenticity'.[44]

Here, the law students interviewed were exposed to professional role models, but also evaluated identities by comparing themselves to law school peers. Most had clear ideas about their possible future 'lawyer' identity but for several interviewees the 'internal assessment' caused concern about whether their sense of self was congruent with their possible future identity.[45] For some, this was due to fellow law students:

> I don't feel I really fit in with anyone who studies law . . . especially like the [student] law society. . . . It is for a very specific crowd . . . middle-class, white, female crowd and I am not middle-class, white.
>
> (W22)

42 Student interviewees were allocated a code for the purpose of quotation: those starting with 'W' were law students and comprise the majority of the students quoted within this chapter. Where non-law students are quoted, this is made explicit.

43 Herminia Ibarra, 'Provisional Selves: Experimenting with Image and Identity in Professional Adaptation' (1999) 44 *Administrative Science Quarterly* 764, 771–772.

44 Ibid 779.

45 See further, Andrew Francis, 'Legal Education, Social Mobility, and Employability: Possible Selves, Curriculum Intervention, and the Role of Legal Work Experience' (2015) 42 *Journal of Law and Society* 173, 199.

This is significant because, according to Ibarra, an individual's identity is partly formed with reference to who they see reflected back at them, when they look at an arena they would like to enter.[46] Gender, ethnicity and social class may all impact on students' socialisation and identity formation during their undergraduate years,[47] particularly when considering entry into the professions.[48] Law students commented on the type of person they thought of as belonging in the legal profession, mostly when they considered themselves 'other' to that traditional image:

> [The Bar] is still dominated by that Old Boys, white middle class who know each other from Harrow-type environment.
>
> (W27)

> There is like an unspoken culture which you kind of have to get . . . and if you didn't grow up in that [middle-class] atmosphere . . . there are just things that you need to pick up.
>
> (W22)

The result of feeling 'other' may affect a law student's sense of self, interactions with their social environment and feelings about their future. They may try to adapt to fit desired identities, as suggested by Reich, who refers to law students wearing a 'social mask' and acting as they thought was expected of them by society,[49] or eventually 'discard a specific combination of self-presentation tactics, as well as the underlying possible self those tactics represent'.[50]

Academic achievement identity

The university's entrance requirements mean that most students have previously experienced significant academic success.[51] It was evident in interviews across the sites that undergraduates had entered university with a strong 'high academic achiever' personal identity, and law was no different:

> I am someone that prided myself on my academic achievement. That was the only thing I really had. That is all you have.
>
> (W22)

46 Ibarra (n 43) 781.
47 Kaufman (n 22).
48 Goldie (n 33).
49 Stephen Reich, 'California Psychological Inventory: Profile of a Sample of First Year Law Students' (1976) 39 *Psychological Reports* 871, 872, cited in Susan S Daicoff, 'Lawyer, Know Thyself: A Review of Empirical Research on Attorney Attributes Bearing on Professionalism' (1997) 46(5) *American University Law Review* 1337.
50 Ibarra (n 43) 783.
51 The School of Law's standard admission criteria for the law program is AAA, placing it amongst the highest entry requirements in England and Wales. Requirements are comparable in the other research project sites.

However, new situational interactions in the learning environment challenge these 'self-avowals' of high academic achiever as the identity is not reflected back by others as it was pre-university.[52] In keeping with many undergraduate students, students from this sample were often used to being the highest achievers in their school[53] and had to adjust their personal identity at university, where they were amongst other academically able individuals. A significant number of the interviewees across the non-law sites described redefining their academic identity and expectations. For example, in keeping with some findings from other sites, one geography student described 'academic success' as achieving consistent grades and wanting other people to think well of her in ways not solely concerned with grades.

Law students encountering similar challenges to their academic identity described a different response. The majority of law interviewees described academic success primarily in terms of achieving high marks, and it was evident that, for many, notions of present success were linked to past 'high academic achiever' identities. Where interviewees experienced academic challenge, this served as a threat to that identity:

> The problem is that I've never not really done well academically.
>
> (W30)

> I've always wanted to get the top grades because that's what I've got before coming to university, but coming to university sometimes makes me feel very average.
>
> (W21)

Although there were examples of modifications of self-expectations (e.g. 'I've set myself more achievable goals which has made a lot of difference to my life' (W32)), this was unusual. The more common outcome was a negative impact on their approach to challenge. For example, W33 struggled to move on from averaging 69% in her first year; 'every time I decide not to read something I can't forget about this 1% and how gutted I would be to finish second year with something that close'.[54]

Ideas about the future appear to reinforce law students' need to retain their academic achiever identity to a much greater extent than other students. Two disciplines which arguably share career competitiveness with law are medicine and mechanical engineering. Students of those disciplines were largely pragmatic about their future career prospects. An engineering student, for example, described being nervous about an internship interview because they can lead to future employment, but later stated: 'I was unsuccessful and that really got me

52 Kaufman (n 22).

53 See Armstrong and Sanson (n 11) 21, 39.

54 At the University of Leeds, an average of 69% would put a student within 1% of achieving the highest possible banded grade.

down but I thought "You know what I'm only in the second year of my degree, I've got plenty of time to get another one."' (G28).

Medical students also reflected upon what they wanted from their degree in a pragmatic manner, for example:

> I want to do academically well, but I also want to have a good time on the way. (E33)

Law students, in contrast, were focused upon their academic achievement, and how this was – in their view – inextricably linked with their future career:

> I don't want to put too much pressure on myself, but I know that soon I'm going to have to because firms recruit two years in advance. (W24)

> I think when people employ you they will look at your degree, your results first. (W34)

Differences between the disciplines must, however, be acknowledged: the majority of the mechanical engineering and medicine students had two and three years respectively remaining of their degree. The law students were largely in their penultimate year of study, with the summer between second and third year regarded by many as a prime opportunity to gain crucial work experience. Graduate prospects are mixed. Medicine students are largely guaranteed future employment. In contrast, law students joining the legal profession in the UK (and around the world) are entering a saturated job market: in the UK in 2016–17, there were 5719 new traineeships registered, and 15896 students graduating from law degrees.[55] This context might explain some of the differences between the students, but does not account for the extent to which law students' concern with academic identity (drawn from their past) was continuing as a present focal point. This focus, when combined with ideas about the requirements of their target industry and future identity, was impairing their capacity to adapt to changes in, and feedback from, the university environment and to consider how they might develop as individuals, both at university and beyond.

Implications

The significant past and future identities served to shape and 'squeeze' interviewees' present identity as law students, which has implications for their well-being – particularly if they have to (or want to) deviate from that identity. A law student

55 The Law Society, *Trends in the Solicitors' Profession: Annual Statistics Report 2017* (Law Society, 2018).

who wants to be a lawyer finds aspects of their identity to be prescribed, including concern with (narrowly defined) achievements. Any perceived 'failures' to reach the standards they set themselves can challenge their present and future selves and may result in negative emotion.[56] The fixed view of the future lawyer identity can cause distress to students who feel 'other' and result in disengagement or demotivation; experiences of difficulty can be interpreted as meaning a desired identity is unachievable and not 'the real me', and should be abandoned.[57] Law students may not take advantage of their undergraduate years as a time to 'play' safely with their identity, and perhaps discover personal and professional identities which feel congruent, or develop multiple, distinct identities which provide protection at times of stress.[58]

The preoccupation with achievement was apparent in hyper-sensitivity to their positioning vis-à-vis other law students. Law students might justifiably be labelled as competitive,[59] and several students referenced this phenomenon:

> It is a very competitive environment.
>
> (W22)

> Someone mentioned oh, so and so got a training contract . . . everyone was like . . . 'oh, I see, I've got to up my game now.'
>
> (W35)

However, what was more evident were comparisons between students:

> Everybody else seemed like they were doing ok . . . I know I'm supposed to ask for help but I can't shake the feeling that I'm supposed to know these things, like I shouldn't be struggling with these things.
>
> (W23)

> When I first came to uni I was a bit, like, 'Oh, do I deserve to be here?' because you sit there and everyone in your seminar . . . is talking about really complicated things and I'm just, like, 'Oh, what's going on?.'
>
> (W21)

> A lot of people in law . . . they all seem very confident . . . they all seem like they've done it before . . . it wasn't until I saw that girl coming out of the office crying and I was like 'wow, maybe people are finding it difficult.'
>
> (W36)

56 Stryker and Burke (n 21).
57 Oyserman and Destin (n 23).
58 Linville (n 38).
59 See Helen Stallman, 'A Qualitative Evaluation of Perceptions of the Role of Competition in the Success and Distress of Law Students' (2012) 31 *Higher Education Research and Development* 891.

Although concern with performance and achievement as compared to others was not unique to law, it was the site where comparisons between students were the most frequent and most pronounced. Notably, through those comparisons, law students consistently found themselves to be deficient in some way. The recurring comparisons appeared partly connected to sustained academic identities, but were also linked to the future lawyer identity. As seen previously, students regarded the legal profession as requiring extraordinarily high standards – and potentially internalised such messages as being part of their own future professional identity. Such messages can be observed and absorbed by students in a variety of ways. For example, messages from the legal sector itself about the competitive nature of the industry can be easily observed,[60] and similar messages can be seen within law schools – for example, around the discussion of assessment marks and application forms for future employment. This has well-being implications. Sheldon and Krieger, for example, argue that one effect of law school and the pressure within it is to redirect the attention of law students from intrinsic motivation (whereby engagement in an activity is undertaken because of inherent enjoyment and interest in doing so)[61] to those which are extrinsic, i.e. 'undertaken as a means to an end' and focused upon external reward and recognition.[62] Although they argue that 'extrinsic motivations are not necessarily detrimental, provided that they have been internalized – that is, provided the person identifies with the rationale and value behind the behavior',[63] if behaviour is being dictated by external pressures this is more likely to be associated with lower subjective well-being. Conversely, if behaviour is motivated by intrinsic factors, this is more likely to have a positive subjective well-being effect.[64] Sheldon and Krieger's studies found that law students moved towards extrinsic values, including 'specifically pursuing their goals less for reasons of interest and enjoyment, and more for reasons of pleasing or impressing others'.[65] Although they are cautious not to equate causation with correlation,[66] the notion that intrinsic motivation and subjective well-being are linked remains a theme within self-determination theory literature.

Of further threat to law student well-being is the sense of being different to what is required by a desired future identity. For some law students this was

60 See for example Monidipa Fouzder, 'How to Get a Training Contract' *Law Gazette* (8 September 2014) <www.lawgazette.co.uk/features/how-to-get-a-training-contract/5042860.article> accessed 7 May 2019; 'How to Get a Job in a Law Firm' *Chambers Student* (December 2014) <www.chambersstudent.co.uk/where-to-start/newsletter/how-to-get-a-job-in-a-law-firm> accessed 7 May 2019; Law Society Junior Lawyers Division, 'Finding a Training Contract' (27 June 2014) <http://communities.lawsociety.org.uk/junior-lawyers/advice-and-features/finding-a-training-contract/5046490.fullarticle> accessed 7 May 2019.

61 Sheldon and Krieger (n 1) 263.

62 Ibid 263. See further Massimiliano Tani and Prue Vines, 'Law Students' Attitude to Education: Pointers to Depression in the Legal Academy and the Profession' (2009) 19 *Legal Education Review* 3.

63 Sheldon and Krieger (n 1) 263.

64 Ibid 264.

65 Ibid 281.

66 Ibid.

experiencing threats to their identity as a high achiever which in turn could be a profound challenge to their notion of future selves (which requires them to be the very best). For others, aspects of social identity (e.g. class, ethnicity) were at odds with their view of 'a lawyer'.[67] Many interviewees saw themselves as different to those working within the legal profession, even those who had received prior exposure to that profession (for example, through family who were members of the profession, or through work experience); [68] this has the potential to demotivate them and impact negatively upon their well-being. Skead and Rogers, for example, found that a higher sense of belonging to peers and university was associated with less anxiety.[69] It is difficult to believe you 'belong' if those around you, and your professional role models, seem to be so different to you.

Such challenges to identity might result in a modification of one's self-perception. However, we might question whether such a reformulation of expectations, and therefore of personal identity, is readily achievable by law students (particularly for those intending to enter the legal profession). It is arguable that students entering a law program quickly find their time to experiment with their identity is squeezed because of external pressures: law school staff will be familiar with students wanting to get legal work experience within their first semester, or expressing disappointment with what are, objectively, a good set of marks. Such pressures mean they do not have the opportunity to play with their identity as a student. Ibarra and Petriglieri state that identity play (defined as 'the crafting and provisional trial of immature (i.e. as yet unelaborated) possible selves')[70] is a way of individuals trying out potential identities to which they have not yet fully committed.[71] This focus upon 'play' has important implications for how the person reaches their destination:

> A primary objective of identity work . . . is acting and looking a part, so as to be granted the claimed identity. . . . In play, the primary drivers of behaviour are enjoyment and discovery rather than goals and objectives. . . . Play, however, requires a relatively safe space to try out new and untested behaviour.[72]

They suggest individuals who are focused upon play are more likely to take a circuitous route to a particular destination, with less of a focus upon an ultimate

67 This finding replicates those of Goldie (n 33) 645, in the medical student context, and Hilary Sommerlad in the law student context: Hilary Sommerlad, 'Research and Theorizing the Process of Professional Identity Formation' (2007) 34 *Journal of Law and Society* 190.

68 See further Sommerlad (n 67) 200–202 on how students might typically view lawyers in narrow – often corporate – terms.

69 Skead and Rogers (n 5) 86. On the importance of a sense of belonging, see further Tracy Levett-Jones and Judith Lathlean, 'Belonginess: A Prerequisite for Nursing Students' Clinical Learning' (2008) 8 *Nurse Education in Practice* 103.

70 Herminia Ibarra and Jennifer L Petriglieri, 'Identity Work and Play' (2010) 23 *Journal of Organizational Change Management* 10, 13.

71 Ibid 11.

72 Ibid 12.

desired outcome.[73] However, taking such a 'circuitous' route requires time, and the feeling of inhabiting a safe environment in which risk-taking and experimentation are permitted. Ibarra and Petriglieri observe that 'some professional settings require highly standardized identities, and hence, allow, individual role holders less scope for playing with identities'.[74] The focus within higher education upon graduate attributes and employability has been criticised by Daniels and Brooker on a similar basis: rather than encouraging students to focus upon their current identities as students, the pressures of employability metrics compel universities to focus students' attentions upon their future identities from an early stage of their careers within higher education.[75] It could be argued that law school is a setting in which a focus (whether overtly or otherwise) on the requirement to professionalise within a short period of time, shunning the student identity in favour of more quickly forming the professionalised identity of a future lawyer, can have a profound effect upon how they see themselves, and how they see their future possibilities. Pressures, whether actual or perceived, to adopt such a future identity can, according to Lairio et al., actually inhibit the ability of those students to become employable, and to navigate working life:

> Reflection on one's own professionalism also includes examination of personal identity and the self because in considering professionalism individuals take a broader look at their own strengths and actions in relation to work and to developing professional identity . . . it is important that university students have opportunities to construct their identity, especially professional identity, during their studies in order to better navigate into the working life.[76]

Recommendations and conclusion

In summary, law students compared themselves with those around them and with those occupying positions which they regarded as desirable: in both comparisons, many regarded themselves as 'different' (and in some way lacking), which could represent a challenge to their identity as high-achieving law students, and future lawyers. The past identity of law students as academically able also persists for a significant period of time during university. There are potential consequences for the individual's well-being as a result:

> Emotional discomfort arises when people are unable to draw a continuous link between old and new selves, leaving them feeling inauthentic . . . or

73 Ibid 13.
74 Ibid 15.
75 Jeannie Daniels and Jennifer Brooker, 'Student Identity Development in Higher Education: Implications for Graduate Attributes and Word-Readiness' (2014) 56 *Educational Research* 65, 74.
76 Marjatta Lairio, Sauli Puukari and Anne Kouvo, 'Studying at University as Part of Student Life and Identity Construction' (2013) 57 *Scandinavian Journal of Educational Research* 115, 116.

devoid of an enduring sense of self. . . . Emotive dissonance also results from the discrepancies between what people really feel and the images they feel compelled to convey in social interactions.[77]

Such emotional discomfort could partly explain the trends seen within law participants. Focus upon academic success as a continuation of their past identity, combined with a belief that requirements of their future desired identity would be high, left students challenged and uncertain. There are, however, steps which can be taken by law schools to guide students through such challenges.

Firstly, law schools can make identity part of curricular or extra-curricular discussions. This would potentially help to create an environment in which identities can more readily be discussed. Such work is already being explored within certain settings. Field and Duffy, for example, reflect upon a (now compulsory) module at QUT Law School which explicitly engages students in reflections on, and discussions of, a 'positive sense of professional identity'.[78] For many UK law schools, content within the course is driven by the current demands of the professional regulator and, although clinical legal education programs provide an opportunity for students to experiment with a future identity and to adapt to what will be required of them within that profession,[79] that is only one such future identity (namely, a lawyer). We might question whether this is sufficient when we are concerned with whether law students have a sufficiently broad future identity in mind.

Secondly, law schools can better influence the messaging received by students, and its effects. Rawson and Vaughan argue that students 'opt-out' of 'applying to law firms where they perceive there is no supplementary fit between themselves and the law firm',[80] e.g. on the basis of differences in social class, educational background and ethnicity. Convincing students that there could be further opportunities for them can partially be achieved through the selection of a broad range of 'role models' for students to encounter (e.g. through volunteering activities or careers events run by the school). Within our study, for example, one student reflected upon visualising herself within an organisation on the basis of such role models:

One thing that I like to see at . . . networking events is to see the diversity myself rather than read your annual report and see the really disappointing

77 Herminia Ibarra and Roxana Barbulescu, 'Identity as Narrative: Prevalence, Effectiveness and Consequences of Narrative Identity Work in Macro Role Transitions' (2010) 35 *Academy of Management* 135, 140.

78 Rachael Field and James Duffy, 'Better to Light a Single Candle Than to Curse the Darkness: Promoting Law Student Well-Being through a First Year Law Subject' (2012) 12 *Queensland University of Technology Law and Justice Journal* 133, 148.

79 See Colin James, 'Seeing Things as We Are: Emotional Intelligence and Clinical Legal Education' (2005) 8 *International Journal of Clinical Legal Education* 123; Colin James, 'Lawyers' Wellbeing and Professional Legal Education' (2008) 42 *The Law Teacher* 85.

80 Eleanor Rowan and Steven Vaughan, '"Fitting In" and "Opting Out": Exploring How Law Students Self-Select Law Firm Employers' (2018) 52 *The Law Teacher* 216, 229.

> figures. Because even if the figure is disappointing, if I see it for myself then I know it is achievable.
>
> (W22)

Finally, we can all desist from viewing resilience as individualised. A person's capacity for resilience and for healthy well-being is not static and only about them: it is in large part about their relationships with those people around them, including family, friends and university staff. To that end, law schools should encourage students to think about how they can support themselves and each other, for example through self-care activities and through maintaining or developing interests unconnected with their law degree.[81]

The research project upon which this chapter draws was funded by the Leeds Institute for Teaching Excellence.

81 Lovell (n 11 and n 12); Skead and Rogers (n 5); Penelope Watson and Rachael Field, 'Promoting Student Well-Being and Resilience at Law School' in Sally Kift et al. (eds), *Excellence and Innovation in Legal Education* (Lexis Nexis Butterworths, 2011) 301.

Index

Note: Page numbers in **bold** indicate tables.

FSC
www.fsc.org
MIX
Papier | Fördert
gute Waldnutzung
FSC® C083411

Kolibri 360 GmbH
Ferdinand-Jühlke-Straße 7
99095 Erfurt, Deutschland
produktsicherheit@kolibri360.de